Democrats and Autocrats

TRANSFORMATIONS IN GOVERNANCE

Transformations in Governance is a major new academic book series from Oxford University Press. It is designed to accommodate the impressive growth of research in comparative politics, international relations, public policy, federalism, and environmental and urban studies concerned with the dispersion of authority from central states up to supranational institutions, down to subnational governments, and sideways to public–private networks. It brings together work that significantly advances our understanding of the organization, causes, and consequences of multilevel and complex governance. The series is selective, containing annually a small number of books of exceptionally high quality by leading and emerging scholars.

The series targets mainly single-authored or co-authored work, but it is pluralistic in terms of disciplinary specialization, research design, method, and geographical scope. Case studies as well as comparative studies, historical as well as contemporary studies, and studies with a national, regional, or international focus are all central to its aims. Authors use qualitative, quantitative, formal modeling, or mixed methods. A trademark of the books is that they combine scholarly rigor with readable prose and an attractive production style.

The series is edited by Liesbet Hooghe and Gary Marks of the University of North Carolina, Chapel Hill, and the VU Amsterdam, and Walter Mattli of the University of Oxford.

Multi-Level Governance Below the State

Liesbet Hooghe, Gary Marks, Arjan H. Schakel, Sandra Chapman, Sara Niedzwiecki, and Sarah Shair-Rosenfield

Multi-Level Governance Above the State

Liesbet Hooghe, Gary Marks, Tobias Lenz, Jeanine Bezuijen, Besir Ceka, and Svet Derderyan

Scale and Community

Liesbet Hooghe and Gary Marks

Organizational Progeny: Why Governments are Losing Control over the Proliferating Structures of Global Governance

Tana Johnson

Democrats and Autocrats

Pathways of Subnational Undemocratic Regime Continuity within Democratic Countries

Agustina Giraudy

OXFORD
UNIVERSITY PRESS

Great Clarendon Street, Oxford, OX2 6DP,
United Kingdom

Oxford University Press is a department of the University of Oxford.
It furthers the University's objective of excellence in research, scholarship,
and education by publishing worldwide. Oxford is a registered trade mark of
Oxford University Press in the UK and in certain other countries

© Agustina Giraudy 2015

The moral rights of the author have been asserted

First Edition published in 2015

Impression: 2

All rights reserved. No part of this publication may be reproduced, stored in
a retrieval system, or transmitted, in any form or by any means, without the
prior permission in writing of Oxford University Press, or as expressly permitted
by law, by licence or under terms agreed with the appropriate reprographics
rights organization. Enquiries concerning reproduction outside the scope of the
above should be sent to the Rights Department, Oxford University Press, at the
address above

You must not circulate this work in any other form
and you must impose this same condition on any acquirer

Published in the United States of America by Oxford University Press
198 Madison Avenue, New York, NY 10016, United States of America

British Library Cataloguing in Publication Data

Data available

Library of Congress Control Number: 2014950702

ISBN 978-0-19-870686-1

Printed and bound by
CPI Group (UK) Ltd, Croydon, CR0 4YY

Cover image: © andipantz/iStockphoto.com

Links to third party websites are provided by Oxford in good faith and
for information only. Oxford disclaims any responsibility for the materials
contained in any third party website referenced in this work.

Para Marco

Acknowledgments

This book began to take shape many years ago as I was putting together my dissertation prospectus. During the long process of researching and writing this book, I have incurred many intellectual and personal debts. First and foremost, I am deeply grateful to my outstanding teachers at the University of North Carolina at Chapel Hill. I owe Jonathan Hartlyn, who chaired my dissertation committee, immense gratitude for his intellectual support, encouragement, and guidance throughout the process of writing my doctoral dissertation and this book. I acknowledge profoundly his enthusiasm and rigorousness in supervising a research project on subnational and territorial politics, a subfield that was not related to his main area of expertise. Evelyne Huber not only graciously read and commented on early drafts of different chapters, but above all provided exceptional intellectual and professional guidance since I began my Ph.D. studies. Lars Schoultz and John Stephens also provided much needed supervision as I was completing this project. Finally, Todd Eisenstadt, at American University, went beyond the call of duty to provide academic advice and support before and after fieldwork.

I have been very privileged to have an extraordinary group of scholars read and comment on portions of this manuscript at various stages. For insightful academic feedback I thank Jorge Domínguez, Kent Eaton, Tulia Falleti, Kelly McMann, Richard Snyder, and Lily Tsai. Other senior scholars, including, Catherine Boone, Grzegorz Ekiert, Frances Hagopian, Steven Levitsky, and Gerardo Munck, provided thoughtful and constructive advice. Jenny Pribble and Hillel Soifer deserve special mention for their willingness to read and make invaluable comments on the whole manuscript. Finally, two anonymous manuscript reviewers at Oxford University Press provided excellent and careful feedback, which has helped to improve the book greatly.

I must also give credit where credit is most due: my interest in subnational undemocratic regimes would not have arisen if not for the work of Edward Gibson. His original article on boundary control lit that first light bulb in my head while I was in my second year of grad school. I have learned tremendously from his writings and thinking on subnational democracy and subnational politics more broadly, and as importantly, from his commitment to doing extensive and rigorous fieldwork in the periphery.

Acknowledgments

I am also indebted to the numerous politicians, officials, and social organizers, who in Buenos Aires, Mexico City, Puebla, Oaxaca, La Rioja, and San Luis generously shared their time with me and helped me understand the politics of subnational undemocratic regime continuity. Without them this research simply could not have been possible. While conducting fieldwork in Mexico and Argentina, many people opened doors for me. Andreas Schedler, and my former undergraduate mentor, Catalina Smulovitz, warmly welcomed me at CIDE and Universidad Torcuato Di Tella, respectively. They not only provided institutional affiliation but, above all, sound academic advice in the very first stages of this research project. In Argentina, I was fortunate to benefit from the thoughtful academic advice of Carlos Gervasoni, Alejandro Bonvecchi, Lucas González, Germán Lodola, Marcelo Leiras, Julieta Suárez-Cao, and Virginia Oliveros. Ernesto Calvo, a dear professor and a much-admired scholar, Juan Pablo Micozzi, and Fred Solt graciously shared hard-to-find data with me. Conversations with Eugenia Giraudy, my beloved sister and colleague, and with Florencia Guerzovich were critical to refining several parts of this book's argument. Allyson Benton, Joy Langston, and Julio Ríos Figueroa were also a great source of knowledge and advice while I was conducting fieldwork in Mexico.

I also want to express my deepest gratitude to the phenomenal friends and colleagues I have made throughout the years of writing this book. Each of them have enriched (and continue to do so) my understanding of important political phenomena of Latin American and beyond. They have also, directly and indirectly, helped me improve my thinking about subnational undemocratic regimes in crucial ways. Juan Bogliaccini, Mireya Dávila, Juan Pablo Luna, Sara Niedzwiecki, Indira Palacios, and Jenny Pribble deserve special mention for their companionship and intellectual support both during the wonderful but stressful years in Chapel Hill and since graduation. In Cambridge, I benefitted enormously from the intellectual and emotional support of my friends Anne Clement, Candelaria Garay, Harris Mylonas, and Hillel Soifer. During the months of fieldwork in Mexico, Alejandra Armesto, Juan Olmeda, Matt Ingram, Sandra Ley, and Jason Lakin contributed critically to helping me understand and analyze Mexican subnational politics. The friendship I have with each of these colleagues is by far one of the most valuable "unintended consequences" of graduate school and of this research project.

This book could not have been researched nor written without the support of several institutions. Fieldwork in Argentina and Mexico during 2007 and 2008 was funded by generous fellowships sponsored by The Horowitz Foundation for Social Policy, the Inter-American Foundation with the Institute of International Education, the Graduate School at the University of North Carolina at Chapel Hill, as well as the Mellon Foundation. The writing

Acknowledgments

of this manuscript was supported by a Dissertation Completion Fellowship from the Graduate School at University of North Carolina at Chapel Hill, which allowed me to complete the dissertation writing-up phase during the 2008–9 academic year. A generous postdoctoral fellowship from the Harvard Academy for International and Area Studies provided the much needed time and resources to turn my doctoral dissertation into a book manuscript. I acknowledge fondly the support of Larry Winnie during the time I spent in Cambridge. I would also like to thank American University, my home institution, and, in particular, my senior colleagues at the School of International Service, for protecting my time during the final stages of this research project. Finishing this book without this invaluable time and without their collegiality would have been exceedingly more difficult. Last, but certainly not least, I would like to extend my sincere thanks to Liesbet Hooghe, Gary Marks, and Walter Mattli—editors of the *Transformations in Governance Series* with Oxford University Press—for their longstanding interest in this project. It has been a real privilege to work with Dominic Byatt. He has proven to be a phenomenal, rigorous, and extremely professional editor. I am very grateful for his enthusiastic encouragement and guidance.

This book has benefitted enormously from the work of several outstanding, hard-working, and very talented research assistants and PhD students. I thank Paula Bonessi, Diane Kuhn, Sara Lacy, James Loxton, Victoria Paniagua, Cécile Sánchez, Paulina Sánchez, and Mercedes Sidders for improving this book with their rigorous and meticulous work.

Perhaps the most important support I have received throughout these past years has come from my family. My parents, Verónica Flynn and Justo Giraudy, have always been there, encouraging me to accomplish my personal goals, providing at all times much needed emotional support, even so during the difficult times of my dad's illness. Every time I visit them in Bariloche (Patagonia, Argentina), and converse with them at the dinner table, I reaffirm why I became interested in subnational politics. I am extremely fortunate to have three unconditional, dedicated, and smart sisters who over the years worked hard to keep our camaraderie growing despite long distance. I am grateful to Jimena, Celina, and Eugenia for supporting me, in their own respective ways, to (finally!) complete this manuscript. I wrote this book in the company of my two daughters, Chiara and Sofia. Raising them while writing this book has been one of the most difficult challenges I have ever faced. For the last three years, there has been very little energy left for work on this manuscript. However, and paradoxically, these past three years have been revitalizing. I have been blessed by Chiara's and Sofia's energy and my life is immeasurably better for that.

I dedicate this book to my husband, Marco Cerletti. He has unquestionably been my greatest source of emotional and intellectual support. His "far

Acknowledgments

peripheral vision" and his commonsense were crucial during the innumerous times that I could not see the forest for the trees. Over these past years, Marco made every effort possible to accommodate his professional goals and career so that I could have the opportunity to move across countries to research and write this book. Still more important, he accompanied me despite the solitary moments he had to spend while I was working on this project. My debt to him is enormous. For his companionship, his patience, his sense of reality, and his love, without which I would have not been able to complete this book, I will be forever grateful.

Contents

List of Figures xv
List of Tables xvii
List of Abbreviations xix

1. Introduction 1
   A New Perspective on the Study of SURs within
      Democratic Countries 3
   Contributions to the Study of SURs in Democratic Countries 5
   Definitions and Argument's Scope Conditions 7
   Research Design, Case Selection, and Organization of the Book 9

2. Explaining Within-Country Pathways of Subnational
   Undemocratic Regime Continuity 14
   Approaches to the Study of SUR Continuity 15
   The Argument 18
   Synthesis of the Argument 31

3. Conceptualizing, Measuring, and Mapping Subnational
   Undemocratic Regimes 33
   SUR Conceptualization and Measurement 34
   Varieties of Subnational Undemocratic Regimes 44
   Conclusion 52

4. Presidential Power in Argentina and Mexico: Fiscal and Partisan
   Instruments of Cooptation 54
   Fiscal Instruments of Presidential Power 55
   Partisan Instruments of Presidential Power 67
   Assessing Sources of Presidential Power—Fiscal vs.
      Partisan Resources 72
   Conclusion 74

5. SUR Reproduction from Above in Argentina and
   Mexico: Quantitative Evidence 76
   SUR Reproduction from Above: Hypotheses and Conditions of
      Presidential Control 77

Contents

Mechanisms of SUR Reproduction from Above	80
Measures of the Dependent and Independent Variables	81
Data and Analytic Technique	84
Results and Discussion	85
Conclusion	90

6. Subnational Undemocratic Regime Continuity in Argentina:
   La Rioja and San Luis — 92
   Subnational Case Selection — 94
   La Rioja: A Case of SUR Reproduction from Above — 97
   Capacity of Presidents to Wield Power over Autocrats and
      La Rioja's SUR — 102
   Prospects for Obtaining Cooperation of La Rioja's Autocrats — 107
   Presidential Action vis-à-vis La Rioja's SUR — 110
   San Luis: A Case of SUR Self-Reproduction — 111
   Capacity of Presidents to Wield Power over Autocrats and
      San Luis's SUR — 116
   Prospects for Obtaining Cooperation of San Luis's Autocrats — 120
   Presidential Actions vis-à-vis San Luis's SUR — 121
   Conclusion — 125

7. Subnational Undemocratic Regime Continuity in
   Mexico: Puebla and Oaxaca — 126
   Subnational Case Selection — 127
   Puebla: A Case of SUR Reproduction from Above — 131
   Capacity of Presidents to Wield Power over Autocrats and
      Puebla's SUR — 138
   Prospects for Obtaining Cooperation of Puebla's Autocrats — 140
   Presidential Action vis-à-vis Puebla's SUR — 142
   Oaxaca: A Case of SUR Self-Reproduction — 144
   Capacity of Presidents to Wield Power over Autocrats and
      Oaxaca's SUR — 151
   Prospects for Obtaining Cooperation of Oaxaca's Autocrats — 154
   Presidential Action vis-à-vis Oaxaca's SUR — 155
   Conclusion — 159

8. Conclusion — 161
   Summary of Findings — 163
   Assessment of the Argument's Validity in Cases of
      SUR Breakdown — 167
   Lessons from Argentina and Mexico — 174

Appendix	179
I: Subnational Democracy	179
II: SURs' Patrimonial State Structures	183
References	189
List of Interviews	205
Index	211

List of Figures

1.1	Argument of the book	4
2.1	Within country pathways of SUR continuity	19
2.2	Conditions for effective fiscal and partisan presidential power	27
3.1	Dimensions of subnational democracy	39
3.2	Levels of subnational democracy in Argentina (1983–2009)	40
3.3	Levels of subnational democracy in Mexico (1997–2009)	41
3.4	Dimensions of patrimonial state structures	47
3.5	SUR state structures in Argentina (1983–2009)	48
3.6	SUR state structures in Mexico (1997–2009)	49
3.7	SUR fiscal autonomy in Argentina (1996–2009)	51
3.8	SUR fiscal autonomy in Mexico (1997–2009)	52
4.1	Share of coparticipation distributed across levels of government in Argentina	60
4.2	Export and import duties as a percentage of tax revenues (Argentina)	61
4.3	Percentage of funds subject to sharing across levels of government in Mexico	64
4.4	Gini coefficients of presidential PNS in Argentina and Mexico	71
6.1	Levels of subnational democracy and fiscal autonomy in the Argentine provinces (average 2003–9)	95
6.2	Geographic location of case studies	96
6.3	Percentage of export/import duties as a share of total central government's revenues	104
6.4	La Rioja: income sources (2002–9)	105
6.5	La Rioja: type of federal revenues as a share of total federal revenue (2002–9)	105
6.6	La Rioja: total income—total expenditures (1997–2009)	106
6.7	La Rioja: debt as percentage of provincial GDP (2001–9)	106
6.8	San Luis: income sources (2002–9)	117

List of Figures

6.9	San Luis: type of federal revenues as a share of total federal revenue (2002–9)	118
6.10	San Luis: debt as percentage of provincial GDP (2001–9)	119
7.1	Levels of democracy and type of state structure in the Mexican states (average 2000–9)	129
7.2	Geographic location of case studies	130
7.3	Puebla: *participaciones, aportaciones,* and other federal revenues as a share of total federal revenue	142
7.4	Oaxaca: *participaciones, aportaciones,* and other federal revenues as a share of total federal revenue	156
A1	A necessary and sufficient concept structure of subnational democracy	180
A2	A family resemblance concept structure of patrimonial state structure	185

List of Tables

1.1	Summary of subnational case selection	13
4.1	Legally prescribed revenue shares for the federal government and the provinces	58
4.2	Major changes in the rules that regulate revenue-sharing systems in Argentina and Mexico	67
4.3	Presidential power: fiscal and partisan instruments of cooptation	73
5.1	Variable description and data sources	82
5.2	Determinants of ATN, PAFEF, and funds for public works with robust cluster standard errors	87
6.1	La Rioja's indicators of democracy	98
6.2	San Luis indicators of democracy	112
7.1	Puebla's indicators of democracy	132
7.2	Percentage of municipalities under PAN, PRD, and PRI rule	135
7.3	Oaxaca's indicators of democracy	145
7.4	Percentage of municipalities under PAN, PRI, and PRD control	152
A1	Indicators of subnational democracy	181
A2	State newspapers used to code clean elections	184
A3	Indicators of patrimonial state structure	186

List of Abbreviations

AFS	Auditoría Superior de la Federación (Federal Superior Audit)
APPO	Asamblea Popular del Pueblo de Oaxaca (Popular Assembly of the People of Oaxaca)
ATN	Aportes del Tesoro Nacional (National Treasury Funds)
CEE	Comisión Electoral Estatal (State Electoral Commission)
CIDH	Comisión Internacional por los Derechos Humanos (International Commission for Human Rights)
CL	Ley de Coparticipación (Coparticipation Law)
CNDH	Comisión Nacional de Derechos Humanos (National Commission of Human Rights)
CONAGO	Confederación Nacional de Gobernadores (National Confederation of Governors)
CROC	Confederación Regional de Obreros y Campesinos (Regional Confederation of Workers and Peasants)
ENP	effective number of parties
ENPL	effective number of parties in the legislature
EU	European Union
FC	Fondo de Compensación (Fund for Compensation)
FDR	Fondo de Desarrollo Regional (Fund for Regional Development)
FEIEF	Fondo de Estabilización de los Ingresos de las Entidades Federativas (Fund for the Stabilization of the States' Revenues)
FEIP	Fondo de Estabilización de los Ingresos Petroleros (Fund for the Stability of Oil Revenues)
FFM	Fondo de Fomento Municipal (Fund for Municipal Promotion)
FGP	Fondo General de Participaciones (General Fund of Participations)
FIES	Fideicomiso para la Infraestructura de los Estados (Trusteeship for States' Infrastructure)
FpV	Frente para la Victoria (Front of Victory)
GDP	Gross Domestic Product
IPF	Inversión Pública Federal (Federal Infrastructural Development)

List of Abbreviations

LCF	Ley de Coordinación Fiscal (Law of Fiscal Coordination)
LPRH	Ley de Presupuesto y Responsabilidad Hacendaria (Law of Budgetary and Fiscal Responsibility)
LSFF	Ley de Fiscalización Superior de la Federación (Law of Federal Fiscal Oversight)
MPN	Movimiento Popular Neuquino (Popular Movement of Neuquén)
PAFEF	Programa de Aportaciones para el Fortalecimiento de las Entidades Federativas (Aportaciones Program for the Enhancement of the Federal States)
PAN	Partido de Acción Nacional (National Action Party)
PEMEX	Petróleos Mexicanos
PIS	Plan de Inclusión Social (Social Inclusion Plan)
PJ	Partido Justicialista (Peronist Party)
PNS	Party Nationalization Score
PR	proportional representation
PRD	Partido de la Revolución Democrática (Party of the Democratic Revolution)
PRI	Partido Revolucionario Institucional (Institutional Revolutionary Party)
PRONASOL	Programa Nacional de Solidaridad (National Solidarity Program)
PT	Partido Trabajador (Workers Party)
RPI	Régimen de Promoción Industrial (industrial promotion regime)
Sedesol	Secretaria de Desarrollo Social (Ministry of Social Development)
SMD	single-member district
SUR	subnational undemocratic regime
UC	usos y costumbres (indigenous customs)
UCR	Unión Cívica Radical (Radical Party)

1

Introduction

"This is my state," yelled José Murat (1998–2004), the Oaxacan governor from the Institutional Revolutionary Party (PRI) to one of the federal officials held hostage in "his" state, "and I decide who meets with whom, and whether or not you hold meetings in Oaxaca" (interview Lepine, see also *Periódico Reforma*, August 23, 2002). In August 2002, two years after Mexico's national democratization took place, a group of federal officials from the Ministry of Social Development (Sedesol) were kidnapped in the Oaxacan city of Mitla. The federal officials had traveled south from Mexico City to answer the claims advanced by the handful of National Action Party (PAN) mayors ruling in Oaxaca, who argued that the PRI state government was not distributing Sedesol programs according to eligibility criteria. Instead, the mayors claimed that the PRI was allocating program funds to political and partisan allies, and consequently funds were not reaching PAN-ruled mayoralities. The kidnapping occurred when the group of PAN Sedesol officials and PAN mayors were holding a meeting to discuss strategies to ameliorate the discretional distribution of social programs in Oaxaca. "All of a sudden," as one of the kidnappees reported, "the doors of the meeting room were opened and Ulises Ruiz [then, federal senator of Oaxaca, and subsequently governor of the state (2004–10)], leading a crowd of 100 PRI mayors, burst into the room, violently apprehended us, and took us away in a pickup truck. The kidnappers held us hostages for one day" (interview Lepine; see also *Periódico Reforma*, August 23, 2002). The governor's aim, as the interviewee reported, "was to demonstrate [to] my boss [Josefina Vázquez Mota, Secretary of Sedesol, 2000–6], that PAN federal officials could not meddle in Oaxacan politics, much less dictate to the governor how federal social programs should be distributed" (interview Lepine). Indirectly, Murat also wanted to send a clear message: PAN President Vicente Fox (2000–6) was not to encroach upon the governor or the state of Oaxaca. Shortly after this episode, the federal government refused to sign subsequent Convenios de Desarrollo Social (treaties of social development)[1] and took other actions to oppose and weaken the regime. Despite efforts from the federal government at undermining Oaxaca's subnational undemocratic regime (SUR), Murat, and his successor Ulises Ruiz, managed to keep the regime alive by relying on a sturdy local coalition of support, which rested primarily on the backing of local party elites.

This episode, which vividly illustrates the persistence of subnational incumbents' undemocratic practices after Mexico's national democratization in 2000, also reveals important aspects of the relationship between democratic presidents and some subnational autocrats. For one, it shows the president's incapacity to wield power over one of Mexico's most recalcitrant undemocratic rulers as well as the president's inability to discipline and obtain the governor's cooperation. From another perspective, the episode highlights the governor's disposition and capacity to challenge the authority of a democratically elected president as well as his capacity to sustain an undemocratic regime despite federal attempts to undermine its foundations.

A different pattern of intergovernmental relations between a democratic president and a subnational autocrat was observed during Fox's presidency in Oaxaca's neighboring state, Puebla, which is also one of the least democratic states of Mexico (see Chapter 3). Unlike Oaxaca, the political presence of the PAN in this traditionally PRI-ruled state has always been significant. Whereas in Oaxaca an average of 9.64 percent of the municipalities between 1998 and 2007 were ruled by the PAN, in Puebla an average of 19.47 percent of municipalities were ruled by the PAN during the same time period.[2] The greater number of PAN-ruled municipalities, which, as discussed in Chapter 7, resulted from a less patrimonial exercise of state power, posed a challenge to the capacity of PRI *poblano* governors to, in Edward Gibson's (2005, 2013) terms, carry out strategies of boundary control. In the era of PAN presidencies (2000–12), the larger presence of the PAN in Puebla's municipalities became critical to facilitate PAN presidents' capacity to wield power and control—via their local party organization—over the state and its subnational autocrat. Greater control over *poblano* governors, in turn, was decisive

---

[1] Every year each Mexican state signs these treaties with the federal government in which both parties stipulate which social programs will be co-financed by the state and the federal government.

[2] Oaxaca's percentage is calculated on the basis of the 152 municipalities where political parties compete in local races. The remaining 418 Oaxacan municipalities have, since the 1990s, adopted a system of indigenous customs (known in Spanish as *usos y costumbres* or UC). Customary law-observing communities use a mix of Western and traditional electoral means: citizens elect federal and state authorities according to standard liberal electoral processes of secret ballot and universal suffrage, and they elect municipal authorities via indigenous customs (see Eisenstadt and Yelle 2012).

Introduction

for inducing and ultimately obtaining political cooperation from Puebla's autocrats. As a result of the presidential leverage that resulted in cooperative *poblano* governors, autocrats in Puebla, unlike their Oaxacan counterparts, were regarded as key political allies of PAN presidents. Furthermore, in contrast to Oaxaca's SUR, Puebla's SUR was rarely seen as threatening. On the contrary, PAN presidents saw fit to sustain and reproduce the Puebla political regime despite its undemocratic characteristics.

A New Perspective on the Study of SURs within Democratic Countries

These two examples reveal important aspects of the relations between (national) democrats and (subnational) autocrats and shed light on the causes of SUR continuity *within* nationally democratic countries. First, contrary to conventional wisdom, SURs within democratic countries maintain different—and at times opposed—relations with the federal government. Whereas some of them can be subjugated to the will of democratically elected presidents, others can become powerful opponents of national incumbents, so much so that they can prevent federal officials from implementing federal policies in their territories. Second, the case of Puebla shows that, despite the fact that democratic presidents breach state-level borders and penetrate undemocratic enclaves by striking alliances with local oppositions, SURs continue to exist. In other words, contrary to conventional wisdom, the existence of "boundary opening" strategies does not necessarily trigger SUR change. Third, the cases reveal that the prospects of wielding effective presidential power over subnational autocrats figures prominently in national democrats' calculations regarding their actions to oppose or sustain SURs. Where presidential power is effective to obtain the acquiescence and cooperation of subnational autocrats, (national) democrats help the latter to strengthen their SURs. Where this presidential power is not effective, presidents favor SUR weakening by, for instance, denying social programs. Yet, despite regime-destabilizing attempts, some SURs continue to stay in power.

The Mexican examples pose important and puzzling research questions for the study of SUR continuity within nationally democratic countries. What explains different pathways of SUR continuity within nationally democratic countries? Why is the pattern of center–SUR relations different within countries? Why do some autocrats and SURs prevail despite presidents' strategies to weaken SURs? Why do democratic presidents support some autocrats and SURs, even when they are from the opposition? Why do presidents support undemocratic regimes even when subnational autocrats cannot carry out strategies of boundary control? Under what conditions do democratically elected presidents endorse or combat (opposition and/or copartisan) autocrats and SURs?

These are the central research questions addressed in this study. In brief, the book argues that there are two alternative within-country pathways to SUR continuity. What sets SURs onto distinct pathways of reproduction is the capacity (or lack thereof) of national incumbents to wield effective power over (opposition and/or copartisan) autocrats and their regimes, which in turn is critical to facilitate (or discourage) the cooperation of subnational undemocratic rulers with the president's agenda. Where national incumbents can wield effective power over and obtain the acquiescence and political cooperation of (opposition and/or copartisan) subnational autocrats, the former have incentives to strengthen and sustain subnational undemocratic regimes from above. When this occurs, *SUR reproduction from above* ensues. Conversely, where presidents fail to exert power over (opposition and/or copartisan) autocrats, and are in turn incapable of obtaining the latter's cooperation, the former have incentives to carry out actions to weaken SURs. Nonetheless, the capacity of subnational autocrats to maintain party elite unity and to elicit the support of the local masses allows autocrats to maintain the status quo and keep their regimes alive. When this occurs, *SUR self-reproduction* ensues. Figure 1.1 graphically summarizes the book's argument.

These two diverging pathways of SUR continuity within countries are the subject of this book's investigation. Specifically, the study seeks to unravel different causal conditions and combinations of variables leading to a similar regime outcome, i.e. SUR continuity, within countries.

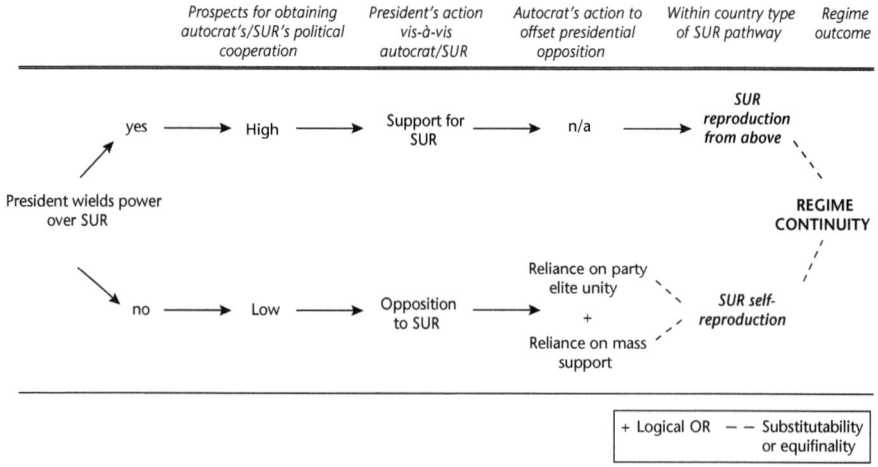

Figure 1.1. Argument of the book

Contributions to the Study of SURs in Democratic Countries

The argument advanced in this book fundamentally challenges the assumption that there is one single pathway to SUR continuity within countries. It shows instead the existence of multiple (within-country) paths to the same political outcome (i.e. regime continuity).[3] The study is premised on the notion that SURs within countries not only differ among themselves but that they maintain different relations with the federal government, which is why they are reproduced differently.[4] The book thus revives a promising line of research, initiated by Richard Snyder (1999, 2001a) more than a decade ago, whose focus on within-country regime differences as well as their varied interactions with the federal government contributed to a better understanding of subnational political processes.

The acknowledgment that there are regime differences—which propel a variety of SUR–center interactions, and, in turn, trigger alternative pathways of SUR continuity within countries—helps advance the study of SURs in national countries in several ways. First, recent scholarship on SUR continuity has found that the factors that perpetuate these regimes in power may be quite different across countries (Gibson 2013). In his path-breaking book, Gibson (2013) argues that, given that the factors that reproduce SURs are intrinsic to a given configuration of national variables, we should see that different combinations of national variables trigger varying patterns of SUR continuity *across* countries. As a result, SUR reproduction in country *x* should differ from the type of reproduction observed in country *y*, which in turn should contrast with the pattern of SUR continuity seen in country *z*. This view, while acknowledging the likelihood of alternative types of regime reproduction, overlooks the possibility that SURs *within a single country* may be sustained by a combination of different causal factors. This book complements existing works that focus on different cross-national trajectories of SUR reproduction by showing that these trajectories can also be dissimilar *within* countries.

Second, the book's acknowledgment of SUR differences and varying types of SUR–federal government interactions within countries invariably shifts the focus of SUR study from single subnational case studies to within-country subnational comparisons. This shift from subnational case study analysis

---

[3] In other words, it reveals the existence of equifinality (George and Bennett 2005). The phenomenon of equifinality is also referred to as "multiple causality" or "multiple conjunctural causation" in Charles Ragin's books, *The Comparative Method* (1987) and *Fuzzy-Set Social Science* (2000).

[4] While there are works that underscore the existence of within-country SUR variation (see, for instance, Gervasoni 2011; Saikkonen 2011), none of them has argued that these differences play a key role in regime continuity.

(which has been the norm so far[5]) to within-country comparative subnational analysis (which is at the core of this book) breaks new ground in the study of SURs in new democracies, and consequently offers a new perspective to assess the continuity of these subnational regimes.

Third, the book departs from existing works on SUR continuity by shifting the focus of attention to presidents rather than governors. Most of the more influential theories on SUR continuity focus on the capacity of subnational autocrats to control borders, but they seldom analyze the sources that allow democratic presidents to wield effective power over SURs and their rulers. This book not only examines the conditions under which this presidential power is possible and effective, but argues that its presence, rather than the power and control exerted by SUR incumbents over the areas they rule, is the key causal mechanism through which democratic presidents engage in strategies of SUR reproduction from above.

The focus on presidential power also importantly fills an important analytical void of existing scholarship on SUR reproduction. Most of the studies on SURs that adopt an intergovernmental approach (see Chapter 2) have argued that democratic presidents tolerate SURs because the latter can provide key political benefits to the former. This quid pro quo is usually seen as mechanical and it is assumed to apply to the universe of SURs within a given country. This book shows, instead, that democratic national incumbents tolerate, and ultimately help to reproduce, only the SURs upon which they can wield effective (fiscal or partisan) power. Likewise, the book shows that subnational autocrats' political cooperation, their acquiescence, as well as their subordination to national democrats take place only to the extent to which presidents wield effective (political and/or fiscal) power over subnational autocrats. In the absence of this presidential power and control, subnational autocrats have few incentives to deliver political benefits that could favor national incumbents. In sum, this study contributes to the literature on SUR reproduction by fleshing out the mechanisms that account for presidents' ability and incentives to further sustain undemocratic regimes in the periphery. This study elucidates as well the factors that propel (copartisan or opposition) subnational autocrats to deliver political goods to national democrats.

Fourth, the study moves past existing assumptions that presidents only help reproduce SURs that are ruled by copartisans. This book, for example, does not take for granted that presidents' capacity to obtain the cooperation of subnational autocrats is higher or more likely when national incumbents and autocrats belong to the president's political party or share the same political ideology. Rather, it assumes that both opposition and

---

[5] For a notable exception, see McMann (2006).

Introduction

copartisan autocrats can deliver important political benefits to the presidential cause, and, in turn, be sustained from above, when disciplined by the watchful eye of democratic presidents. By challenging the relevance of national–subnational copartisanship, the book helps open up new research frontiers in the study of SUR reproduction in nationally democratic countries.

Finally, while the book builds on existing works by stressing the importance of variables at both the national and subnational levels of government, it argues that new variables need to be taken into account in order to address SUR continuity in democratic countries. The book shows that the territorial extension of national political parties, the nature of state structures prevailing in each SURs, as well as the capacity of SUR incumbents to maintain local party elite unity and to elicit mass support, are key factors for the sustainability of SURs. The focus on national and subnational variables that have so far been overlooked contributes to complementing existing works on SUR continuity within democratic countries.

Definitions and Argument's Scope Conditions

What is a SUR?

The SURs analyzed and referred to in this book are not municipal, local regimes; instead, they are provincial or state-level, second-tier political regimes. Following McMann (2006) and Gervasoni (2010a, 2010b), this study defines provincial/state-level SURs as civilian electoral regimes that are neither fully authoritarian nor fully democratic.[6] As discussed in greater detail in Chapter 3, SURs can be clearly distinguished from subnational authoritarian regimes because they hold regular, multiparty elections, and, unlike authoritarian regimes, opposition groups and parties are not legally barred from competing in subnational elections. What distinguishes SURs from subnational democracies is the fact that the actual opposition's capacity to defeat subnational autocrats (and/or their parties) in elections is significantly handicapped. Through a variety of undemocratic, illegal, and informal actions, such as electoral fraud, restriction of political and civic rights and liberties, electoral violence, and/or periodic changes in electoral rules and political institutions, incumbents systematically prevent the opposition from gaining access to state positions—hence SURs cannot be regarded as democratic.

---

[6] For a discussion and justification of why these regimes are not referred to as hybrid or any other subtype of hybrid regimes, such as competitive authoritarian regimes (Levitsky and Way 2010), see Chapter 3.

SUR Continuity and SUR Change

The focus of inquiry of this book is SUR continuity, rather than SUR origins or SUR change. Accordingly, the study centers both on the provinces/states that continue to be or became undemocratic and remained so in the period under study (i.e. 1983–2009 in Argentina, and 1997–2009 in Mexico), and the factors that helped perpetuate these regimes in power. The primary reason for focusing on regime continuity rather than regime origins and change is that, as shown in Chapter 3, SURs are stable. The evidence presented in this book indicates that, once in place, the vast majority of SURs remain for long periods of time, with only few of them making strides towards subnational democracy. For this reason, the task of this book is to understand the specific mechanisms that enabled SURs and their autocrats to cling to power for so many years, thus turning these regimes (and their rulers) into durable and "sticky" undemocratic polities (autocrats). Accordingly, the subnational cases selected for in-depth analysis will be cases where undemocratic regimes were in power for decades.

In the concluding chapter, however, positive cases, i.e. subnational regimes that remained undemocratic, are contrasted with cases of SUR change, i.e. negative cases. This contrast is meant to show that the conditions hypothesized to be crucial for producing SUR continuity in the positive cases were absent, or not all present, in the negative cases that experienced SUR breakdown. The analysis presented in Chapter 8 reveals that the two hypothesized conditions, ineffective presidential (fiscal or partisan) power in the first place, and the incapacity of autocrats to rely on a sturdy local coalition of support (i.e. inability to build party elite unity and obtain mass support), in the second place, were present in Oaxaca and Puebla after 2009. The absence of these two conditions explains why these two SURs experienced party alternation in 2010, ten years after Mexico's national transition to democracy. In sum, this analysis reveals that the theoretical model presented in this book offers the possibility of predicting SUR breakdown.

Federal and Unitary Countries

Unlike previous works on subnational undemocratic regimes, this book develops an explanation of SUR continuity that can travel beyond federal democratic countries. In general, works on this topic have produced theories whose core premises are only to be found in federations or highly decentralized democratic countries (Gibson 2005, 2013; Gervasoni 2010a, 2010b, 2011; Mickey 2013). As a result, these theories can only explain SUR continuity in these settings. The core building blocks of this book's argument, in contrast, can be found in both unitary and federal democratic countries. According to

Introduction

the argument presented here, presidents' capacity (or lack thereof) to wield effective (fiscal or partisan) power, their ability to obtain the cooperation of subnational autocrats, and undemocratic rulers' ability to neutralize presidential power are the three key factors that account for various trajectories of SUR continuity within democratic countries, and they are not exclusive to federal polities.[7] The implications of this book's explanation should apply in all countries where a democratic national government coexists alongside an undemocratic subnational government.

Research Design, Case Selection, and Organization of the Book

The explanation of SUR continuity advanced in this book is tested in contemporary Argentina and Mexico, two of the largest Latin American countries. Three aspects make Argentina and Mexico particularly suitable for this study. First, as shown in Chapter 3, Argentina and Mexico have a considerably large number of SURs. Second, as demonstrated in Chapter 3, Argentine and Mexican SURs vary widely regarding the institutional and fiscal factors that shape presidential power over SURs, and in turn, in the factors that determine alternative pathways of SUR continuity within each country. This variation is needed to test the validity of the book's argument. Third, as shown in Chapter 5, Argentina and Mexico differ in terms of the instruments presidents have used to wield power over, and obtain the cooperation of, subnational autocrats and their regimes. Whereas Argentine presidents have generally exercised power through fiscal means, their Mexican counterparts have resorted to partisan instruments to win over undemocratic governors. Despite differences in the way in which presidential power has been exerted in each country, the trajectories of SUR continuity within countries have been similar. That is, where national incumbents have been able to wield effective power over autocrats, SUR reproduction from above has resulted in both countries. Where, by contrast, national incumbents have been incapable of exercising authority over recalcitrant undemocratic governors, presidents have undertaken actions of SUR weakening. The study of Argentina and Mexico thus reveals that, in spite of dissimilar strategies of presidential encroachment upon autocrats, the logic of the argument holds across countries, thus validating the generalization of the explanation.

In terms of the methodology, the book employs a multi-method approach that includes both quantitative and qualitative methods, as well as cross-national

---

[7] That two federal countries are selected as the primary cases of study in this book does not invalidate this claim.

and within-country comparisons of two SURs in each country (La Rioja and San Luis in Argentina; Oaxaca and Puebla in Mexico). The qualitative analyses examine the 2003–9 period in Argentina and the 2000–9 period in Mexico, spanning four presidencies in two countries. In Argentina, the presidency of Néstor Kirchner (2003–9) and the first half of Cristina Fernández de Kirchner's administration are analyzed. The Mexican presidency of Vicente Fox (2000–6) and the first half of Felipe Calderón's administration are examined in Mexico. The quantitative analyses, in turn, cover the mid-1990s–2009 period in Argentina and the 2000–9 period in Mexico.

The book is divided into one theoretical and six empirical chapters. Chapter 2 outlines the theory of within-country pathways of SUR reproduction. The first part of the theoretical chapter discusses existing approaches to the study of SUR continuity. Against that framework, the second section of the chapter presents this book's argument and lays out its core building blocks. As noted, one of the major contentions of the book is that effective presidential power over subnational autocrats determines within-country pathways of SUR continuity. Accordingly, Chapter 2 theorizes about the conditions under which this presidential power is likely. Building on the idea that presidents' power over autocrats is not absolute but distributive, the chapter explores the institutional and economic resources available to presidents in order to coopt and to obtain the acquiescence of subnational autocrats. Likewise, the chapter analyzes the institutional and economic resources that subnational autocrats have to resist presidential power. Drawing on the insights provided by the literature on political parties' territorial structures and fiscal federalism, the chapter argues that presidents usually employ two major resources to control autocrats: their party organizations and/or federal funds that are allocated to subnational jurisdictions. Subnational autocrats, for their part, make use of two different resources to prevent encroachments of national incumbents: their fiscal autonomy vis-à-vis the central government, and the nature of local state structures that facilitate the concentration of authority in the hands of the ruler. Given that these resources vary across SURs in a given country, some autocrats are in a position to neutralize presidential power, whereas others easily succumb to it. This variation in the capacity of subnational autocrats to resist encroachments from the central government accounts for the different within-country pathways of SUR continuity within democratic nations.

Chapter 3 advances a careful characterization and operationalization of subnational political regimes, and measures the level of democracy in all Argentine and Mexican provinces over time. In doing so, the chapter "maps the terrain" of SURs, spells out more clearly what these regimes are all about, and provides a systematic assessment of subnational political regimes across time and space in two of Latin America's biggest countries. The conceptual

Introduction

and operational definitions of SURs, as well as their measurement and results, are presented in the first part of this chapter. The second part is devoted to uncovering and systematizing SUR variation. The chapter distinguishes between regimes that have or lack patrimonial state structures, and those that have or lack fiscal autonomy from the national government. In so doing, the chapter provides a systematic empirical analysis of SUR variation in all Argentine provinces and Mexican states over time. The data presented and analyzed in Chapter 3 also help to eliminate/weaken the explanatory power of alternative theories of SUR continuity. Specifically, the data challenge the validity of theories that argue that SUR continuity is determined by geographic location, cultural heritage, and levels of socioeconomic development.

Testing the explanation advanced in this book requires a two-stage strategy. The first stage occurs at the country level, and is focused on identifying the instruments available to presidents to exert effective presidential power over SURs and their autocrats. The second stage explores within-country comparisons and aims to show that pathways of SUR continuity within countries are primarily determined by the capacity (or lack thereof) of national incumbents to wield effective power over autocrats and their regimes, which in turn is critical to facilitate (or prevent) the cooperation of subnational undemocratic rulers with the achievement of the president's cause.

Chapter 4 measures and compares fiscal and partisan instruments of presidential power in Argentina and Mexico. An examination of each of the post-1989[8] presidencies in Argentina reveals that presidents used multiple instruments to exercise power over subnational rulers. While Peronist President Menem employed fiscal and partisan resources to discipline SURs and their autocrats, Peronist Presidents Duhalde, Kirchner, and Fernández de Kirchner wielded power over subnational autocrats using mostly fiscal instruments. By contrast, Presidents Fox and Calderón in Mexico resorted to partisan instruments to exert authority over and obtain the cooperation of SURs and their autocrats.

After establishing the specific instruments of presidential power, the book carries out within-country comparisons to explore whether different trajectories of SUR continuity were contingent upon subnational undemocratic rulers' capacity to resist (or succumb to) presidential power. Chapter 5 tests the more general claim of the book's argument, namely, that effective presidential power over autocrats leads to SUR reproduction from above. To do so, different cross-sectional time-series analyses of all Argentine and Mexican SURs are performed. The chapter analyzes the politics of SUR reproduction

---

[8] Fiscal data for Alfonsín are missing, which is why the assessment of his capacity to wield power over provincial-level authorities is incomplete.

during the administrations of Menem (1989–99), De la Rúa (1999–2001), Duhalde (2002–3), and the Kirchners (2003–9) in Argentina, and the presidencies of Fox (2000–6) and Calderón (2006–9) in Mexico. The quantitative analyses conducted in Chapter 5, which encompass the universe of SURs in the post-transitional period in Argentina and Mexico, help gain inferential leverage and maximize the generalizability of the theoretical claims raised in Chapter 2.

Because quantitative analyses do not permit the testing and substantiation of the specific mechanisms through which the effective exercise of presidential power leads to alternative pathways of SUR reproduction within countries, a qualitative analysis is needed to reconstruct the causal chain that links the cause (presidential power or lack thereof) with the effect (the pathway of SUR continuity that ensues). To meet this goal, *causal process observation* is conducted to identify the pieces of data that provide information about the context, processes, and mechanisms through which the initial case conditions are translated into case outcomes.

Using evidence gathered from over 150 original, in-depth interviews with Argentine and Mexican national and subnational top-ranked officials, journalists, and former politicians, as well as information from archival documents, Chapters 6 and 7 carry out four in-depth, subnational case studies to explore whether the capacity of national incumbents to wield power over autocrats and to obtain their cooperation determines within-country pathways of SUR continuity. Given that SUR pathways are primarily determined by presidents' capacity (or lack thereof) to wield power over SURs, SURs in each country were selected so as to maximize variance along the subnational independent variable (i.e. fiscal autonomy and/or type of state-structure) facilitating or hindering presidential power. Thus, under the presidencies of Kirchner (2003–7), and the first half of the Fernández de Kirchner administration (2007–9) in Argentina, when the main resource of presidential power was fiscal, subnational case selection in this country was determined by SURs' level of fiscal autonomy, as different values on this (subnational) variable are key for either hindering or allowing presidential power and autocrats' cooperation with the national government. The case of La Rioja, an undemocratic fiscally dependent province, and the case of San Luis, an undemocratic, fiscally autonomous province, provide the desired variation. The focus of Chapter 6 is on the administrations of Peronist Governors Ángel Maza (1995–2007) and Luis Beder Herrera (2007–present) in La Rioja, and Peronist Governor Alberto Rodríguez Saá (2003–11) in San Luis.

By contrast, under the presidency of Fox (2000–6), and the first half of the Calderón administration (2006–9), when presidential power was exerted mainly through partisan instruments, subnational cases in Mexico were selected based on their type of subnational state structure—as patrimonial

Introduction

Table 1.1. Summary of subnational case selection

Predominant instrument of presidential power	Country	Relevant SUR attribute to neutralize presidential power	Within-country type of SUR Pathway	
			SUR reproduction from above	SUR self-reproduction
Fiscal	**Argentina** (2003–9)	Fiscal autonomy	**La Rioja**	**San Luis**
Partisan	**Mexico** (2000–9)	Patrimonial state structure	**Puebla**	**Oaxaca**

structures can help neutralize partisan power, while non-patrimonial state structures facilitate it. The case of Oaxaca, where a patrimonial state structure was in place, and the case of Puebla, where a non-patrimonial state structure existed, offer the desired variation. The focus of Chapter 7 is on the administrations of the Party of the Institutional Revolution (PRI) Governors Melquíades Morales (1998–2004) and Mario Marín (2005–2010) in Puebla, and PRI Governors José Murat (1998–2004) and Ulises Ruiz (2004–2010) in Oaxaca. Table 1.1 provides a visual summary of the criteria employed to select national and subnational cases.

The final chapter of the book is divided into three parts. The first part presents a summary of the book's findings and primary contributions. In order to help validate the main claims of this book's argument, the second section of Chapter 8 shows that the conditions hypothesized to be crucial for SUR continuity were not present in Puebla and Oaxaca after the 2010 elections, when SUR breakdown occurred. The chapter concludes with a discussion of the lessons learned from the analyses of Argentina and Mexico, emphasizing the contributions of the book to the literature on subnational undemocratic regimes and intergovernmental relations in multi-level polities.

2

Explaining Within-Country Pathways of Subnational Undemocratic Regime Continuity

As Robert Dahl and Guillermo O'Donnell observed quite some time ago, the unfolding of democracy in different regions of the world and over time has been territorially uneven across levels of government and subnational units (Dahl 1971; O'Donnell 1999). New democracies have not escaped this trend; quite the contrary, one persistent aspect of these new national regimes is the existence of what Edward Gibson (2005, 2013) has referred to as "regime juxtaposition"—that is, the prevalence of subnational undemocratic regimes (SURs) alongside a democratic national government.

Over recent years a wealth of insightful and novel academic works, ranging from in-depth, qualitative single case-studies to medium-N, within-country studies, have provided a detailed documentation of SURs in countries as diverse as India, Russia, Kyrgyzstan, the United States, Argentina, Brazil, Colombia, and Mexico.[1] These works provide empirical confirmation that democratic advancement has been territorially uneven across both levels of government and subnational units. Such works have also provided in-depth descriptions of how these regimes function, as well as of the tactics employed by subnational autocrats to consolidate the regimes that sustain them in power.

As a result of these investigations, we know, for instance, that undemocratic rulers engage in strategies of institutional engineering that limit the number of entrants into the electoral arena and reduce intraparty

---

[1] Fox 1994; Hagopian 1996; O'Donnell 1999; Cornelius 1999; Snyder 1999; Eisenstadt 1999; Heller 2000; Solt 2003; Gibson 2005, 2013; Petrov 2005; Lankina and Getachew 2006, 2011; McMann 2006; Borges 2007; Montero 2007, 2010a; Remington 2009, 2010a, 2010b; Reisinger and Moraski 2010; Giraudy 2010, 2013; Gervasoni 2010a, 2010b, 2011; Durazo-Hermann 2010; Behrend 2011; Saikkonen 2011; Rebolledo 2011; Benton 2012; Mickey 2013; Lankina 2012; Gerring et al. 2013; among others.

factionalism (Calvo and Micozzi 2005; Gibson 2013). Gerrymandering to over-represent rural districts against the more competitive capital districts, on one hand, and changes in electoral rules that alter district magnitudes, on the other, are only some examples of the institutional reforms carried out by incumbents to consolidate their ruling positions. Subnational autocrats also consolidate their power by exerting monopoly power over electoral commissions, most of which are packed with loyalists who act subserviently and help SUR incumbents secure electoral victories by settling electoral and post-electoral conflicts favorably (Ley 2009; Rebolledo 2011). Consolidation of undemocratic regimes is also possible due to the suppression of checks and balances, which generally occurs through the frequent and arbitrary reshuffling of provincial/state-level supreme and lower courts (Leiras et al. 2012; Gervasoni 2011; Castagnola 2012). Suppression of various civil rights, such as freedom of expression and organization (McMann 2006; Gervasoni 2010a, 2010b), as well as the recurrent violation of political rights, such as the incarceration of political opponents (Gibson 2005; Martínez Vásquez 2007), also helps subnational autocrats to entrench themselves and their regimes in power.

Approaches to the Study of SUR Continuity

Another important contribution of this literature has been the identification of the causes of the continuity of subnational undemocratic regimes. Existing works on the causes of SUR continuity have generally emphasized either subnational factors or national–subnational interactions as the main determinants of subnational undemocratic regime durability. Scholars within the "subnational factors" camp argue that variables specific to each subnational unit—such as the economic autonomy of inhabitants, the spatial location of clientelistic machines within SURs, geographic location, citizens' human capital, or the size of electoral districts—are the main predictors of SUR continuity.

For instance, in her analysis of subnational democracy in Russia and Kyrgyzstan, McMann (2006) finds that capitalism, which enhances economic autonomy, enables citizens to engage in politics and to challenge authorities, thus creating conditions favorable to subnational democratization. Similarly, Montero (2011) finds that where small populations, high levels of poverty, and poor communication with more developed urban centers exist, as occurs in Brazil's Northeastern undemocratic states, local bosses and conservative party leaders of SURs have greater leeway to isolate clients (voters), tie them into enforceable vote-buying contracts, and in turn sustain undemocratic regimes. In their analysis of the Indian states, Lankina and Getachew (2012) find that the presence of colonial-era Christian missionary activity, which played a key role in promoting education and, in turn, in augmenting human capital, spurred social inclusivity and propelled social reform movements leading to the toppling of SURs in the post-colonial era. Gerring et al. (2013) further argue that the size of an electorate has a positive impact on levels of subnational democracy. Specifically, they show that smaller districts are less competitive (i.e. more undemocratic). The reasons for this, they contend, hinge on three factors: lower diversity of preferences, lower organizational density, and a smaller pool of potential challengers. Analyzing the Russian regions, Lankina and Getachew (2006) show that the geographic location of subnational districts shapes the prospects for SUR continuity. They demonstrate that geographic proximity to the West encouraged neighboring Western actors to pursue targeted subnational democratization efforts through European Union (EU) direct financial aid. Finally, Lankina (2012) contends that pre-communist human capital affects variations in current human capital and democracy in Russia's regions. She finds that pre-communist education is a predictor of post-communist modernization, which, in studies of Russian regions, is linked to regional democratic variation (Lankina and Getachew 2006; Petrov 2005; Remington 2009, 2010a, 2010b; Moraski and Reisinger 2003). Pre-communist education may also positively and significantly affect post-communist democracy. In sum, according to this first approach, a variety of subnational factors specific to each subnational unit accounts for the persistence of SURs.

Explanations within this analytical camp, while greatly improving our knowledge of the causes of SUR durability, are problematic for the following reasons. First, the wide variety of factors that account for SUR continuity have expanded the scope of theoretical disagreement to such an extent that it has become difficult to adjudicate empirically among competing claims, preventing, in turn, the accumulation of knowledge about the subnational causes that sustain SURs in power. Second, explanations within this approach implicitly assume that subnational units are autonomous jurisdictions independent from the politics that unfold at the national level of government. As a result, they rule out the possibility that SUR durability might be shaped by national factors. This is particularly problematic in cases where SURs, such as the ones analyzed in this study, are embedded in countries that are democratic at the national level. As discussed in detail in Chapter 3, the wide acceptance of democratic rules at the national level of government strongly shapes subnational actors' actions, incentives, and options towards SUR continuity (Gervasoni 2010b). For these reasons, the "subnational factors" approach is inappropriate for the study of SUR reproduction within national democracies.

The idea that subnational undemocratic units are not isolated from national democratic politics resonates with a well-established tradition within sociology and political science that views subnational political outcomes as a byproduct of the political dynamics that play out at the intersection of national and subnational-level arenas. Works within this second approach, hereafter the "national–subnational interaction" approach, either intuitively or self-consciously build on the premise that, in large-scale systems of territorial governance, political institutions are entangled across space—and precisely for that reason, political action and political outcomes, such as the continued maintenance of SURs, are not limited to a single arena (Rokkan 1970; Tarrow 1978; Rokkan and Urwin 1982, 1983). On the contrary, as Gibson (2005, 2013) underscores, subnational political outcomes are routinely shaped by the regular interventions of national governments and national institutions, such as political parties, territorial regimes, or fiscal arrangements. Hence, a much more appropriate study of SUR continuity in national democracies must be rooted in theories of territorial politics.[2]

Proponents of explanations that focus on national–subnational interactions as the main causal factor of SUR continuity claim that factors such as presidents' strategic behavior towards SURs, national policies, or national institutions shape the prospects for SUR continuity. For instance, in his analysis of Mexico, Snyder (1999, 2001a) shows that policies carried out at the national level, such as the implementation of neoliberal (market) reforms, can contribute to the maintenance and strengthening of SURs. These reforms trigger reregulation projects in the states through which undemocratic incumbents generate rents and resources to consolidate their ruling positions, which is exactly what occurred in Mexico. Similarly, both Cornelius (1999) and Montero and Samuels (2004) argue that policies of decentralization, which swept across Latin America during the late 1980s and 1990s, and which shifted political, fiscal, and administrative power away from the national government toward subnational units, gave undemocratic state-level rulers greater autonomy, resources, and leverage to maintain SURs in power. In a similar vein, Gibson (2005, 2013) claims that national institutions, such as the territorial regime (or type of federal system), shape the strategic options available to subnational autocrats, and in turn their capacity to employ strategies of boundary control. Boundary closers, i.e. subnational autocrats who maximize influence over local politics and deprive provincial oppositions of access to national allies and resources, can maintain their regimes in power effectively. Other national institutions, such as the revenue-sharing systems of federal countries, also shape the prospects of SUR

---

[2] According to Edward Gibson, territorial politics is not about the territory but about how politics is organized and fought out across territory (Gibson 2013: 15).

continuity. As Gervasoni's (2010b) analysis of Argentina shows, provinces that receive disproportionately large central government transfers provide undemocratic incumbents with generous fiscal federalism rents that allow them to restrict democratic contestation, weaken checks and balances, and overall reproduce SURs in power. Finally, as Tudor and Ziegfeld (forthcoming) show, central government intervention, coupled with pre-independence patterns of subnational political competition and caste structures in each state, have a decisive effect on delaying the onset of subnational democratization in the Indian states.

Theoretical disagreement regarding the factors that account for SUR reproduction also affects this second approach. While this prevents adjudication between competing explanations, and thus challenges knowledge accumulation, perhaps a more fundamental shortcoming of this approach is the assumption that SURs are a more or less homogeneous mass of political regimes exhibiting identical interactions with the federal government. This approach therefore assumes that national institutions and national policies will shape undemocratic regime continuity in all SURs in the exact same way. This assumption is problematic for at least two reasons. First, it overlooks the possibility that SURs within a single democratic country may be reproduced differently precisely because they interact with national actors, national institutions, and national policies in a different way. Second, because of this omission, existing theories overgeneralize their scope by assuming that the causes that account for SUR continuity in a given SUR in country x are generalizable to the universe of SURs within that same country.

This book seeks to expand knowledge of SUR continuity within democratic countries by challenging the assumption that national institutions, national actors, and national policies similarly impact different SURs within a given country. The book instead argues that a democratic president maintains different types of relations with SURs (and their autocrats), and that these varied interactions are decisive for triggering multiple routes of SUR durability within a given country. The remainder of this chapter is devoted to developing the building blocks of this new explanation.

The Argument

As I have noted, the general argument of this book is that the capacity (or lack thereof) of presidents to exert control over subnational autocrats triggers different pathways of SUR continuity. This section discusses in more detail (a) the factors that make presidential power important for determining SUR continuity, (b) the instruments to which presidents can resort in order to exert power over subnational autocrats and their SURs, (c) the instruments

Within-Country SUR Continuity

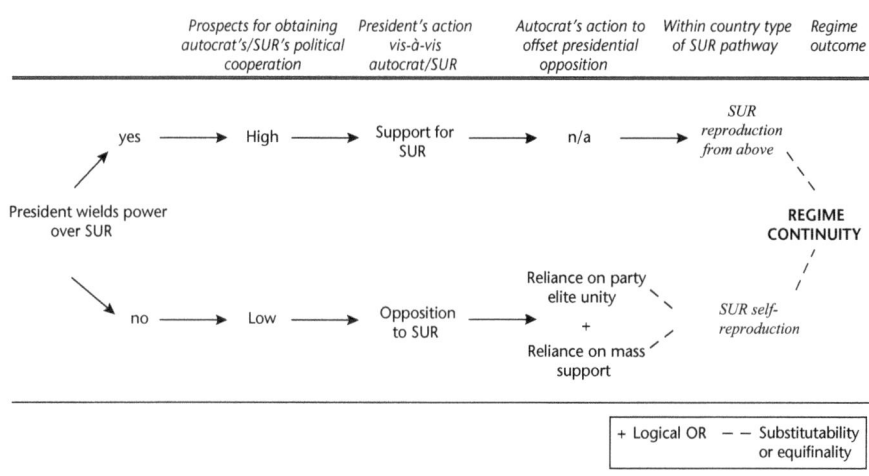

Figure 2.1. Within-country pathways of SUR continuity

which autocrats can employ in order to neutralize this power and to ultimately render it ineffective, (d) the conditions under which two different types of presidential power, i.e. fiscal or partisan, can ensue, and (e) the different pathways of SUR reproduction that result from the capacity (or lack thereof) of presidents to wield power over autocrats and SURs. Figure 2.1 provides a visual summary of this book's argument and its building blocks.

(a) The Importance of Presidential Power for Shaping SUR Continuity

Several studies show that undemocratic governors can be key partners for political coalition-making (Hagopian 1996; Snyder 1999; Gibson 2005; Hunter and Power 2007; Moraski and Reisinger 2003; Reisinger and Moraski 2010; Tudor and Ziegfeld forthcoming). Their political power stems from their privileged position to control local party branches and local party machines, national legislators, voters, and provincial legislatures—and, indirectly, other provincial agencies such as provincial comptrollers, heads and members of provincial electoral commissions, and provincial Supreme Court justices.[3] Monopoly over party elites and party cadres, voters, national and provincial legislators, and provincial state agencies turns subnational autocrats into influential political actors, as they have the means necessary to deny electoral support, refrain from providing national legislative backing

---

[3] Subservient legislatures usually pack monitoring institutions with those loyal to the incumbents, thus hampering their function of adequately checking subnational autocrats (Melo et al. 2009; Pardinas 2005; Rebolledo 2011; Ley 2009; Leiras et al. 2012; Castagnola 2012). As a result, SUR incumbents can, without fear of being sanctioned by oversight agencies, have absolute control over provincial-level politics and actors.

that may be decisive for passing the president's agenda, discredit presidential policies and presidential initiatives, or even challenge presidents' political ambitions. Subnational autocrats who are difficult to discipline can, in sum, become significant stumbling blocks to presidents' political ambitions and agendas.

Yet effective presidential power over SUR incumbents can turn challengers (from either the president's party or the opposition) into allies. Subnational autocrats who are in a vulnerable position vis-à-vis the central government can in fact be very beneficial for a president in need of political support.

For instance, with their tight control over local party machines, as well as their capacity to prevent opposition forces from winning over voters, autocrats from SURs can help deliver votes that have a decisive impact on general and mid-term national elections (Snyder 1999; Gibson 2005; Tudor and Ziegfeld forthcoming). Subnational autocrats can also become attractive coalitional partners due to their capacity to deliver electoral support by engaging in "turnout buying" (Nichter 2008). Their command of the party machine confers on autocrats a powerful instrument to discourage voters' presence at the polls, thus helping national incumbents' parties (if different from the autocrat's party) to win non-provincial electoral races. Furthermore, autocrats' capacity to control local and federal legislators' political careers turns them into valuable coalitional partners, as they have considerable leeway to influence and discipline legislators' voting behavior, and thus secure congressional support for the passage of bills that are central to national incumbents' political projects (De Luca et al. 2002; Gordin 2004; Jones and Hwang 2005; Samuels 2003; Díaz-Cayeros 2006; Langston 2004, 2005; Langston and Aparicio 2008; Rebolledo 2011). Finally, SUR incumbents can become key partners for national governing coalitions given their capacity, for instance, to maintain political stability and manage security threats in areas that are strategic to national security and governability. For instance, recalcitrant autocratic governors, who usually control paramilitary forces, can be charged with the presidential "mission" of managing security threats in key geographic areas (Snyder 1999).[4]

The possibility of exerting effective presidential power over subnational autocrats is not only important to turning challengers into allies, but is also critical to increasing the president's capacity to extract real and credible

---

[4] Not all subnational autocrats, however, can deliver political benefits to presidents (see Giraudy 2010). For instance, not all of them have the capacity to ensure the provision of national legislative support. Because autocrats' capacity to deliver legislative votes depends on their ability to control legislators' political careers, autocrats can only exert leverage over deputies and senators who belong to their own political parties. They cannot, by contrast, influence the voting behavior of opposition legislators. Only autocrats who control a sizeable share of deputies and senators can ensure the delivery of legislative support.

inter-temporal political concessions and support from subnational autocrats. In the absence of effective presidential power, it is possible for some subnational undemocratic incumbents to renege on their promises to provide political support.

The capacity to wield effective presidential power over SURs and their autocrats—or otherwise stated, SUR/autocrats' vulnerability vis-à-vis national incumbents—figures prominently in presidents' calculations regarding the reproduction of SURs. Presidents who can exercise effective power over (copartisan or opposition) autocrats have high incentives to contribute to the reproduction of the regimes that sustain them in power. By contrast, presidents who are prevented from wielding effective power over subnational autocrats should opt to oppose rather than support SURs in power, even when these regimes are ruled by copartisans. In sum, copartisan/opposition vulnerable subnational autocrats who have real power to deliver secure political returns should receive the support of democratic presidents. Conversely, invulnerable copartisan/opposition subnational autocrats, who have the actual power to challenge presidential authority, are expected to suffer political retaliation from presidents who are likely to seek to undermine the foundations of the subnational regimes.[5]

Before specifying the conditions that render presidents powerful vis-à-vis SURs, some clarifications about presidential power are in order. Presidential power over subnational autocrats and subnational regimes can be exercised directly or indirectly. Direct leverage over (opposition or copartisan) undemocratic governors materializes when presidents can induce subnational incumbents to concede political spaces that they would otherwise not concede, such as: pressuring national politicians to endorse candidates whom the former would otherwise not endorse (this includes mobilizing voters to vote for the president's endorsed candidate), legislative support for bills that run counter to the governor's/province's/partisan interests, and general support (manifesting as assistance for public rallies and public declarations) for policies enacted by the national government that are not in accord with a governor's agenda and/or ideological stand.

Indirect presidential power over (some aspects of) subnational politics/arenas materializes when democratic presidents trespass provincial borders and broadcast their authority and power (through their own provincial party

---

[5] The contention that presidents opt to back vulnerable autocrats as well as their regimes does not rule out the possibility that federal incumbents might choose to support copartisan/opposition subnational democratic rulers who can also deliver political support. This possibility is not explored in this book given that the focus of inquiry is the continuity of SURs rather than the reproduction of subnational *democratic* regimes. It is possible that, all things equal, faced with the trade-off of supporting SURs over subnational democratic regimes, presidents should choose to reproduce the former over the latter. This is because subnational autocrats, who have absolute control of provincial politics, are in a better position to deliver political support.

branches), in order to strike alliances with municipal leaders or local opposition groups (Gibson 2005, 2013; Dickovick 2007; Fenwick 2010) and to circumvent or undermine undemocratic autocrats' territorial and electoral power. Hereafter, this type of presidential power is referred to as "presidential power from within" because it is exerted through municipal politicians or local opposition groups loyal to the president.[6]

Finally, two additional issues must be considered in order to specify the conditions under which national incumbents exercise power over SURs. First, presidents are endowed with different resources (fiscal, military/police, institutional, symbolic, etc.) for controlling the territory they govern, and it is the availability of these resources that determines the actual capacity of presidents to exert power over territory and society. Second, presidential power is not absolute but relative (Mann 1986). Therefore, in order to wield power over subnational undemocratic arenas/autocrats, subnational rulers' capacity to resist this pressure needs to be low relative to the power of democratic presidents.

Given these considerations about the relative strength of presidents to exert power over SURs, the first step in analyzing different pathways of SUR continuity is to evaluate both the resources that are at the disposal of national incumbents to wield authority over subnational autocrats, and those that are available to subnational undemocratic incumbents to neutralize presidential power. Building on different bodies of literature, it is possible to identify two particularly important resources available to presidents—fiscal and partisan—and two resources available to subnational autocrats—fiscal and institutional.

(b) *Instruments of Presidential Power*

FISCAL INSTRUMENTS

Numerous works show that fiscal resources enable presidents to exert power over subnational autocrats (Eaton 2004; Wibbels 2005; Díaz-Cayeros 2006; Falleti 2010; Bonvecchi and Lodola 2011). Presidential fiscal power over subnational rulers is likely to be higher in countries where intergovernmental transfers are not channeled using automatic and formula-based criteria, but rather occur on a discretionary basis (Bonvecchi and Lodola 2011). Presidential fiscal power should also be greater where the rules that regulate the distribution of intergovernmental transfers, as well as the amount of intergovernmental transfers, are easily changeable. Flexible fiscal arrangements that enable presidents to increase the share of resources that remains at the

---

[6] In Gibson's (2005) terms, this type of presidential control would be possible where SUR incumbents are prevented from carrying out strategies of boundary control.

federal level of government, thus decreasing the proportion of funds that is sent to subnational levels of government, increase presidential leverage over subnational autocrats.

Likewise, presidential fiscal power over subnational autocrats may be higher depending on the availability and percentage of taxes that are not subject to being shared with subnational governments. In almost all federal countries, there are taxes, such as import/export duties or oil revenues, that are collected by the federal government and not distributed to the provinces. These taxes, which in some countries comprise a large bulk of a country's total revenue, are generally administered at the discretion of the federal government. Consequently, the taxes offer national incumbents an additional tool with which to increase their fiscal discretion, power, and control over subnational governments.

PARTISAN INSTRUMENTS

National political parties and, more specifically, political parties' organizational structures, constitute powerful means through which national-level politicians can discipline subnational rulers. Different strands of literature within political science have long recognized the crucial role played by national political parties in domesticating and controlling local potentates and subnational politicians. The literature on state building and party system formation, for example, has viewed political parties as instruments crucial to exercising political influence over the peripheries, as well as to undermining local potentates' authority (Caramani 2004; Rokkan 1970; Tilly 1990; Keating 1998). Similarly, the literature on federalism has highlighted the importance of political parties and partisan structures as means of obtaining the cooperation of subnational incumbents (Mainwaring 1999; Jones et al. 2000; Stepan 2000; Willis et al. 1999; Samuels 2003; Wibbels 2005; Levitsky 2003; Leiras 2006). Strong, cohesive, institutionalized, and disciplined parties are viewed as facilitators of the central government's ability to discipline and obtain the cooperation of subnational *copartisans*.[7]

Presidential parties that are territorially extended and electorally viable in subnational districts also help increase presidential leverage over *opposition* subnational incumbents. Despite the fact that presidents lack (internal) partisan mechanisms to discipline opposition rulers at the subnational level—simply because these incumbents do not belong to their parties—the organizational presence of presidents' parties in any given subnational unit

---

[7] The mechanisms through which parties control subnational copartisans are manifold and depend on their internal organizational structures. The literature, however, has identified two main mechanisms of control over subnational copartisans: via coat-tails effects (Wibbels 2005; Rodden 2003), and via the selection, nomination, and appointment of candidates (Samuels 2000; Wibbels 2005; Willis et al. 1999).

increases electoral performance (Van Dyck 2013), thus allowing them to put pressure on subnational incumbents and eventually obtain their cooperation. For instance, national incumbents can take advantage of their local networks of offices, activists, and members to strengthen on-the-ground electoral mobilization in order to co-opt subnational regime supporters, win over municipal governments, and/or forge opposition coalitions with disgruntled local elite members, local dissatisfied journalists, other local opposition activists (Gibson 2005, 2013), or mayors (Dickovick 2007; Fenwick 2010). If presidential parties can effectively challenge subnational incumbents' electoral power within districts and in turn threaten their territorial control, they can be used as a tool to exert presidential power from within. For instance, presidents can obtain the cooperation of subnational rulers by lessening electoral pressure in exchange for political cooperation. Conversely, when presidents lack partisan organizations, and thus have a shortage of networks of brokers, activists, and community organizers, it is more difficult for them to forge national-local coalitions to undermine provincial subnational incumbents' power, and in turn, to obtain the incumbents' cooperation.

In sum, presidential partisan power, i.e. the capacity to obtain copartisan and/or opposition subnational incumbents' compliance through party leverage, should be greater where (a) presidential party organizations, and the rules and procedures that regulate relations between the party leadership and lower-level branches are highly routinized,[8] and (b) the president's party has an electoral foothold in all of subnational units. By contrast, it should be lower where (a) the presidential party's organization is weakly routinized, and (b) it is electorally viable in only one district.

(c) Subnational Autocrats' Instruments of Autonomy

FISCAL INSTRUMENTS

Financial autonomy of subnational rulers from the central state is one major resource through which lower-tier incumbents can neutralize presidential power and, in turn, encroachments from the center (Boone 2003; Wibbels 2005). The greater subnational incumbents' reliance on local taxes (that are not part of revenue-sharing systems), the lower their fiscal deficits, and the lower their levels of indebtedness, the greater their potential for counterbalancing presidential power and gaining more autonomy. By contrast, greater financial dependence upon the central government creates structural

---

[8] According to Levitsky (2003) internal (formal or informal) routinization is one dimension of party institutionalization. It can be defined as "a state in which the rules and procedures within an organization are widely known, accepted, and complied with" (2003: 18). Nonroutinization, by contrast, is a state in which (formal or informal) rules and procedures are fluid, contested, and routinely circumvented or ignored.

conditions conducive to the subjugation of subnational ruling elites vis-à-vis the center (Wibbels 2005; Díaz-Cayeros 2006).

It is worth emphasizing that in federal countries where revenue-sharing systems exist, all subnational governments are, formally speaking, dependent on the national government, given that the main (domestic) taxes are collected by the federal government and then channeled to subnational levels of governments.[9] In this book, financial autonomy is conceived of as being a byproduct of subnational governments' fiscal deficits, levels of indebtedness, and capacity to raise subnational taxes. The ability of subnational governments to avoid financial mismanagement is of particular importance for increasing financial autonomy vis-à-vis the central government, and thus increases the chances of neutralizing presidential control. As various works show, financially reckless governors who run fiscal deficits and are highly indebted often turn to the central government for financial aid and bailouts (see Sanguinetti 1999; Hernández Trillo et al. 2002; Wibbels 2005; Rodden 2006). Given the discretion with which presidents decide whom to bail out, profligate governors can easily become political hostages of central incumbents and vulnerable to presidential control.

INSTITUTIONAL INSTRUMENTS

Provincial institutions, and more specifically the provincial state structure, constitute the second resource available to subnational undemocratic incumbents to neutralize presidential power. As Evans (1994) and Ertman (1997) note, state structures establish the rules and procedures through which incumbents exercise power, thus creating different capacities for rulers' action vis-à-vis presidents and local actors. A well-established tradition within political science has distinguished between state structures that (a) centralize power in the hands of the ruler, blur public and private interests and purposes within the state administration, reduce the autonomy of followers by generating ties of loyalty and dependence, and appropriate state resources for private economic or political gain, versus state structures that (b) limit incumbents' power, establish and allow for a clear distinction between the private and public domains, confer autonomy to societal groups, and minimize rulers' appropriation of state resources (Evans 1994; Migdal 1992, 1994; Bates 1981, 2008; Ertman 1997; Hartlyn 1998; Mazzuca 2007, 2010). Whilst receiving different conceptual labels, these state structures can be subsumed into two generic terms: patrimonial versus non-patrimonial.[10]

---

[9] Revenues are distributed in two rounds. In the first round, taxes are split into two (not necessarily equal) parts between the federal government and the subnational. In the second round, the subnational share is distributed among all provinces/states according to country-specific formulas.

[10] As Max Weber (1976 [1925]) noted, patrimonial state structures are ideal types, and as such can rarely be found in practice.

Patrimonial state structures can play a decisive role in shaping the capacity of subnational autocrats to resist co-optation from the central government. In subnational jurisdictions where patrimonial state structures prevail, autocrats stand in a strong position to centralize authority in order to maximize political control over their domains. Consequently, they are better positioned to close subnational territorial borders and prevent presidential control from within. Where these state structures exist, as Gibson (2005, 2013) describes, subnational autocrats can easily carry out strategies of boundary control, whereby they seek to maximize national influence over local politics and deprive provincial oppositions of access to national allies and resources.

The opposite holds true where non-patrimonial state structures exist. In such institutional settings, state structures prevent subnational autocrats from centralizing authority, and from exercising tight control over state resources, territory, and opposition parties/groups. As a result, autocrats are virtually powerless to circumvent local-national pro-democratic coalition-making, or in Gibson's (2013) words, to thwart boundary control situations. Accordingly, presidents in non-patrimonial SURs have greater ability to infiltrate these regimes. It is through coalition-building with local groups and subnational opposition leaders that presidents can penetrate SURs and, in turn, challenge and co-opt subnational autocrats from within. Hence, presidential power (from within) should be enhanced where non-patrimonial state structures prevail.

(d) *Prospects for Fiscal and Partisan Presidential Power*

Since presidential power is distributive, presidents can only obtain the acquiescence of autocrats if subnational incumbents are unable to neutralize presidential power. Accordingly, a combination of national and subnational variables needs to be present in order for presidents to wield effective power over SURs/autocrats. The clusters of variables located in the left-hand column of Figure 2.2 indicate two possible and particularly common combinations of variables that are, in theory, conducive to the maximization of effective presidential power. The clusters are made up of the already-mentioned instruments of power available to presidents and subnational autocrats' instruments of autonomy. Clusters of variables result in two different types of presidential power: *fiscal* and *partisan*.[11]

Effective fiscal presidential power materializes when the main instrument available to presidents is fiscal, i.e. when they enjoy high levels of fiscal discretion and when partisan power is low, i.e. where (a) the presidential party's

---

[11] A third type of presidential power, fiscal-partisan, is also possible. It occurs when the fiscal and partisan types are combined.

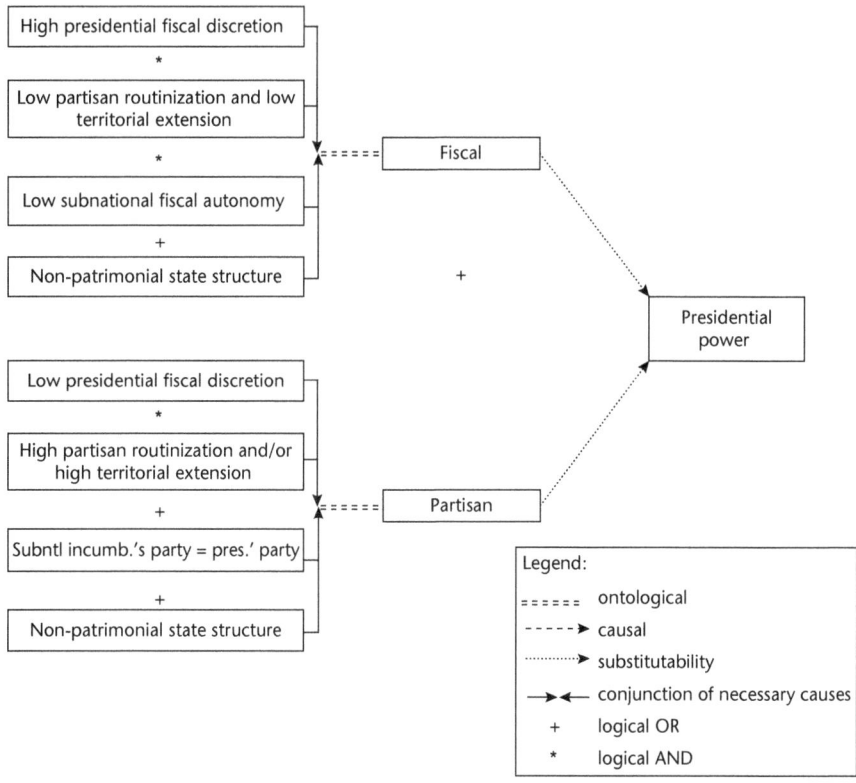

Figure 2.2. Conditions for effective fiscal and partisan presidential power

organization is weakly routinized, and (b) it is electorally viable in only one district. In this scenario, effectively inducing the cooperation of subnational autocrats is only possible when subnational rulers are fiscally dependent on the central government. If such dependence does not exist, fiscally responsible and economically sound subnational incumbents are in a position to neutralize presidential power, no matter how much fiscal discretion presidents have.[12]

Conversely, effective partisan presidential power materializes when presidents have low levels of fiscal discretion and, at the same time, (a) their party organizations, as well as the rules and procedures that regulate relations between the party leadership and lower-level branches, are highly routinized, and (b) their party has an electoral foothold in all subnational units. For this to happen, one of the following two subnational variables must be

---

[12] Presidential fiscal power can also become effective if subnational units have a non-patrimonial state structure. Despite the fact that this variable is not necessary for this type of presidential power (thus the sign "+"), such a state structure allows fiscally powerful national incumbents to funnel funds to local oppositions, thus increasing the possibilities of building national–local alliances through which they may wield power over autocrats from within.

present: (a) undemocratic incumbents' membership in the presidents' party, which enables presidents to exert direct partisan control from above, or (b) subnational autocrats' membership in an opposition party, whereby a non-patrimonial state structure must be in place—as this type of institution facilitates the subsistence of local opposition forces and subnational opposition groups, with whom the center can ally in order to pressure and challenge subnational autocrats' authority from within.

(e) *Within-Country Pathways of SUR Reproduction*

A FIRST PATHWAY OF SUR CONTINUITY: SUR REPRODUCTION FROM ABOVE

Regardless of the type of presidential power employed to discipline subnational undemocratic arenas/rulers, presidents who can wield effective power over subnational autocrats, and who can in turn induce their routine political cooperation, stand to gain much from the perpetuation of SURs in power. As a result, nationally democratic incumbents have strong incentives to invest in the continuity and stability of regimes that are likely to deliver regular political support. When this occurs, a first pathway of SUR continuity, i.e. *SUR reproduction from above*, ensues.

How can democratically elected national incumbents contribute to reproducing SURs from above? Presidents resort to a variety of formal and informal mechanisms in order to help these SURs stay in power. They can veto legislation seeking to dismiss undemocratic incumbents from office. They can also strengthen SURs by exerting pressure over members of federal agencies of control, such as Supreme Court justices or federal comptrollers, in order to deter them from sanctioning subnational autocrats for their abuses of power and financial misdoings. Another form of support from the central government occurs when presidents help subnational autocrats secure the economic resources they need to consolidate their regimes. These resources may stem from special subsidies, such as tax-incentives programs, as well as from bailouts or central bank rediscounts (see Bonvecchi and Lodola 2011). They can also come in the form of earmarked funds for housing programs, public works, conditional cash transfers, or federal government authorization for a wide range of initiatives. [13] Earmarked funds for housing and public works, as well as special permits to implement various programs, may contribute to improving public service delivery, and, in turn, may be used by subnational autocrats as an instrument to boost their popularity among the local population. Access to conditional cash transfers may also help increase SUR incumbents' capacity

---

[13] These permits could include, among others, authorization to open radio stations, build airports, or produce medicines in SUR laboratories.

to reward loyalists with handouts, and to in turn obtain the support of some voters. Presidents can also contribute to SUR reproduction by consciously choosing not to endorse opposition candidates (including candidates from the president's own party) who may eventually challenge SUR incumbents in provincial-level electoral races. Finally, autocrats and their regimes can be maintained simply due to national executive inaction and inattentiveness.

A SECOND PATHWAY TO SUR CONTINUITY: SUR SELF-REPRODUCTION

Yet, as noted earlier, not all subnational autocrats cooperate with presidents. Unlike incumbents from SURs who are disciplined by presidential power, undemocratic rulers from unruly subnational regimes may become strong challengers to presidents' authority and key opponents of presidential political decisions. The incapacity of presidents to discipline entrenched and recalcitrant subnational incumbents, and the consequent failure to obtain routine political support (or gain it at a very high premium), raises the costs for national incumbents of supporting SURs, and their rulers, in power. The lower political returns yielded by uncontrollable SURs, coupled with subnational incumbents' capacity to threaten presidential authority, gives presidents incentives to oppose these regimes.

Presidents can resort to a variety of tactics to destabilize regimes and autocrats. For instance, presidents can commission federal audits to investigate SUR incumbents' misdoings or file claims against incumbents with federal Supreme Courts. Alternatively, they can delay or suspend agreements to promote specific federal programs in a given SUR. Other presidential initiatives to challenge SURs include the transfer of funds that grant subnational incumbents little discretion to manage public money in attempts to entrench themselves in power or to buy off challengers to the regime; as well as flooding SURs with resources during electoral campaigns and elections, to threaten incumbents' prospects of winning elections.

These initiatives, while useful to discrediting subnational undemocratic incumbents and undermining the foundations of their regimes, may be necessary but not sufficient to destabilize SURs and their autocrats' power. Indeed, presidential strategies to oppose SURs can be neutralized if subnational autocrats rely on a sturdy coalition of support. In particular two variables endogenous to SURs, i.e. party elite cohesion and mass support, are critical to maintaining a sturdy and durable ruling coalition, and thus central to ensuring the regime's long-term survival.[14]

---

[14] The next paragraphs draw heavily on the literature on varieties of national-level nondemocratic regimes. Illustrative works of this line of research include among others, Way 2005; Lazarev 2005; Magaloni 2006; Levitsky and Way 2010; Brownlee 2007; Magaloni and Kricheli 2010; Slater 2010; and Falleti 2011.

Autocrats, as Brownlee (2007) observes, do not rule completely alone—they depend on coalitions of party elites for their stability. Ambitious and disgruntled party elites who no longer see the benefits of siding with the regime, and who, as a result, defect from the ruling party, can become one of the main sources of regime breakdown, especially if they are driven into the opposition's ranks. Maintaining the unity of party elites is thus critical to keeping SURs in power, even more so when subnational incumbents are embattled with presidential policies aimed at undermining their power.

The possibility for party elite defection is especially high in SURs because these regimes exist within a context of national democratic politics. The existence of a national democratic political system with alternative and viable national political parties increases the chances of subnational party elite desertion, as party detractors can build and advance their political careers at the national level (Benton 2011). Moreover, by joining national parties, potential party elite defectors may be able to side with national advocates of subnational democratization, or obtain access to national political and economic resources in the country's capital through which they can maneuver to topple SURs from above (Gibson 2005, 2013).

How can party elites remain loyal to subnational autocrats? How can party elite defection be prevented? Cohesive political parties, as noted by the literature on national-level autocracy and competitive authoritarianism, constitute one of the main institutions through which party elite unity can be maintained (Levitsky and Way 2010). Cohesive political parties regulate elite conflict by generating collective benefits for the coalition's members and by reducing individual insecurity and assuaging fears of prolonged disadvantage (Brownlee 2007). Formal and informal rules of appointments and promotions within (provincial) ruling parties, for instance, allow incumbents to make credible intertemporal power-sharing deals with potential elite detractors (Magaloni 2006; Magaloni and Kricheli 2010). As Magaloni and Kricheli (2010: 127) put it, party elites "will support the regime rather than seek to conspire against it only if, in exchange, they can expect to be promoted into rent-paying" or ruling positions. When they do not expect such credible power sharing, party elites split and instability becomes more likely (Magaloni 2006). Where, by contrast, ruling parties are not cohesive, party elites see fewer guaranteed opportunities for political advancement from within and are thus more likely to seek power from outside the regime (Levitsky and Way 2010). "Such party elite defection," Levitsky and Way (2010: 62) note, "is often a major cause for regime breakdown."

Likewise, to stay in power, subnational autocrats, like their national counterparts, need to win elections as well as avoid instability and social unrest between electoral races (Magaloni 2006). They therefore need to build mass support to obtain the acquiescence of the electorate both during and between elections (Magaloni 2006; Magaloni and Kricheli 2010; Levitsky and Way 2010). To elicit political support from the masses, subnational autocrats must implement policies and programs that are popular among voters. Unlike undemocratic presidents who usually entice the electorate's support by implementing economic programs that are popular with the masses (Magaloni 2006), SUR incumbents, who have virtually no control over macroeconomic policy (Wibbels 2005; Falleti 2010), appeal to voters by delivering provincial public goods—such as public works, social programs, housing subsidies, scholarships, tax deductions, and other similar goods. It does not matter whether SUR incumbents distribute public goods programmatically among the local population or whether they dispense clientelistic handouts. What is relevant is that incumbents in SURs are forced to deliver goods so as to give citizens a vested interest in the perpetuation of the regime (Magaloni 2006; Geddes 2006, 2008).

Where subnational incumbents are able to either ensure party elite unity (which results from maintaining party cohesion) or deliver (programmatically or clientelistically) public goods to obtain mass political support—or to do both—*SUR self-reproduction* should take place. Given that this regime trajectory occurs in the presence of presidential strategies to oppose and weaken SURs, maintenance of party elite unity and mass support is essential to counterbalance potential exogenous (national) destabilizing forces.

Synthesis of the Argument

The core premise of this study is that the capacity (or lack thereof) of national incumbents to wield (fiscal/partisan) power over SURs and autocrats in order to obtain their political cooperation explains alternative trajectories of SUR continuity within nationally democratic countries. The book puts forward a two-step argument. The first step centers on the capacity of presidents to exert power over autocrats and to induce their acquiescence. Effective presidential power is likely where province-specific variables are present. If presidents are fiscally strong, they can wield effective authority over SURs/autocrats whose economies are highly dependent on the national government. Likewise, if national incumbents maintain territorially extended and highly institutionalized partisan structures, they can infiltrate SURs and wield power over autocrats either directly from above or from within to obtain their political cooperation. For this type of presidential power to be possible, one of the following two variables must be present: subnational autocrats must belong to the president's party, and thus be subject to direct presidential partisan control from above; or, if autocrats belong to an opposition party, a non-patrimonial state structure must be in place—as these institutions facilitate the subsistence of local opposition forces and subnational opposition groups, with whom the center can ally in order to infiltrate SURs to challenge and control subnational autocrats from within.

The second step of the argument focuses on the consequences for regime continuity that derive from the capacity (or lack thereof) of presidents to exert power over SURs and autocrats. When presidents have the resources to induce cooperation from subnational autocrats and thus secure credible and routine political support, the former have strong incentives to invest in the continuity and stability of undemocratic provincial regimes and autocrats. Under these circumstances, SUR reproduction from above, the first pathway of SUR continuity, takes place. Conversely, where democratic presidents fail to exert effective power and are prevented from disciplining subnational undemocratic rulers via fiscal or partisan means, they will implement policies to oppose and weaken SURs and their rulers. Presidential opposition to SURs and autocrats, which in part takes place as a result of presidents' aversion to supporting autocrats who could eventually pose a serious challenge to a president's political, legislative, and economic ambitions, does not necessarily lead to SUR breakdown. Endogenous variables, such as subnational autocrats' capacity to ensure party elite unity and mass political support, not only determine autocrats' ability to counterbalance presidential attempts at destabilizing SURs, but also the resources at their disposal to maintain the status quo and keep their regimes alive. Where this occurs, SUR self-reproduction, a second pathway of SUR continuity, should take place.

The remainder of this book is devoted to testing the argument advanced in this chapter. Before evaluating its validity, the universe of SURs to which the explanation will be applied needs to be defined. To this end, the next chapter conceptualizes, operationalizes, and measures SURs in contemporary Argentina and Mexico.

3

Conceptualizing, Measuring, and Mapping Subnational Undemocratic Regimes

As noted in Chapter 2, there is a considerably large body of literature devoted to the study and analysis of subnational undemocratic regimes (SURs) in democratic countries.[1] The proliferation of works on SURs, however, contrasts sharply with the scarce attention devoted to issues of conceptualization, operationalization, and measurement of SURs.[2] Most works on subnational undemocratic regimes do not offer, for example, clear conceptual definitions of these regimes' dimensions, subdimensions, indicators, and their aggregation. Moreover, these works rarely provide rules for coding democratic versus undemocratic subnational units, and only some of them measure the degree of democracy across *all* subnational units *over time* in a given country. Complicating things further, analysts of SURs use a variety of conceptual forms, such as hybrid, authoritarian, neopatrimonial, or "closed-game" to refer to subnational political regimes that are not democratic. Each of these labels, in turn, is generally employed to denote a different set of empirical cases, thus adding to conceptual confusion.

A second problem of existing works on SURs is that they assume unit homogeneity across the subnational regimes that do not qualify as democratic. As noted in the preceding chapters, much writing on SURs has treated these polities as identical, especially with regard to the interactions and relations they maintain with national rulers or national institutions. However, while sharing important political characteristics, such as low levels of democracy, these subnational regimes vary considerably from one another. For instance,

---

[1] See Fox 1994; O'Donnell 1999; Cornelius 1999; Snyder 1999; Eisenstadt 1999; Solt 2003; Gibson 2005, 2013; Petrov 2005; Lankina and Getachew 2006; McMann 2006; Montero 2007, 2010a; Giraudy 2010, 2013; Gervasoni 2010a, 2010b, 2011; Durazo-Herrmann 2010; Behrend 2011; Rebolledo 2011; Benton 2012; Mickey 2013; among others.

[2] Exceptions are Solt 2003; McMann 2006; Gervasoni 2010b, 2010a; Saikkonen 2011; Rebolledo 2011.

subnational regimes can be differentiated by the power bases of incumbents within states as well as rulers' distinct styles of leadership (Snyder 1999), and, as this chapter shows, they can also be distinguished by their state structure and level of fiscal autonomy vis-à-vis the central government.

The goal of this chapter is to address these two deficits in studies of regime juxtaposition. To do so, the chapter advances a characterization and operationalization of subnational political regimes, and measures the level of democracy in Argentine and Mexican provinces across time and space in all of the countries' subnational units. In doing so, the chapter "maps the terrain" of SURs, conceptualizes these regimes more clearly, and provides a systematic measurement and quantitative assessment of subnational political regimes in two of Latin America's biggest countries. The conceptual and operational definitions of SURs, as well as their measurement and results, are presented in the first part of this chapter. The data reported and analyzed in this section also help to rule out the explanatory power of alternative theories of SUR continuity. Specifically, the data challenge the validity of theories that argue that SUR continuity is determined by geographic location, cultural heritage, and levels of socioeconomic development. The second part of this chapter is devoted to uncovering and systematizing SUR variation. The chapter distinguishes between regimes that have or lack patrimonial state structures, and those that have or lack a fiscally autonomous relationship with the national government. In so doing, the chapter provides a systematic empirical analysis of SUR variation in all Argentine provinces and Mexican states, making a substantial empirical contribution through the generation of new longitudinal, cross-provincial data on varieties of subnational political regimes.

SUR Conceptualization and Measurement

What are Subnational Undemocratic Regimes?

SURs are civilian electoral regimes that are neither fully authoritarian nor fully democratic. The subnational regimes analyzed in this book coexist alongside a national democratic regime. Because they are embedded in a national democracy, they are not, and neither can they become, blatant subnational authoritarian regimes. The following aspects of the national democratic regime prevent subnational incumbents from ruling in a fully authoritarian manner. SURs in democratic countries hold regular, multiparty elections, and, unlike subnational authoritarian regimes, opposition groups and parties are not legally barred from contesting elections. Parties exist and are often affiliated with or constitute the provincial branches of national parties that are competitive at the national level. The existence of constitutional federal penalties for violations of provincial democratic procedures—such as the prerogative of federal intervention that can result in incumbents' dismissal, as well as the wide acceptance of democratic rules at the national level of government—operate as powerful deterrents for provincial incumbents' open violations of democratic procedures (Gervasoni 2010a; Gibson 2013). In addition, long-established democratic practices at the national level, such as the existence of a free national media, can discourage subnational autocrats from ruling in a fully authoritarian manner. For instance, as Gervasoni (2010a) asserts, the possibility that the national free media could expose nondemocratic governors and threaten their prospects for advancing careers in national politics, discourages subnational undemocratic rulers from violating basic political and civic rights of opponents, from unconstitutionally closing provincial legislatures, or from suspending or banning provincial (or municipal) elections.

Unlike subnational electoral authoritarian regimes, where electoral results are certain, elections in SURs can be, at times, uncertain. The links that subnational opposition parties maintain with their respective national party inevitably increases the uncertainty of subnational elections. Local oppositions often resort to the national party branch in order to boost their electoral clout. It is, for instance, the access to material resources or to the national media that allows subnational opposition parties to increase their chances of winning office. Hence, unlike fully subnational authoritarian regimes, in SURs incumbents' fear of electoral defeat can be real and justified. In sum, SURs differ from fully subnational authoritarian regimes because in the former elections are regular, sometimes competitive, and uncertain; regime adversaries' political and civic rights are minimally protected; and parties are allowed to compete seriously in free multiparty elections.

What distinguishes SURs from subnational democracies is the fact that the actual opposition's capacity to defeat incumbents (and/or their parties) in elections is significantly handicapped. In SURs, regime challengers effectively compete in elections but incumbents win by employing a variety of undemocratic and illegal tactics. In many SURs, rulers lose the vote but resort to fraudulent tactics to win the counting procedure, thus preventing the opposition from assuming office. Likewise, control over various electoral commissions, most of which are packed with loyalists who act subserviently, helps SUR incumbents secure electoral victories by settling electoral and post-electoral conflicts in ways that favor incumbents (Ley 2009; Rebolledo 2011). Similarly, in most SURs, the mass media are not free. By contrast, they are linked to the governing party, either because incumbents own newspapers, radio, and/or TV stations, or because the media are bought off through generous advertising contracts signed with incumbents to bias coverage in favor of the ruling party (McMann 2006; Giraudy 2009; Gervasoni 2011; Behrend 2011). Periodic electoral and institutional engineering, which may include alteration of electoral rules, gerrymandering, and reforms to the provincial constitutions, enables SUR incumbents to restrict the entrance of competitors into the electoral race or underrepresent them in legislative bodies (Calvo and Micozzi 2005; Gibson 2005, 2013). Co-optation via economic means and intimidation are also common tactics used by SUR incumbents to limit and control the electoral participation of opposition parties and dissidents. In sum, it is through the use of these tactics that subnational autocrats manage to turn opponents into weak competitors, and by so doing prevent them from defeating incumbents and, consequently, from accessing governing positions and/or controlling majorities in legislative bodies. This distinctive feature of SURs places them at the polar opposite end of subnational democracies, which paraphrasing Przeworski (1991: 10) are "system[s] in which parties lose in multiparty elections."

To recapitulate, the regimes analyzed in this book are neither authoritarian nor democratic. SURs are civilian, electoral regimes that protect basic political and civic rights—which is why they are not encompassed by the concept "authoritarianism." However, through a variety of undemocratic, illegal, and informal actions, incumbents systematically prevent the opposition from gaining access to state positions—hence they cannot be regarded as democratic.

Subnational Undemocratic Regimes vs. Subnational Hybrid Regimes

Several authors of subnational regimes have employed the concept of "hybrid regimes" to denote subnational political regimes that are neither democratic nor fully authoritarian (McMann 2006; Gervasoni 2010b; Behrend 2011). As noted elsewhere (Giraudy 2013), the concept of a hybrid regime implicitly rests on an expanded definition of democracy, which combines attributes that denote both the access to public office and the exercise of political power (Mazzuca 2010).[3] Subnational regimes that fail to meet one, many, or all attributes comprised by either the access and/or exercise dimensions are regarded as hybrid. As a result, the term "hybrid" has been used to denote cases in which individuals lack freedom to form and join organizations (as McMann (2006) finds in Russia and Kyrgyzstan), in which local incumbents control business opportunities, the local judiciary, and clientelistic networks

---

[3] According to Mazzuca (2007, 2010), access to political power involves the efforts of groups in society to gain control over state positions. In a democracy, actors access power through clean, fully contested, and regular elections. Exercise of state power, by contrast, refers to the patterns followed by rulers in the management of the resources under their control (Mazzuca 2007). State power can be exercised with or without adherence to the rule of law and established procedures, with or without universalistic criteria, with or without corruption, with or without abusing political authority.

Conceptualizing, Measuring, and Mapping

(as Behrend (2011) finds in Argentina and Durazo-Herrmann (2010) finds in Mexico), or in which incumbents control national legislators, labor unions, business organizations, and NGOs (as noted by Gervasoni (2010a) in Argentina).

One of the main problems with the concept of hybrid regimes is that, even though this term reveals that regimes are not authoritarian, it cannot tell us what specific aspect of the access or the exercise dimensions they are missing. In other words, it is hard to say if the subnational regime is hybrid because it prevents individuals from forming and joining organizations or because its rulers control the local judiciary and distribute clientelistic handouts. As a result of this conceptual stretching, scholars have difficulty agreeing on the specific domain of empirical cases that are encompassed by this term. A hybrid regime, as described by Sartori (1970), becomes applicable to a variety of very different empirical cases, and is stretched beyond recognition.

The term subnational *undemocratic* regimes employed in this book, instead, delimits (and denotes) cases that only fare poorly on the access to office dimension. Specifically, these are cases where actors cannot access office because elections are *not* free, competitive, or clean. The term SUR, which focuses on elections exclusively, denotes that the underlying notion of democracy employed in this book is the electoral (procedural, minimal, or Schumpeterian) (Collier and Levitsky 1997; Diamond et al. 1999; Mainwaring et al. 2007; Munck 2004, 2009; Munck and Verkuilen 2002).

To sum up, the cases in this book referred to as SURs are neither democratic nor authoritarian, and they are considered as undemocratic for their deficit with regard to the access/electoral dimension. Unlike hybrid regimes, however, which denote cases that fail to meet a wide variety of access and exercise attributes, SURs only fail to meet one or more of the attributes of electoral democracy, including regular, free, competitive, and clean elections.

Measurement and Operationalization of Subnational (Electoral) Democracy

Before operationalizing subnational democracy, a word is in order about the approach adopted to measuring democracy in this book. Scholars who study and measure political regimes can be divided in two camps: those who take a dichotomous view of regimes versus those who view political regimes in terms of gradations (see Collier and Adcock 1999). The first camp treats regimes as democracies or non-democracies (Sartori 1987; Linz 1975; Huntington 1991; Przeworski et al. 1996; Geddes 1999); the second group, by contrast, views regimes in terms of levels or degrees of democracy (Dahl 1971; Bollen and Lennox 1991; Coppedge and Reinicke 1991; Vanhanen 2000; Gervasoni 2010b). Given that the findings of research are influenced by the conception of political regimes as dichotomous or in terms of gradations, it is important to explicitly note which approach is taken to measuring political regimes.

This book follows Giovanni Sartori's recommended two-step procedure to measure electoral democracy. As Collier and Adcock write:

> Sartori argues that regimes must first be classified as democracies or nondemocracies. Then, only as a second step, a further set of criteria can be applied to those regimes deemed democratic by the initial dichotomy. Only with regard to these cases should scholars inquire as to how democratic they are (1987: 182–83). Sartori asserts that "unless the two problems are treated in this order, the oxen may well wreck the cart rather than pull it (1987: 156)." (1999: 548)

As already noted, subnational political regimes that are embedded in a national democratic system cannot be regarded as authoritarian (or non-democracies), as they meet most of the minimal criteria of democratic regimes, such as regular, competitive, and multiparty elections, basic protection of civic rights, and universal suffrage. Consequently, the cases that this book seeks to study have, by definition, passed the first rule of Sartori's two-step procedure. By treating democracy as a continuous variable—that is, by endorsing Sartori's second rule—this book follows a well-established tradition that advocates for measuring democracy in terms of degrees or levels (Dahl 1971; Bollen and Lennox 1991; Coppedge and Reinicke 1991; Vanhanen 2000; Gervasoni 2010b). In practical terms, this means that subnational jurisdictions that obtain the lowest scores on the subnational electoral democracy scale must be regarded as SURs.

In this book, subnational electoral democracy is conceived in the tradition of Przeworski et al. (1996). Their definition of democracy requires the selection of the chief executive and the legislature through contested elections, the presence of more than one political party, and the actual rotation of the incumbents out of office after a reasonable interval.[4] This definition of electoral democracy, however, is silent with respect to the quality of the electoral process. Consequently, Przeworski et al.'s definition is specified in the following terms: "democracy is a political regime in which those who govern are selected through contested and *clean* elections exclusively, and lose office." In sum, as outlined in Figure 3.1, subnational electoral democracy is conceived of as having three essential and constitutive dimensions: (a) fully contested elections (for both legislative and executive posts), (b) clean elections, and (c) alternation (turnover) in office.[5]

---

[4] It should be stressed that Przeworski et al. (1996) endorse a dichotomous approach to measuring electoral democracy. Again, because this book focuses on subnational electoral democracy in nationally democratic systems, there are good reasons to measure subnational democracy in terms of levels.

[5] The Appendix provides a discussion and justification of the turnover dimension as a defining trait of democracy. It also describes the individual indicators used to measure each of

Conceptualizing, Measuring, and Mapping

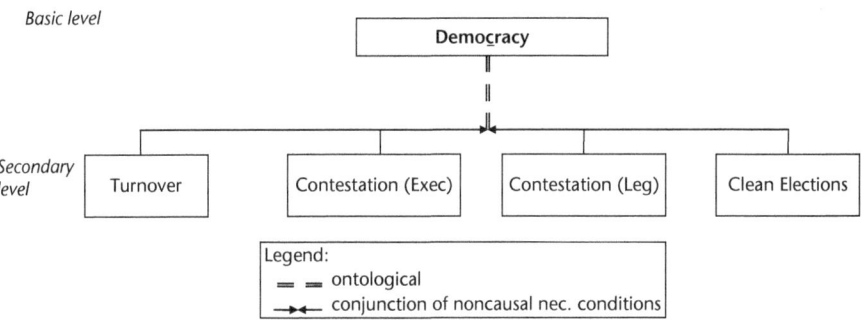

Figure 3.1. Dimensions of subnational democracy

Results and Discussion

The dataset used to measure subnational democracy encompasses 24 provinces in Argentina and 32 states in Mexico. Databases span the 1983–2009 period in Argentina and the 1997–2009 period in Mexico. Time intervals in each country start with the most recent transition to democracy at the national level, as these transitions paved the way for "regime juxtaposition" (Gibson 2005). The onset of democratization in Argentina is set in 1983, when military rule was replaced by a democratically elected civilian government. In Mexico, it is set in 1997 since, according to prominent Mexican scholars, this year marked the onset of democratization in the country at the federal level (see e.g. Magaloni 2005). In 1997, the Institutional Revolutionary Party (PRI) lost its majority in the lower chamber of Congress, and consequently its hegemony in the legislative arena. Time intervals in each country end in 2009, when mid-term national elections were held.

As noted, one of the goals of this chapter is to map the terrain of SURs in order to make a systematic assessment of where these regimes exist and for how long. Figures 3.2 and 3.3 reveal the wide variance in the levels of subnational democracy in Argentina and Mexico, and more importantly show that, consistent with findings obtained in previous small-N case studies, many provinces in Argentina and a high number of states in Mexico show a sustained democratic deficit, even after national democratization. SURs exist in provinces and states that obtained scores close to zero for more than 12 consecutive years or three consecutive terms. As will be discussed in detail, many of those cases remained undemocratic until 2009.

---

dimension of subnational democracy, their aggregation procedure, and provides detailed information about the sources for each individual indicator.

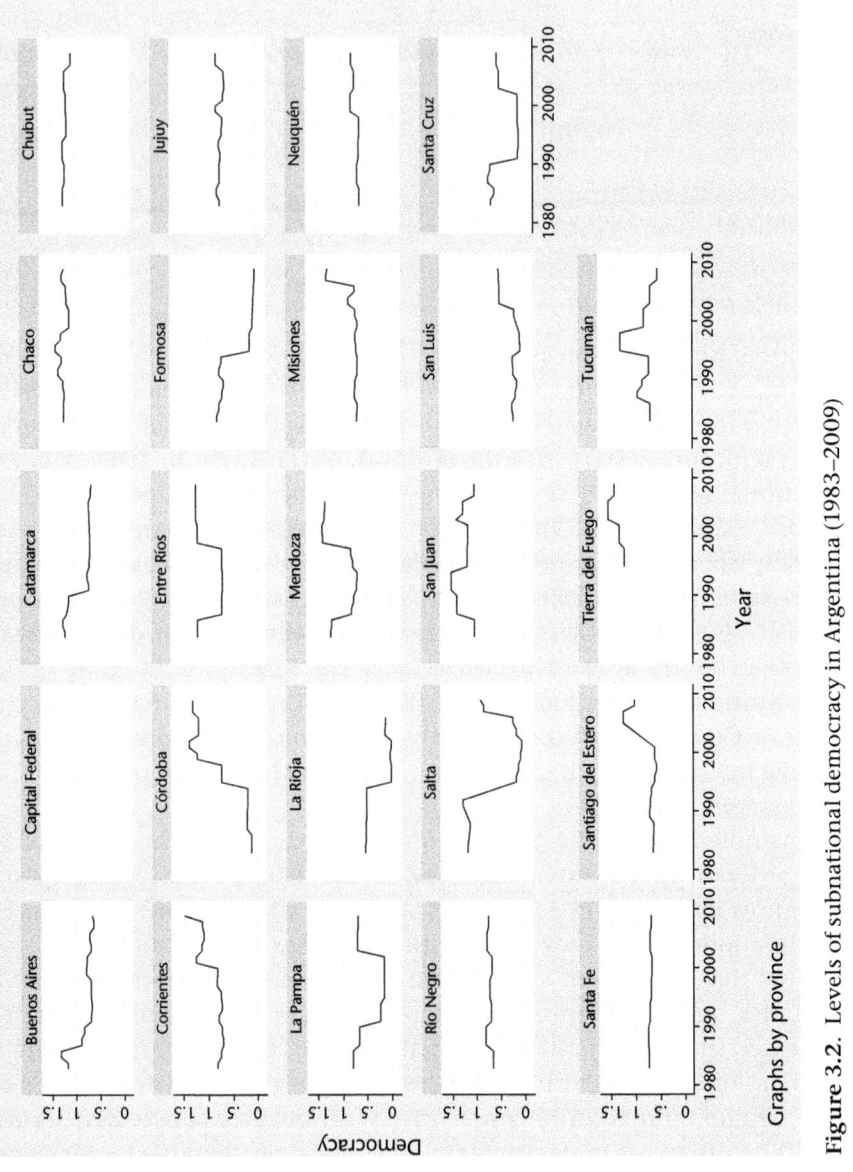

Figure 3.2. Levels of subnational democracy in Argentina (1983–2009)

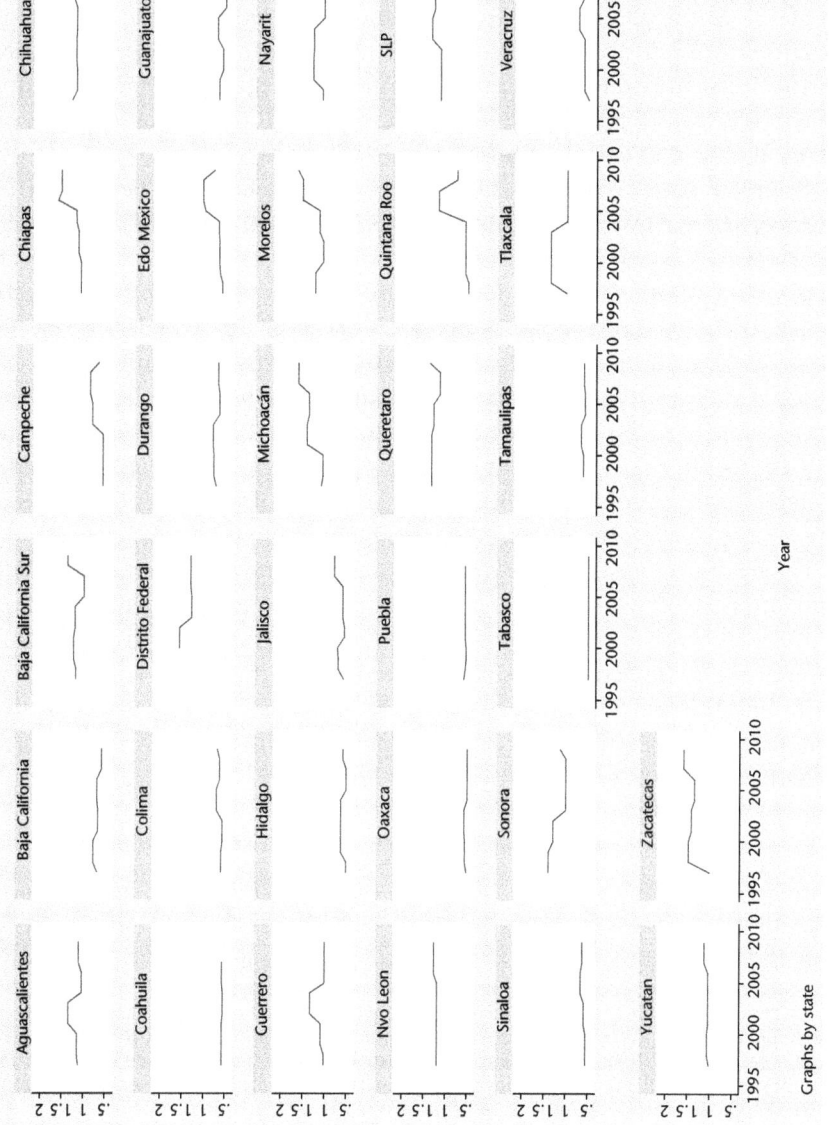

Figure 3.3. Levels of subnational democracy in Mexico (1997–2009)

In both Figures 3.2 and 3.3 higher values indicate higher levels of subnational democracy. Zero and near-zero scores denote subnational undemocratic regimes (SURs).

As Figure 3.2 shows, at least five out of 24 provinces (20.83 percent)—i.e. La Rioja, San Luis, Santa Cruz, Formosa, and La Pampa—can be considered as SURs.[6] Autocrats in these provinces have resorted to a variety of tactics, ranging from redistricting to constitutional reform, reengineering electoral institutions, and exerting systematic control over legislative bodies, in efforts to win elections by large margins of victory. In all these provinces, incumbents managed to curtail opposition parties' access to office.

A similar pattern of subnational democratic deficit can be observed in Mexico, where at least 15 out of 32 states (46.87 percent) remained undemocratic after national democratization. In the states of Baja California, Campeche, Coahuila, Colima, Durango, Guanajuato, Jalisco,[7] Hidalgo, Oaxaca, Puebla, Sinaloa, Tabasco, Tamaulipas, Veracruz, and Yucatán, levels of democracy have been very low for more than two uninterrupted terms (see Figure 3.3). In each of these states, while alternation of incumbents has been possible, due to a no-reelection clause, incumbent parties have stayed in power for more than two consecutive terms—always exerting tight control over legislative bodies, systematically winning elections by large margins of victory, and/or by resorting to post-election fraud to prevent opponents from taking office.

The evidence presented in Figures 3.2 and 3.3 reveals interesting within- and cross-country differences. First, whereas in Argentina there seems to be a discernible relationship between SURs and partisanship, this association disappears in Mexico. Argentine SURs in La Rioja, San Luis, Formosa, Santa Cruz, and La Pampa have been ruled by the Peronist party (or PJ) since 1983.[8] The partisan pattern observed in the Mexican SURs, however, is different, as SURs have been governed by the PRI and the PAN. Specifically, PRI-ruled

---

[6] Santiago del Estero, the stronghold of Peronist caudillo Carlos Juárez, has been usually regarded as a SUR. It is not enumerated in this list because, in 2004, there was an intervention there by President Néstor Kirchner. Elections were held in 2005, and since then the province has been governed by the Radical Party (UCR). It is still too soon to assess whether Santiago del Estero will become undemocratic again. The reason why Salta and Córdoba are not regarded as SURs despite obtaining scores that are close to zero is because their governors did not stay in power for more than 12 consecutive years or three consecutive terms.

[7] Regime coding for this study starts in 1997, when Mexico experienced the first signs of transition to democracy. Hence, cases such as Guanajuato and Jalisco, where the PRI was ousted from office before 1997, but which has remained ruled by the same party since 1997, have, technically speaking, not experienced alternation. Apart from technicalities, the National Action Party (PAN), the newly incumbent party has governed with a hegemonic-like style, and has resorted to informal practices to undermine the power of opposition parties.

[8] Highly democratic provinces, such as Entre Ríos, Mendoza, Chubut, have also been ruled by the PJ for many consecutive years. Similarly, provinces that score low on the democratic scale, i.e. in-between SURs and highly democratic provinces, such as Río Negro or Neuquén, have been ruled by non-PJ parties, such as the UCR and the Popular Movement of Neuquén (or MPN), respectively. These data indicate that, excluding SURs, there is not a clear correlation between levels of subnational democracy and partisanship.

SURs such as Oaxaca, Veracruz, Puebla, and Tabasco have coexisted with PAN-ruled SURs in Jalisco and Guanajuato. It should be stressed, however, that in PRI-ruled states, the incumbent party has been in office for more than 80 years, whereas in PAN-governed states, the incumbent party has controlled the governorship and the legislature for no more than 16 consecutive years.[9] Despite these differences, the findings of this chapter reveal an interesting regime pattern of subnational politics in Mexico: the dominance of hegemonic party rule. The hegemony held by the PRI in all Mexican states until 1989 has given way to the dominance of the PAN. Still, despite the existence of PAN undemocratic states, the PRI has the largest number of SURs.

Second, the results indicate that SURs can be found in diverse geographic areas, thus casting doubt on extant assertions about the relationship between SURs and geographic location. Previous scholarship has found a positive correlation between low levels of democracy and provinces located in north-central Argentina (Sawers 1996), and states in the southern regions of Mexico (Cornelius 1999; Ward and Rodríguez 1995). The results presented in Figures 3.2 and 3.3 indicate that these correlations are unwarranted and misleading, as SURs abound in different locations of Argentina and Mexico. Argentine SURs exist in the northeastern part of the country (La Rioja), in the southern Patagonian region (La Pampa and Santa Cruz), in the northwest (Formosa), and in the central part of the country (San Luis). Likewise, Mexican SURs are found in the center-western part of Mexico (Jalisco), in the southern states (Oaxaca and Puebla), on the US–Mexican border (Baja California), and on the Gulf coast (Veracruz).

The fact that SURs in both countries are located in multiple geographic locations—which differ in terms of their culture, religion, colonial heritage, local traditions, ethnicity, and thus with regard to mass attitudes and values—reveals that (local) cultural, religious, anthropological, and ethnographic explanations factors are not decisive determinants of subnational democracy. This finding is especially relevant in light of recent works analyzing subnational democracy in India that found a statistically significant effect of geographically different colonial legacies—religious influences, specifically—on levels of democracy (Lankina and Getachew 2012). The results of this chapter are also significant because they contrast sharply with the trend observed in other regions of the world, such as Russia, where geographic location acts as a decisive determinant for subnational democracy (Lankina and Getachew 2006). Specifically, proximity to Europe facilitates the diffusion of Western influences in Russia's localities and increases their political openness. In addition, these findings are important because they contradict the results of national-level theories of democracy that have associated national democracy with a specific set of values (i.e. self-expression values) (Inglehart

---

[9] Coding of post-electoral conflicts conducted for this study also reveals that elections have not been clean in Jalisco.

and Welzel 2005) or mass attitudes (Diamond et al. 1999) that are determined by cultural, traditional, religious, and ethnic factors.

Third, the existence of SURs in Argentina and Mexico is not necessarily related to levels of economic development. Provinces with medium-high levels of economic development, such as Santa Cruz and San Luis in Argentina, and Jalisco and Guanajuato in Mexico, are as undemocratic as the least economically developed Argentine provinces of La Rioja and Formosa, and the Mexican states of Oaxaca and Puebla. This finding, which is consistent with results advanced in other studies of subnational democracy (Gervasoni 2010b; McMann 2006), indicates that the association between democracy and economic development is not linear, thus undermining the explanatory power of a widely accepted theory of national democracy (such as modernization theory) to account for SUR continuity. This finding further buttresses Gibson's contention that "the study of subnational democratization should not be seen as a theoretical derivative of national democratization, wherein the main challenge lies in identifying which theories developed for the study of countries can be transferred to the study of provinces" (2013: 9).

One undisputable conclusion that can be drawn from the results presented in this chapter is that SURs in Argentina and Mexico differ considerably from one another, especially regarding their geographic location, levels of socioeconomic development, and party ideology. These results strongly suggest that these regimes should not be seen as a set of homogeneous political regimes. Treating them as homogeneous units could potentially lead to invalid theoretical assumptions about how these regimes originate, how they operate, and how they manage to endure and change. Specifically, the assumption of SUR homogeneity increases the risk of obscuring the existence of different causal mechanisms that may account for SUR origins, functioning, continuity, and even change. In contrast, by acknowledging regime variation, scholars can gain more analytic leverage on the causal mechanisms that explain regime origins, continuity, and change within and across SUR types. The next section explores regime variation along two specific variables, i.e. SURs' fiscal autonomy vis-à-vis the central government and SURs' state structures, as they have the potential to shed important light on the functioning and continuity of these subnational regimes.

Varieties of Subnational Undemocratic Regimes

The discussion advanced so far reveals that, despite the existence of SUR differences, partisan, economic, geographic, cultural, and ethnic dissimilarities cannot account for the continued existence of undemocratic subnational regimes in Argentina and Mexico. Indeed, as the evidence presented in Figures 3.2 and 3.3 indicates, both democratic and undemocratic regimes are spread throughout various regions of Argentina and Mexico, where economic, partisan, cultural, and ethnic differences exist. As noted in Chapter 2, however, other cross-SUR differences, such as the type of provincial state structure or levels of fiscal autonomy from the federal government, shape the opportunities presidents have to co-opt and subjugate subnational autocrats, and in turn uncover the existence of different causal mechanisms that account for various trajectories of SUR continuity within democratic countries. The remainder of this chapter seeks to empirically demonstrate these differences across SURs in Argentina and Mexico.

SURs' Institutional Variation: Patrimonial vs. Non-Patrimonial SURs

Provincial states vary dramatically in their internal organization and relations to society. Different kinds of state structures establish the rules and procedures through which incumbents exercise power (Evans 1994; Ertman 1997; Hartlyn 1998; Mazzuca 2007, 2010), thus creating different capacities for rulers' action. These differences, in turn, have been decisive in shaping a wide variety of outcomes, ranging from policy-making implementation (Snyder 2001a; Falleti 2011), to promotion of economic and industrial growth (Evans 1994), and even to the sustainability of political regimes (Hartlyn 1998).

A well-established tradition within political science has distinguished between state structures that (a) centralize power in the hands of the ruler, blur public and private interests and purposes within the state administration, reduce the autonomy of followers by generating ties of loyalty and dependence, and appropriate state resources for private economic or political gain, on one hand, and state structures that (b) limit incumbents' power, establish and allow for a clear distinction between the private and public domains, confer autonomy on societal groups, and minimize rulers' appropriation of state resources, on the other (Ertman 1997; Hartlyn 1998; Evans 1994; Migdal 1992, 1994; Bates 1981, 2008; Mazzuca 2007, 2010). Whilst receiving different conceptual labels, these state structures can be subsumed into two generic terms, patrimonial vs. non-patrimonial.[10]

As noted in the previous chapter, patrimonial state structures can play a decisive role in shaping the capacity of subnational autocrats to resist co-optation from the central government.[11] In subnational jurisdictions where patrimonial state structures prevail, autocrats stand in a strong position to centralize

---

[10] As Max Weber (1976 [1925]) noted, patrimonial state structures are ideal types, and as such can rarely be found in practice, and thus may not apply in all particular cases.

[11] They also play a central role in policy-making design and implementation (Snyder 2001a; Niedzwiecki 2012).

authority and thus maximize political control over their domains. For instance, by easily appropriating state resources and distributing them according to particularistic criteria, they can reduce the autonomy of followers and prevent the emergence of powerful opposition forces, which might eventually challenge autocrats' power. Consequently, subnational rulers acting within these institutional settings are better positioned to close subnational territorial borders both for the purpose of hindering local actors from striking alliances with national incumbents, as well as for preventing national elites from trespassing provincial/state-level borders in attempts to control local populations. Where these state structures exist, as Gibson (2005, 2013) states, subnational undemocratic incumbents can easily carry out strategies of boundary control, whereby they seek to maximize influence over local politics and deprive provincial oppositions of access to national allies and resources, both of which are theorized as triggers of subnational democratization (Gibson 2005, 2013).

The opposite holds true where non-patrimonial state structures exist. In such institutional settings, subnational autocrats are prevented from centralizing authority, and from exercising tight control over state resources, territory, and opposition parties/groups, thus becoming virtually powerless to avoid local–national pro-democratic coalition-making. Accordingly, presidents in non-patrimonial SURs have greater capacity to infiltrate these regimes. It is through coalition-building with local groups and subnational opposition leaders that presidents can penetrate SURs and, in turn, challenge and co-opt subnational autocrats from within.

As already noted, patrimonial state structures tap into three dimensions: (a) centralization of power in the hands of the ruler, (b) reduction of followers' autonomy through the generation of ties of loyalty and dependence, and (c) appropriation of state resources for private economic or political gain (Ertman 1997; Hartlyn 1998; Evans 1994; Migdal 1992, 1994; Bates 1981; 2008; Mazzuca 2007, 2010). Figure 3.4 systematizes these dimensions.[12] Data used to measure patrimonial state structures cover 21 provinces in Argentina and 31 states in Mexico.[13] Databases span the periods 1983–2009 in Argentina, and 1997–2009 in Mexico.

As Figures 3.5 and 3.6 show, there is considerable variation in terms of state structures across Argentine and Mexican SURs. The state structures found in the Argentine undemocratic provinces of La Rioja and Formosa can be clearly distinguished from the ones existing in the undemocratic districts of Santa

---

[12] Appendix (section II) discusses indicators of patrimonialism and aggregation procedures.
[13] City of Buenos Aires and Mexico City are excluded because, unlike the other provinces/states, they do not possess lower levels of government (aka municipalities). Due to the absence of this second-tier level of government, the secondary-level dimension, "(subnational) rulers' fiscal discretion," is not computed, thus preventing comparability with other districts.

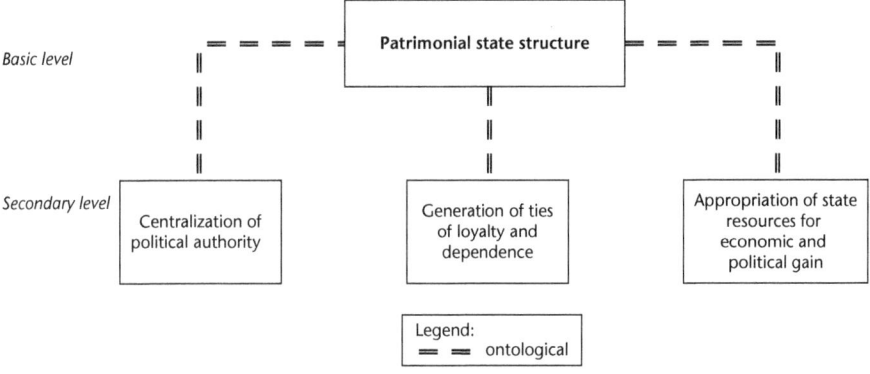

Figure 3.4. Dimensions of patrimonial state structures

Cruz, San Luis, and La Pampa. In the former provinces, the concentration of authority in the hands of autocrats, the reduction of followers' autonomy through the generation of ties of loyalty and dependence, and the appropriation of state resources for private economic or political gain are much more pronounced than in the latter districts.

A similar pattern of SUR variation can be observed in Mexico where the state structures found in the undemocratic states of Oaxaca, Hidalgo, Tamaulipas, Sinaloa, and Coahuila contrast sharply with the ones present in the undemocratic states of Puebla and Tabasco. In Mexico as well as in Argentina, the rules and procedures through which subnational autocrats exercise power differ considerably, thus creating different capacities for action by rulers.

In addition to showing institutional variation across SURs, the evidence presented in Figures 3.5 and 3.6 reveals at least two important insights in tackling the study of SURs in democratic countries. First, contrary to conventional wisdom, a significant number of these regimes exercise state power along fairly non-patrimonial lines, and without necessarily abusing it. This finding supports the idea that SURs can be thought as of pertaining to two general types, patrimonial and non-patrimonial. Acknowledgment of SUR types is not only essential to gaining a more thorough understanding of the specific causal mechanisms that underpin regime continuity within each SUR type, but is also critical to singling out well-defined and independent domains of cases within which analysts can identify causal (unit) homogeneity to thus refine our understanding of these regimes.

Second, the evidence presented in Figures 3.5 and 3.6 shows that levels of economic development and geographic location are good predictors of patrimonial state structures. Non-patrimonial state structures are more likely to be found in Argentine SURs where higher levels of economic development exist. The same pattern can be observed in Mexico, where SURs with higher

Democrats and Autocrats

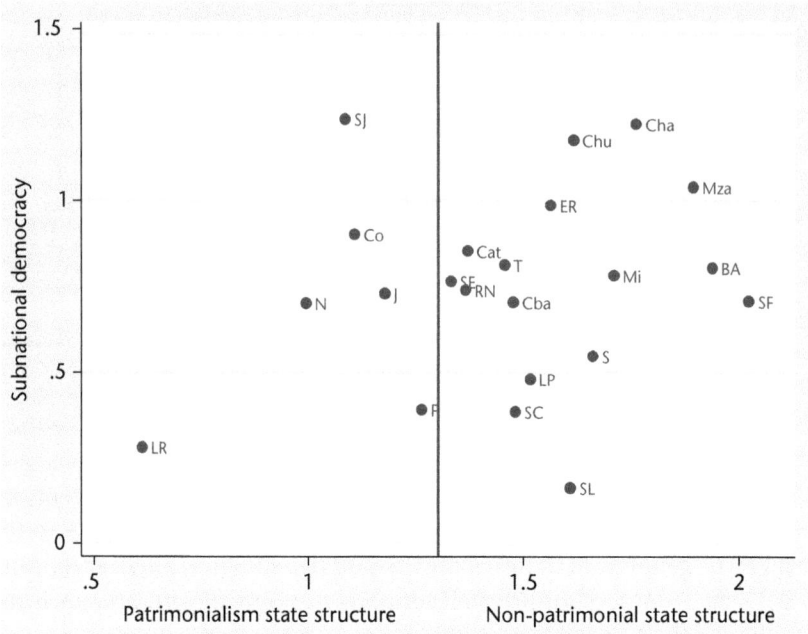

Figure 3.5. SUR state structures in Argentina (1983–2009)

Notes: Values are averaged values for the 1983–2009 period. Y-axis: Higher values indicate higher levels of subnational democracy. Zero and near-zero scores denote undemocratic regimes. X-axis: Lower values denote patrimonial state structures. BA (Buenos Aires), Cha (Chaco), Chu (Chubut), Co (Corrientes), Cba (Córdoba), ER (Entre Ríos), F (Formosa), J (Jujuy), LP (La Pampa), LR (La Rioja), Mza (Mendoza), Mi (Misiones), N (Neuquén), RN (Río Negro), S (Salta), SJ (San Juan), SL (San Luis), SC (Santa Cruz), SF (Santa Fe), SE (Santiago del Estero), TF (Tierra del Fuego), T (Tucumán).

levels of socioeconomic development, such as Tabasco, are characterized by state structures that are less patrimonial. In contrast, the provinces and states where patrimonial state structures are more common are located in the least economically developed and poorest SURs of Argentina and Mexico, such as in La Rioja and Formosa in Argentina or Oaxaca and Hidalgo in Mexico. These findings suggest that Max Weber's classic assertion about the "elective affinity" between capitalist development and non-patrimonial administrations applies to subnational levels of government.[14]

SURs' Fiscal Variation: Fiscally Autonomous vs. Fiscally Dependent SURs

Fiscal autonomy of subnational rulers from the central state is one major resource through which lower-tier incumbents can neutralize encroachments and co-optation from the center (Boone 2003; Wibbels 2005).

---

[14] The same pattern is observed when non-SURs are taken into account. Less economically developed (democratic) provinces and states are more likely to have patrimonial state structures.

Conceptualizing, Measuring, and Mapping

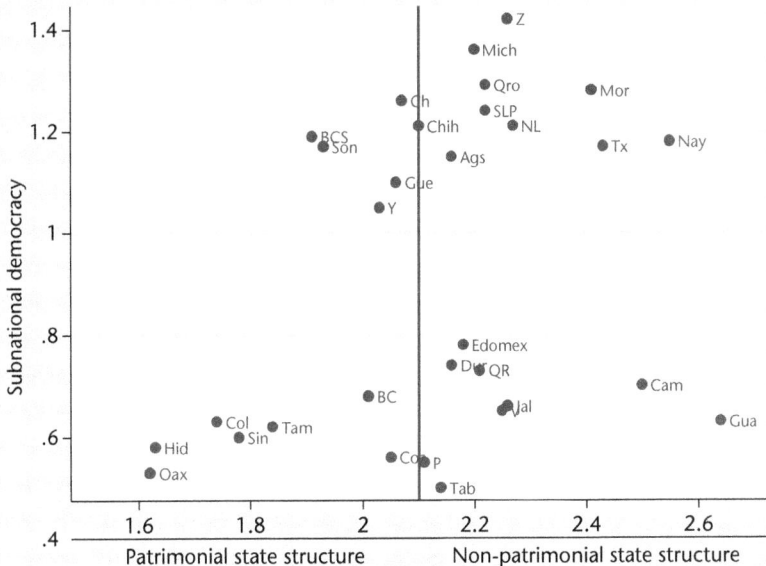

Figure 3.6. SUR state structures in Mexico (1997–2009)

Notes: Values are averaged values for the 1997–2009 period. Y-axis: Higher values indicate higher levels of subnational democracy. Zero and near-zero scores denote undemocratic regimes. X-axis: Lower values denote patrimonial state structures. Ags (Aguascalientes), BC (Baja California), BCS (Baja California Sur), Cam (Campeche), Ch (Chiapas), Chih (Chihuahua), Coa (Coahuila), Col (Colima), Dur (Durango), Edomex (Estado de México), Gua (Guanajuato), Gue (Guerrero), Hid (Hidalgo), Jal (Jalisco), Mich (Michoacán), Mor (Morelia), Nay (Nayarit), NL (Nuevo León), Oax (Oaxaca), P (Puebla), Qro (Querétaro), QR (Quintana Roo), SLP (San Luis Potosí), Sin (Sinaloa), Son (Sonora), Tab (Tabasco), Tam (Tamaulipas), Tx (Tlaxcala), V (Veracruz), Y (Yucatán), Z (Zacatecas).

The greater subnational incumbents' reliance on local taxes, the lower their fiscal deficits, and the lower their levels of indebtedness, the greater their potential for rewiring territorial borders and neutralizing political intrusion from the center. By contrast, greater fiscal dependence upon the central government creates structural conditions conducive to the subjugation of subnational incumbents vis-à-vis the center (Wibbels 2005; Díaz-Cayeros 2006).

It is worth emphasizing that in federal countries where revenue-sharing systems exist, all subnational governments are, strictly speaking, dependent on the national government, given that the main (domestic) taxes are collected by the federal government and then channeled to subnational levels of governments.[15] In this study, and contrary to what other important works

---

[15] Revenues are generally distributed in two rounds. In the first round, taxes are split into two (not necessarily equal) parts between the federal government and the subnational. In the second round, the subnational share is distributed among all provinces/states according to country-specific formulas.

on SURs do (Gervasoni 2010b; Gibson 2013), fiscal autonomy/dependency is not assessed in terms of the subnational autocrats' reliance on this type of funds and transfers but rather as a byproduct of subnational governments' fiscal solvency, which is usually determined by fiscal deficits, levels of indebtedness, and capacity to raise subnational taxes. The decision to assess fiscal autonomy in terms of solvency is justified by Bonvecchi and Lodola's (2011) demonstration that not all intergovernmental transfers expand the capacity of presidents to marshal support from subnational rulers. Transfers such as those stemming from revenue-sharing systems, which flow to subnational jurisdictions automatically and on a pre-established formula, do not confer on presidents a greater capacity to elicit subnational rulers' support—nor do they affect the dependency of subnational incumbents on the national government—because they flow to subnational jurisdictions on a regular and automatic basis.

By contrast, other fiscal variables, such as provincial indebtedness and provincial fiscal deficits, are more accurate determinants of presidents' capacity to elicit subnational rulers' support and cooperation. As various works show, economically reckless governors who run fiscal deficits and are highly indebted often turn to the central government for financial aid and bailouts (see Sanguinetti 1999; Hernández Trillo et al. 2002; Wibbels 2005; Rodden 2006). Given the discretion with which presidents decide whom to bail out, profligate subnational rulers can easily become political hostages of central incumbents and vulnerable to presidential co-optation. Moreover, the prospects of subjugation increase in countries such as Argentina, where not all subnational jurisdictions have the legal and fiscal capacity to buy debt beyond the central government, and thus have to resort to presidential bailouts to maintain solvency.

Fiscal autonomy is measured as the average of the yearly debt and deficit of any given provincial government.[16] Data span the periods 1996–2009[17] in Argentina, and 1997–2009 in Mexico. Debt and deficit data for Argentina were calculated with data obtained from Base de Datos Provinciales del Centro de Investigaciones en Administración Pública (Facultad de Ciencias Económicas, Universidad de Buenos Aires). Debt data for Mexico come from the Unidad de Coordinación con las Entidades Federativas (Secretaria de Hacienda y Crédito Público, or SHCP). Deficit data were calculated with figures of the Sistema Estatal y Municipal de Base de Datos (SIMBAD), INEGI.

As Figures 3.7 and 3.8 show, levels of fiscal autonomy vary considerably across Argentine and Mexican SURs. With their higher levels of fiscal

---

[16] Debt and deficit are expressed as shares of each province's total revenues.
[17] Data on debt for the period 1983–96 were not available.

Conceptualizing, Measuring, and Mapping

dependency on the federal government, the provinces of Formosa and La Rioja in Argentina are more prone to be vulnerable to fiscal manipulation by national officials. A similar prediction can be made for some Mexican SURs, such as Sinaloa, Coahuila, and Hidalgo, among others. Conversely, greater fiscal autonomy from the federal government, as experienced in the Argentine SURs of Santa Cruz, La Pampa, or San Luis, or in Oaxaca and Tabasco in Mexico, should act as a shield vis-à-vis fiscal co-optation, and in turn, offer greater possibilities for neutralizing presidential control.

The information presented in Figures 3.7 and 3.8 sheds important light on one central aspect of SURs and their rulers: subnational undemocratic rule and fiscal profligacy do not necessarily go hand in hand. It could be argued that the potentially high costs of creating dependency on the central government through fiscal mismanagement may act as an important deterrent for subnational autocrats to engage in fiscal profligacy and as a strong incentive to keep SUR economies in check. A fiscally and financially sound provincial economy may not only be effective in preventing presidential co-optation, it

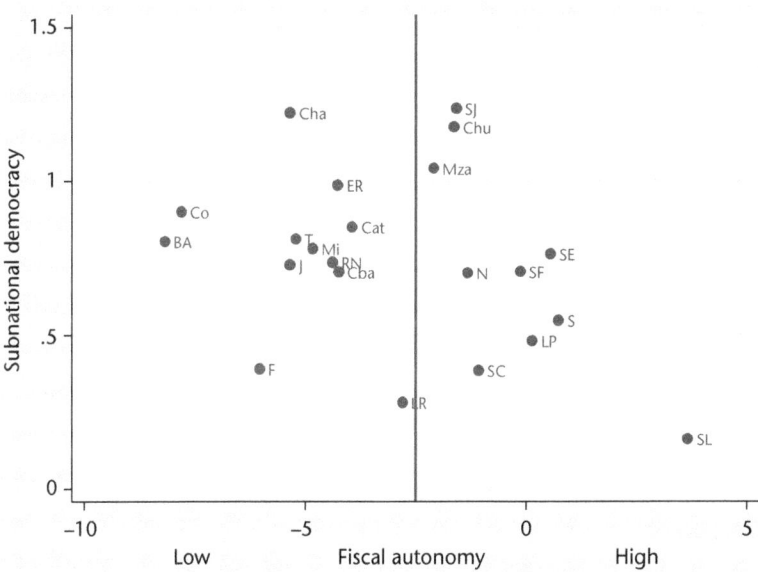

Figure 3.7. SUR fiscal autonomy in Argentina (1996–2009)

Notes: Fiscal autonomy values are averaged values for the 1996–2009 period. Y-axis: Higher values indicate higher levels of subnational democracy. Zero and near-zero scores denote undemocratic regimes. X-axis: Higher values denote higher fiscal autonomy. BA (Buenos Aires), Cha (Chaco), Chu (Chubut), Co (Corrientes), Cba (Córdoba), ER (Entre Ríos), F (Formosa), J (Jujuy), LP (La Pampa), LR (La Rioja), Mza (Mendoza), Mi (Misiones), N (Neuquén), RN (Río Negro), S (Salta), SJ (San Juan), SL (San Luis), SC (Santa Cruz), SF (Santa Fe), SE (Santiago del Estero), TF (Tierra del Fuego), T (Tucumán).

Democrats and Autocrats

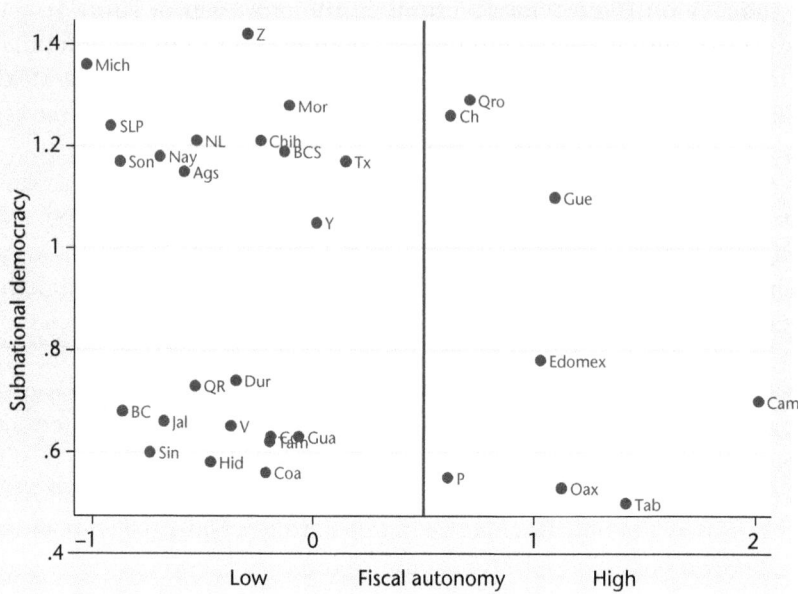

Figure 3.8. SUR fiscal autonomy in Mexico (1997–2009)

Notes: Values are averaged values for the 1997–2009 period. Y-axis: Higher values indicate higher levels of subnational democracy. Zero and near-zero scores denote undemocratic regimes. X-axis: Higher values denote higher fiscal autonomy. Ags (Aguascalientes), BC (Baja California), BCS (Baja California Sur), Cam (Campeche), Ch (Chiapas), Chih (Chihuahua), Coa (Coahuila), Col (Colima), Dur (Durango), Edomex (Estado de México), Gua (Guanajuato), Gue (Guerrero), Hid (Hidalgo), Jal (Jalisco), Mich (Michoacán), Mor (Morelia), Nay (Nayarit), NL (Nuevo León), Oax (Oaxaca), P (Puebla), Qro (Querétaro), QR (Quintana Roo), SLP (San Luis Potosí), Sin (Sinaloa), Son (Sonora), Tab (Tabasco), Tam (Tamaulipas), Tx (Tlaxcala), V (Veracruz), Y (Yucatán), Z (Zacatecas).

may also be crucial for sustaining SURs. Fiscal autonomy can be an important tool for subnational autocrats to neutralize potential economic sanctions of pro-democratizing presidents but it can also help subnational autocrats to deliver goods and benefits that can eventually help to attract local popular support for SURs.

Conclusion

This chapter has argued that SURs are civilian, electoral regimes that are neither authoritarian nor fully democratic. They can be clearly distinguished from subnational authoritarian regimes because they hold regular, multiparty elections, and, unlike authoritarian regimes, opposition groups and parties are not legally barred from contesting elections. These regimes, however, are not democratic. What distinguishes SURs from subnational democracies is the fact that the actual opposition's capacity to defeat incumbents (and/or their parties) in elections is seriously handicapped. In SURs, regime challengers effectively compete in elections but incumbents win systematically by employing a variety of undemocratic tactics.

Drawing on this definition, the chapter provided an operationalization of subnational democracy and a detailed discussion of its dimensions, subdimensions, indicators, and their aggregation. Additionally, unlike previous studies[18] that for the most part do not measure levels of subnational democracy across all subnational jurisdictions, the chapter not only identified the universe of SURs, but also specified the jurisdiction for which theories of regime continuity should not be applied. Finally, the chapter showed that SURs should not be seen as a set of homogeneous political regimes. As the evidence obtained in Argentina and Mexico reveals, these regimes not only differ considerably from one another in terms of their geographic location, levels of socioeconomic development, and party ideology, but also regarding their state structures and levels of fiscal autonomy. The findings thus suggest that the assumption of unit homogeneity, which has dominated studies of SURs, needs to be revisited.

The identification of the universe of SURs, as well as the identification of regime differences analyzed in this chapter, provides the first two elements needed to test the theory advanced in Chapter 2. The next chapter builds on this identification by analyzing and measuring the national variables, i.e. the instruments of presidents' power that are required to complete the process of theory testing.

---

[18] Exceptions are Solt 2003; McMann 2006; Gervasoni 2010b, 2010a; Giraudy 2010, 2013; Saikkonen 2011.

4

Presidential Power in Argentina and Mexico: Fiscal and Partisan Instruments of Cooptation

One of the major contentions of this book is that the possibility of exerting presidential power over subnational autocrats strongly conditions the pathway of subnational undemocratic regime (SUR) continuity. This chapter explores the instruments available to presidents to induce the cooperation and obtain the acquiescence of subnational autocrats. Drawing on the insights provided by scholarship on fiscal federalism and political parties, the chapter argues that presidents usually employ two major resources to subjugate autocrats: their party organizations and/or federal funds that are allocated to subnational jurisdictions. In emphasizing the availability of institutional and economic resources to induce cooperation, the chapter moves beyond much of the recent literature's exclusive focus on presidential use of either fiscal or partisan tools as a means to obtain subjugation.[1]

This chapter also emphasizes the changing nature of presidential power, measured in terms of national incumbents' access to fiscal and partisan resources. The analysis conducted here indicates that the instruments of presidential power used to obtain the cooperation of subnational rulers vary considerably not only across countries, but also within countries and presidential administrations. Whereas some presidents have access to a combination of resources to exert leverage over subnational rulers, others lack access to any of them. In effect, the examination of each of the post-1983 presidencies in Argentina reveals that Peronist Party (or PJ) President Carlos Menem (1989–1999) had access to and employed fiscal and partisan resources to

---

[1] For works focusing exclusively on fiscal resources, see e.g. Solnick 1995; Gibson and Calvo 2001; Bonvecchi and Lodola 2011; Willis et al. 1999. For works analyzing partisan resources, see Ordeshook 1996; Mainwaring 1999; Samuels 2000; Rodden 2003; among others. For works analyzing both resources see Wibbels 2005.

discipline SURs and their autocrats, while PJ Presidents Duhalde, Kirchner, and Fernández de Kirchner leveraged subnational autocrats using only fiscal instruments. By contrast, Alianzist president De la Rúa had limited access to both types of resources. National Action Party (PAN) Presidents Fox and Calderón in Mexico, in turn, resorted to partisan instruments to obtain the acquiescence of subnational autocrats.

This chapter is divided into three sections. The first examines the fiscal instruments of presidential power prevailing in Argentina and Mexico, during 1989–2009[2] and 2000–2009, respectively. After an individual assessment of each country, the section presents a cross-country comparison in order to assess the relative fiscal power of Argentine vis-à-vis Mexican presidents. The second part then analyzes and compares the instruments of partisan power available to Argentine and Mexican national incumbents. Building on the findings of the first two parts, the third part compares and contrasts presidential access to the two instruments in order to assess the primary resource or combination of resources employed by each president in each country.

Before turning to this analysis, a note about the analytical approach adopted in this chapter is in order. Chapter 2 noted that subnational autocrats vary considerably regarding their capacity to neutralize presidential power. In this chapter, however, subnational autocrats and subnational jurisdictions are treated as if they were a homogeneous bloc. The chapter temporarily overlooks subnational differences because its aim is to determine the type of presidential power prevalent under each presidency, and in particular under the administrations of Néstor Kirchner and Cristina Fernández de Kirchner in Argentina, and Vicente Fox and Felipe Calderón in Mexico. Hence, the chapter measures the absolute power that presidents have vis-à-vis subnational rulers, regardless of whether this power is neutralized by specific characteristics of subnational units and subnational incumbents. This means that the indicators selected to assess whether presidents have (or lack) access to either type of resources necessarily have to overlook provincial differences.

Fiscal Instruments of Presidential Power

As argued in Chapter 2, numerous works show that fiscal resources increase presidential fiscal power vis-à-vis subnational rulers and, in turn, increase the potential for obtaining their acquiescence (Eaton 2004; Wibbels 2005; Díaz-Cayeros 2006; Bonvecchi and Lodola 2011; Falleti 2011). Presidential

---

[2] Fiscal data for the Alfonsín (1983–9) administration are missing.

fiscal power is shaped not so much by access to fiscal resources, but mainly by national incumbents' ability to manipulate the distribution of intergovernmental funds. Even in years of economic downturn or international crises, when access to fiscal resources may be scarce, presidential fiscal power may nonetheless increase if transfers sent to subnational jurisdictions are not channeled using automatic and formula-based criteria, but rather on a discretional basis. To the extent that presidents can discretionally determine the timing, amount, and the targeting of a given transfer, they should be in a strong position to easily control and thus induce lower-tier incumbents to give their political support (Bonvecchi and Lodola 2011). Presidential fiscal power should also be greater where the rules that regulate the distribution of intergovernmental transfers, as well as the amount of intergovernmental transfers, are easily changeable. Unstable fiscal arrangements that enable presidents to increase the share of resources that remains at the federal level of government, thus decreasing the proportion of funds that is sent to subnational levels of government, necessarily increase presidential leverage over subnational autocrats. Likewise, presidential fiscal power should be greater where a high percentage of a country's total revenues is not subject to sharing with subnational governments.

In light of these considerations, in what follows presidential fiscal power is gauged along three dimensions: (a) the existence of a revenue-sharing system[3] that allocates transfers across levels of government along automatic (rather than discretional) criteria, (b) the stability of the revenue-sharing system's rules that determine the amount and distribution of transfers that are sent to subnational jurisdictions, and (c) the percentage and distributional criteria of tax revenues that are not transferred to the provinces and which are exclusively administered by the federal level of government.[4]

Argentina

I. EXISTENCE OF REVENUE-SHARING SYSTEM AND STABILITY OF TRANSFERS' DISTRIBUTIONAL RULES/AMOUNTS[5]

Argentina's first-ever automatic revenue-sharing system dates back to 1934, when the first Coparticipation Law (henceforth CL or coparticipation) was passed. The CL represented an agreement between the provinces and the

---

[3] In a revenue-sharing system a country's main taxes are collected by the federal government and distributed automatically in two rounds. In the first round, tax revenues are automatically split in two (not necessarily equal) parts between the federal government and the subnational units. In the second round, the subnational share is automatically distributed among the subnational jurisdictions following strict distributional criteria and formulas.

[4] Dimensions (a) and (b) are analyzed in the same subsection.

[5] The focus of this subsection is on the changes that were introduced to each country's revenue-sharing system. Consequently, the analysis enumerates and describes these changes but does not assess the factors that triggered them.

federal government according to which the provinces would delegate to the national Congress exclusive rights over certain taxes (i.e. sales, excise, and income taxes) in exchange for an automatic share in the revenues collected (Eaton 2004: 68–9). At a time of deep economic crisis, the governors saw great value in shifting the significant administrative and political costs of collecting taxes onto the federal government, despite the fact that the latter appropriated the lion's share, i.e. 82.5 percent of the revenues subject to sharing compared to the 17.5 percent that were sent to the provinces.

The automatic revenue-sharing agreement instituted in 1934 suffered several modifications thereafter regarding the specific taxes that would be subject to sharing. The three most significant changes preceding the latest transition to democracy in 1983 occurred in 1973 with the passage of a new CL. This law not only stipulated that the totality (rather than some) of taxes levied by the federal government, with the exception of import and export duties, should be subject to sharing, but also introduced strict formulas (based on population and regional economic development) to allocate resources across subnational jurisdictions (CECE 1995; Porto 2003). In addition, the new law established that taxes collected by the federal government would be distributed in equal parts (48.5 percent) between the federal government and the provinces.

As Table 4.1 reports, almost every single democratic Argentine president subsequently modified the rules regulating the 1973 revenue-sharing agreement, and altered the share of the revenues that would be sent to the provinces. Overall, these changes progressively sliced off the share of revenues that remained at the national government, and thus curtailed presidential fiscal power.

The equally shared portion of revenues between levels of government, however, was altered during the democratic administration of President Alfonsín (1983–9). Before exiting power in 1983, the military regime of Reynaldo Bignone (1982–3) issued a decree declaring the expiration of the 1973 CL, due at the end of 1983. The incoming democratic government, however, was fragmented along partisan lines and lacked the number of national legislators needed to pass a new CL. During the deadlocked negotiations over a new revenue-sharing law, which lasted three consecutive years—1985, 1986, and 1987—the intergovernmental distribution of tax proceeds subject to sharing did not follow pre-established patterns. As Eaton notes, during those years "the federal government distributed tax revenues to the provinces not according to automatic procedures or transparent criteria but according to ad hoc negotiations in which political factors predominated. . . . According to the dynamic of these years, Alfonsín and his Economy Ministers negotiated the size and timing of revenue transfers directly with the governors" (2004: 146). In so doing, Alfonsín significantly increased presidential fiscal power vis-à-vis the provinces (CECE 1995).

Table 4.1. Legally prescribed revenue shares for the federal government and the provinces

Law #	Year of CL's reform	Federal government	Provinces
12143 and 12147	1934–1946	82.50%	17.50%
12956	1947–1958	79%	21%
14788	1959	66%	34%
	1960	64%	36%
	1961	62%	38%
	1962	60%	40%
	1963	58%	42%
	1964–1966	54%	46%
	1967	59.20%	40.80%
	1968–1972	61.90%	38.10%
20221	1973–1980	48.50%	48.50% (a)
	1981–1984	48.50%	51.50% (b)
	1985–1988	no coparticipation law	
23548	1988–1991	42.34%	57.66% (c)
24130 and 24699	1992–1993*	minimum floor	
25235	1999–2001	fixed sum	
25570	2002	41.24%**	58.76%

(a) Does not include 1.8% destined to City of Buenos Aires and Fund for Regional Development (FDR); (b) includes FDR; (c) includes National Treasury Funds (ATN).
* Porto and Sanguinetti (1993) estimate that 54.07% remained at the federal level of government and 45.3% were transferred to the provinces.
** Does not include the 15% deduction withheld by the federal government.
Sources: CECE #9 (1995, 1997), and Laws 24130, 25535, 25400, 25570.

The 1987 legislative landslide victory of the Peronist party served as a catalyst to pass a new CL. Control over both congressional chambers and of a majority of the country's governorships enabled the Peronist party to pass a new coparticipation system that favored the provinces over the federal government. The newly instituted CL, which considerably curtailed presidential fiscal power, established the federal government's portion of revenues subject to sharing as 42.34 percent, with the provinces receiving the remaining 54.66 percent.[6]

Counterintuitively, these distributional percentages, which greatly benefitted Peronist governors, were changed in a direction favorable to the central government under the Peronist presidency of Carlos Menem (1989–99). Without revoking the 1988 coparticipation law, in 1992, Menem and the governors signed the so-called Primer Pacto Fiscal (Fiscal Pact I), which enabled the president to retain 15 percent of the taxable revenues plus a monthly fixed sum of AR$45,800,000 of the revenues previously subject to sharing

---

[6] The remaining 3% is made up of ATN and special funds for specific provinces.

with the provinces.[7] As importantly, the Fiscal Pact I introduced the first-ever change to the criterion in which the provincial share of the coparticipation pie was calculated. Despite changes in the magnitude of the share that remained at the federal level of government and the portion that was sent to the provinces, during the 1930-91 period, the amount of the revenues flowing to the provinces and remaining at the federal level were determined by the ebb and flow of federal tax receipts (Eaton 2004). Starting in 1992, this practice was abandoned and was replaced by a minimum revenue guarantee, the so-called *piso mínimo* (minimum amount), of US$725 million per month for the provinces. This minimum amount was increased to US$740 million in 1993 with the signing of a new fiscal pact, the so-called Fiscal Pact II. Despite this increase, which modestly benefitted the provinces, the adoption of the minimum revenue guarantee expanded presidential fiscal power. As Eaton (2004) notes, although the 1988 coparticipation law had reduced the federal government's share of revenues to 42.34 percent, the fiscal pacts of 1992 and 1993 effectively increased its share to 50.07 percent.

Menem's two innovations to the revenue-sharing system, namely, the withholding of specific percentages of previously shareable tax revenues and the introduction of the minimum floor, were maintained in place by Alianzist President Fernando De la Rúa (1999–2001). During his administration, fractions of specific taxes included in the revenue-sharing system and subject to sharing were deducted from the coparticipation pie and earmarked to finance specific federal and provincial projects, including education programs, health provision, public works, and housing.[8] Likewise, in 1999, De la Rúa and the governors signed the Compromiso Federal (Federal Compromise), an agreement that set a fixed (instead of a minimum) sum of coparticipation transfers to the provinces. The original amount was set at US$1.35 billion, and it was subsequently increased to US$1.36 billion in 2001. Despite the greater fixed amount of coparticipation funds sent to the provinces, the share of revenues that was allocated to subnational jurisdictions never reached the 54.66 percent established in the 1988 coparticipation law.

Under the presidency of Peronist Eduardo Duhalde (2002–3), the fixed amount and minimum floors were abandoned. After 2002, the share of tax revenues that was sent to the provinces was calculated on the basis of the

---

[7] The deducted revenues were used to finance the national pension system, which at the time was in dire straits.

[8] It is important to note that the introduction of earmarked transfers curtailed the governors' capacity to discretionally employ federal transfers. Unlike the coparticipation funds, which can be allocated as each governor pleases, earmarked transfers have to be destined to finance specific programs and projects. The federal government is responsible for determining the programs and projects that will be financed with earmarked funds.

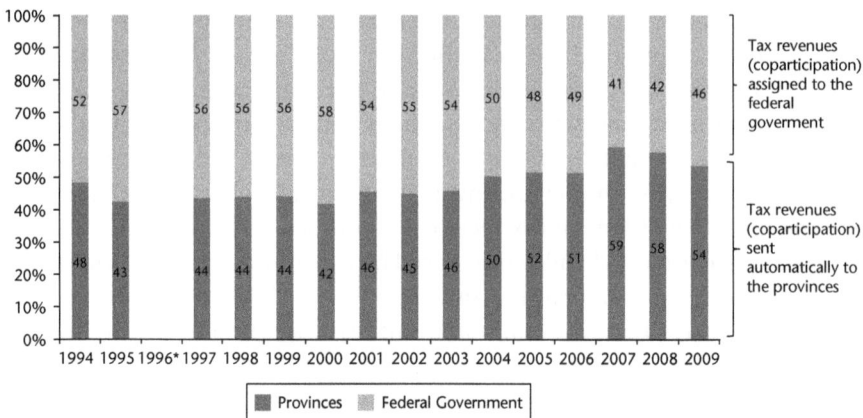

Figure 4.1. Share of coparticipation distributed across levels of government in Argentina

Source: Author's calculations based on data from the Cuenta de Inversión (for the 1994–2009 period), Boletín Fiscal (for 1998).

* Data for 1996 are unreliable.

ebb and flow of federal tax receipts, thus resuming the pre-1992 pattern of computation. Still, unlike the 1988–92 period, the federal government continued to slice off a substantial amount of the coparticipation resources, as the 15 percent deduction, the monthly fixed sum of AR$45,800,000, and all other deductions from specific domestic taxes stood in place. While this latter factor was unbeneficial to the provinces—in that it prevented them from obtaining a larger slice of the coparticipation pie—the overall increase of tax receipts, due in large part to the expansion and stability of the country's economy, as well as the creation in 2009 of the Fondo Nacional Solidario (National Solidarity Fund),[9] resulted in greater absolute amounts of coparticipation for the provinces.

Figure 4.1 demonstrates these trends with statistics. The figure shows that, between 1994 and 2007, the share of taxable revenues sent to the provinces remained well below the 54.66 percent established in the 1988 coparticipation law. In contrast, the share of coparticipation corresponding to the national level of government has remained well above the 42.34 percent established in the CL. Only in 2007 and 2008 did actual coparticipation shares emulate the ones set by the CL. Apart from the non-compliance with the CL guidelines, the statistics presented in Figure 4.1 reveal two interesting patterns about the allocation of automatic transfers in Argentina, and

---

[9] The National Solidarity Fund, instituted during the Fernández de Kirchner administration, established that 30% of the soy duties were to be automatically allocated to the provinces.

Presidential Power in Argentina and Mexico

about presidential fiscal power in particular. First, they indicate that, with the exception of the 1997–2000 period, shares across levels of government changed over time—denoting that the institutions of fiscal federalism in Argentina have been systematically altered, generally to favor presidents over governors. Second, they reveal that presidents were able to retain the bulk of proceeds of the revenue-sharing system and thus limit the amount of money that governors can use with discretion. All in all, these trends underscore that presidents in Argentina enjoyed considerable fiscal power vis-à-vis governors.

II. TAX REVENUES NOT SUBJECT TO SHARING

As noted before, not all taxes and revenues are subject to sharing with subnational jurisdictions. In Argentina, the bulk of these tax proceeds is made up of export/import duties, which according to the constitution are not subject to sharing with the provinces. One of the main characteristics of these tax receipts is that they are administered and allocated as the national government sees fit. Therefore, if these revenues are abundant or make up a large share of a country's total revenues, presidents stand in a strong position to expand their fiscal power vis-à-vis subnational rulers.

As Figure 4.2 shows, in the early and mid-1990s, export/import duties accounted for an average of 6 percent of the taxes collected by the national government. These returns plummeted in the late 1990s as a result of a deterioration of commodity prices. Indeed, between 1999 and 2001, export/import duties reached their lowest point since 1991, i.e. 4 percent. In the

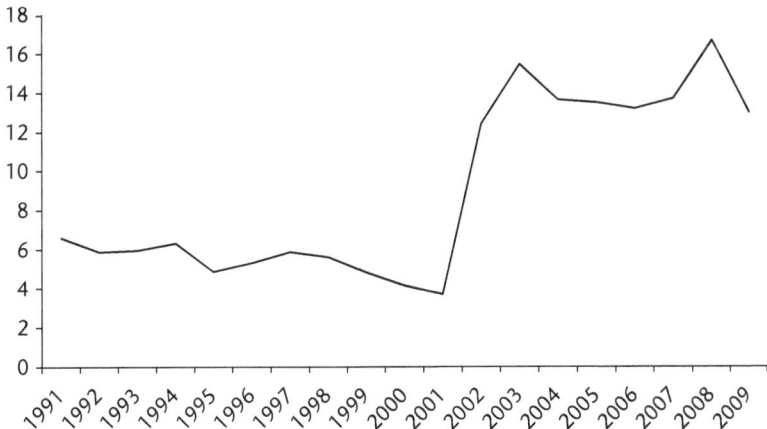

Figure 4.2. Export and import duties as a percentage of tax revenues (Argentina)
Source: Author's calculations based on data provided by Dirección Nacional de Investigaciones y Análisis Fiscal, Ministerio de Economía.

2000s, by contrast, commodity prices increased to unprecedented levels, allowing Presidents Duhalde, Kirchner, and Fernández de Kirchner to retain an average of 14 percent of the country's tax income.

The data presented in Figure 4.2 show that presidential fiscal power, as determined by the proportion of total revenues that are not shared with the provinces, underwent a considerable expansion under the most recent Peronist administrations, reaching unprecedented levels in 2002 and 2008, when export/import proceeds accounted for 15.4 and 16.6 percent of total revenue, respectively. Conversely, presidential fiscal power suffered a considerable cutback under the Alianzist administration of President Fernando De la Rúa. Likewise, a mild decrease in presidential fiscal power was observed in 2009, less due to decreasing export/import tax proceeds than to the creation of the National Solidarity Fund, which stipulated that 30 percent of the proceeds of soy exports, i.e. 2.31 percent of the tax revenues, be allocated to the provinces.

Mexico

I. EXISTENCE OF REVENUE-SHARING SYSTEM AND STABILITY OF TRANSFERS' DISTRIBUTIONAL RULES/AMOUNTS

The Mexican revenue-sharing system was instituted in 1980, with the passage of the Law of Fiscal Coordination (or LCF). The new law was a watershed in the history of Mexico's fiscal federalism. For the first time, states agreed to give up their authority over taxation in return for unconditional revenue-sharing transfers, the so-called *participaciones* (Díaz-Cayeros 2006). With the intention of diminishing presidential discretion and ensuring a steady flow of funds to the states, the new fiscal arrangement tied *participaciones* to explicit formulas that took into consideration population, revenue collected in the past, and indicators of state performance in tax collection (Courchene and Díaz-Cayeros 2000; Díaz-Cayeros 2006). In addition, the LCF stipulated very strict provisions regarding the automaticity of the *participaciones*' allocation, and prescribed strict sanctions to be applied whenever the federal government failed to comply with the criteria set for distribution.

The 1980 LCF stipulated that 17.6 percent of the taxes subject to sharing be assigned to the General Fund of Participations (or FGP), the main subfund making up the *participaciones* fund.[10] In other words, since 1980, 17.6 percent of the taxes subject to sharing flowed automatically to the states and were calculated based on a fixed formula. This percentage was subsequently

---

[10] The other subfunds include: Fund for Municipal Promotion (or FFM), and the Fund for Compensations (or FC).

increased to 18.26 percent in 1989, 18.51 percent in the early 1990s, and 20 percent in 1997 (SHCP 2007).[11]

In contrast to the pattern observed in Argentina, the amount of *participaciones* in Mexico (including all subfunds and special taxes) has remained considerably stable over time, accounting for an average of 25 percent of the total shareable revenue between 1998 and 2009 (Secretaría de Hacienda y Crédito Público: Unidad de Coordinación con Entidades Federativas, <http://www.shcp.gob.mx/Estados/Participaciones/Paginas/Presentacion.aspx>). Additionally, unlike the Argentine tradition, increases in the FGP and in the other *participaciones* subfunds moved in the same direction; namely, they helped to curtail presidential fiscal power, as the federal government was forced to automatically transfer a greater proportion of tax revenues to the states.

In 1997, within the broader context of public services' decentralization and the implementation of the so-called Nuevo Federalismo (New Federalism program), President Zedillo (1994–2000) introduced another major change in the Mexican revenue-sharing system. Most of the funds/programs that were distributed by the federal government through a myriad of federal agencies before 1997—and that were earmarked for specific purposes at both the state and municipal level, such as the conditional cash transfer program known as the National Solidarity Program (or PRONASOL), the fund for Federal Infrastructural Development (or IPF), and funds destined to the payroll of teachers and the provision of health care—were incorporated into the LCF.

The PAN administrations of Vicente Fox (2000–6) and Felipe Calderón (2006–12) incorporated additional funds into the *aportaciones* subfund. In 2003, for instance, the federal government began to automatically distribute on a fixed formula the so-called Trusteeship for States' Infrastructure (or FIES), which transfers revenues from oil surpluses to the states. Likewise, in 2007, the Calderón administration altered the distribution criteria of the so-called Program for the Enhancement of the Federal States (or PAFEF). The program, which had been subject to discretional allocation since its inception in 2000, was incorporated into the *aportaciones* subfund, thus becoming an automatic transfer sent directly to the states.

The creation of the *aportaciones* subfund, as well as its expansion, meant that the allocation of transfers destined to assist with social, welfare, and

---

[11] If to that one adds the remaining *participaciones* subfunds, roughly 23% of Mexico's total shareable revenues have been automatically channeled to the states. In addition to these subfunds, several specific taxes and economic incentives are also subsumed under *participaciones*, such as the property tax on automobiles (*tenencia*) and tax on new cars (ISAN). Like all the *participaciones* subfunds, these additional taxes are calculated on arithmetic formulas and transferred automatically to the states.

Democrats and Autocrats

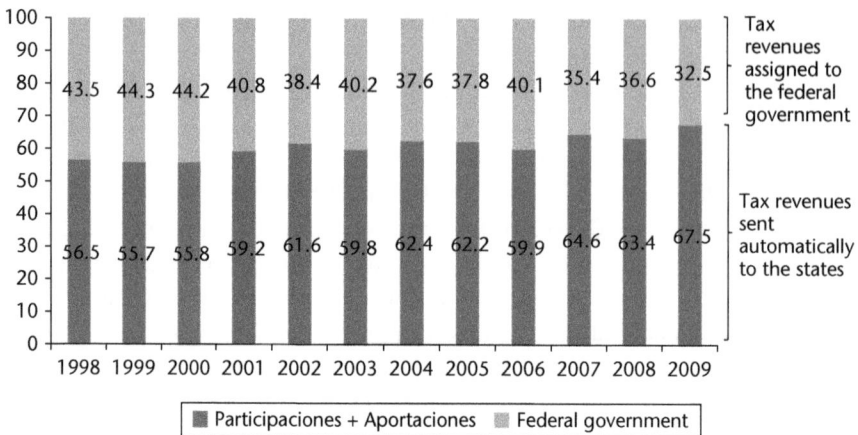

Figure 4.3. Percentage of funds subject to sharing across levels of government in Mexico

Source: 1997–2002: Diagnóstico de la Secretaria de Hacienda y Crédito Público 2007; 2002–9: SHCP—Unidad de Coordinación con Entidades Federativas.

infrastructure development—which between 1998 and 2009 accounted for an average of 28 percent of the revenues subject to sharing[12]—became automatic and subject to distributional fixed formulas rather than to the discretion of each federal agency and president. As a result, since 1997, presidents in Mexico have experienced a steady and sustained reduction in presidential fiscal power.

Figure 4.3 reports the percentages of the distribution of Mexico's shareable revenues across levels of government. As can be observed, the share of revenues that has remained at the federal level of government has decreased dramatically (almost 12 percentage points) since the transition to democracy in 2000. This evidence clearly reveals that presidential fiscal power, as defined by revenue shares, has suffered considerable setbacks in the last decade.

II. TAX REVENUES NOT SUBJECT TO SHARING

As already discussed, not all tax revenues are subject to sharing with subnational jurisdictions. If these proceeds are abundant or make up a large share of a country's total revenues, presidents stand in a strong position to expand their fiscal power vis-à-vis subnational rulers. Therefore, to fully estimate the extent of presidential fiscal power, this subsection assesses the post-2000 evolution of the tax receipts left out of the LCF.

---

[12] Data to calculate this percentagee were obtained from the Secretaría de Hacienda y Crédito Público: Unidad de Coordinación con Entidades Federativas <http://www.shcp.gob.mx/Estados/Participaciones/Paginas/Presentacion.aspx>.

In Mexico, around a third of the country's total revenue is obtained from oil exports. The Secretaría de Hacienda y Crédito Público[13] reports that, between 2000 and 2003, oil returns accounted for 31.5 percent of the country's revenues, and for 36.7 percent between 2004 and 2007. Even though a portion of these revenues is transferred to the states in the form of *participaciones* and *aportaciones*, another part—the extraordinary revenues from oil—is not shared with subnational jurisdictions. These proceeds, which are equivalent to Argentina's export/import duties, in that they remain at the federal level of government and can be used by the president with absolute discretion, are decisive in increasing or decreasing presidential fiscal power.

The extraordinary revenues from oil result from unpredicted increases in oil prices, and are calculated as the difference between underestimated and actual oil prices. Because extraordinary oil revenues are not assigned to any budgetary item, and they are easier to manipulate, Mexican presidents have adopted the tradition of underestimating oil prices to increase their fiscal leeway (FUNDAR 2006; CEFP 2007).[14] The extraordinary returns from oil account for a considerable share of Mexico's income. For instance, during the administration of Vicente Fox, the unpredicted returns stemming from oil exports reached 439,288 million Mexican pesos (i.e. around US$40 billion) (FUNDAR 2006).

Reports by FUNDAR show that, between 2003 and 2006, when oil prices reached unprecedented levels, and when extraordinary revenues from oil peaked, proceeds were used with ample discretion (FUNDAR 2006). In 2004 and 2005, for instance, President Fox employed returns to finance current expenditures, including increases in teachers' wages, and specific public projects in selected states. This discretional use of oil receipts was offset in 2006, when the Law of Budgetary and Fiscal Responsibility (henceforth LPRH) was passed. The law set clear guidelines for the allocation of extraordinary proceeds, and obliged the federal government to distribute returns according to the following criteria: 40 percent for the Fund for the Stability of Oil Revenues (or FEIP), 25 percent for the Fund for Stabilization of the States' Revenues (or FEIEF), 25 percent for the state-run company Petróleos Mexicanos' (PEMEX) Stabilization Fund for Investment in Public Infrastructure, and 10 percent for investments in the states' public infrastructure. Between 2006 and 2009, as a result of these new guidelines, President Felipe Calderón experienced a considerable decrease in presidential fiscal power.

---

[13] <http://www.apartados.hacienda.gob.mx/contabilidad/documentos/informe_cuenta>.
[14] It should be noted, however, that while presidents may deliberately underestimate oil prices, an accurate estimation of oil proceeds is hard to make given the intrinsic volatility of oil prices.

Presidential Fiscal Power in Comparative Perspective

A comparison between Argentina and Mexico along the three dimensions analyzed in the previous sections[15] reveals that, up to 2009, presidents in Argentina enjoyed greater fiscal power than their Mexican counterparts. This holds true despite the fact that the bulk of intergovernmental fiscal transfers in both countries is regulated by a well-established revenue-sharing system that operated along the principle of automaticity.

Up to 2009, presidential fiscal power was greater in Argentina than in Mexico because the Argentine revenue-sharing system's rules were unstable and frequently altered to benefit presidents over governors. Indeed, with the exception of Alfonsín between 1988 and 1989, every Argentine president changed the rules regulating the revenue-sharing system. The suspension and modification of the Argentine revenue-sharing system, as well as its detrimental effects on provincial fiscal autonomy, contrast sharply with the pattern observed in Mexico. Since the transition to democracy, and up to 2009, Presidents Fox and Calderón did engage in major legal alterations of the revenue-sharing system's rules, and when these alterations occurred they curtailed, rather than expanded, presidential fiscal power. Table 4.2 summarizes the major changes to the rules of the revenue-sharing system as well as the effect of presidential fiscal power.

The greater share of transfers that were retained by Argentine presidents than their Mexican counterparts is a second major cause of the greater fiscal power observed in Argentina. A comparison of Figures 4.1 and 4.3 shows that Argentine presidents retained, on average, 48 percent of the total amount of shareable revenues, whereas Mexican national rulers held an average of 39.3 percent.

Presidential fiscal power in Argentina was also greater than that in Mexico due to the fact that over time, these resources continued to be allocated in a discretional manner. With the exception of the National Solidarity Fund instituted in 2009, which set clear criteria to distribute 30 percent of the proceeds of soy exports, there were no attempts to earmark revenues from export/import taxes. By contrast, Mexican presidents saw a significant curtailment of presidential fiscal power from 2003 (and up to 2009), when extraordinary revenues from oil began to be earmarked.

---

[15] Dimensions include: (a) the existence of a revenue-sharing system that establishes the automatic allocation of transfers across levels of government, (b) the stability of the revenue-sharing system's rules that determine the amount of and distribution of transfers that are sent to subnational jurisdictions, and (c) the percentage and distributional criteria of revenues that are not transferred to the provinces and which are administered by the federal level of government.

Table 4.2. Major changes in the rules that regulate revenue-sharing systems in Argentina and Mexico

Country	Year when rule was changed	Description of change	Effect of change on presidential fiscal power
ARGENTINA	1983	Suspension of CL	expansion
	1988	New CL is passed	retrenchment
	1992	Fiscal Pact I sets a minimum floor to be sent to the provinces 15% and US$45,800,000 are deducted from the provincial coparticipation pie	expansion
	1992	Fiscal Pact II increases the minimum floor	no effect*
	1999	*Compromiso Fiscal* sets a fixed sum to be sent to the provinces	expansion
	2001	*Compromiso Federal por el Crecimiento y la Disciplina Fiscal* increases fixed sum	no effect*
	2002	Coparticipation percentages are put back in place (but 15% and $45,800,000 are deducted from the provincial coparticipation pie)	no effect**
MEXICO	1980	*Participaciones* fund is created	retrenchment
	1997	*Aportaciones* fund is created	retrenchment
	1999	Additional sub-funds are included in the *aportaciones* fund	retrenchment
	2003	FIES fund is created	retrenchment
	2007	PAFEF is transformed into an *aportaciones* sub-fund	retrenchment

* No effect despite increase because transfers are still made automatically, thus maintaining presidential fiscal power stable
** No effect despite introduction of coparticipation percentages because coparticipation continues to be sliced off

On the whole, the country comparisons indicate that, between the latest transition to (national) democracy and 2009, greater stability in the rules egulating revenue sharing and the shares accruing to subnational levels of government, coupled with lower availability of revenues subject to sharing, offered Mexican presidents less fiscal discretion/power than their Argentine counterparts.

Partisan Instruments of Presidential Power

As noted in Chapter 2, different strands of literature within political science have long recognized the crucial role played by political parties to induce the cooperation and obtain the acquiescence of subnational *copartisans* (Mainwaring 1999; Levitsky 2003; Jones et al. 2000; Garman et al. 2001). Using a variety of internal party procedures, including the selection, nomination, and appointment of subnational candidates, presidents can effectively discipline and obtain the cooperation of subnational incumbent copartisans (Willis et al. 1999; Samuels 2000; Wibbels 2005).[16]

Presidential parties that are electorally viable in subnational districts also help increase presidential leverage over *opposition* subnational incumbents. Despite the fact that presidents lack (internal) partisan mechanisms to discipline opposition rulers at the subnational level—simply because these incumbents do not belong to their party—the organizational presence of the presidents' party in any given subnational unit increases electoral performance (Van Dyck 2013), thus allowing them to inflict pressure on subnational rulers and to eventually obtain their cooperation. For instance, national incumbents can take advantage of their local networks of offices, activists, and members to strengthen on-the-ground electoral mobilization,[17] co-opt subnational regime supporters, win over municipal governments, and/or forge opposition coalitions with disgruntled local party elites, local dissatisfied journalists, or other local opposition activists. If presidential parties are able to challenge subnational incumbents' electoral power within districts and hence threaten their territorial control, they can be used as powerful tools to obtain the cooperation of subnational rulers, as presidents can choose to lessen electoral pressure in exchange for political cooperation. Conversely, when presidents lack partisan organizations, and thus have a shortage of networks of brokers, activists, and community organizers, it is more difficult for them to forge the national–local coalitions needed to undermine provincial incumbents' power, and in turn, to obtain the acquiescence of subnational rulers.

Presidential partisan power, or the capacity to obtain copartisan and/or opposition subnational incumbents' compliance through party leverage, should be greater where (a) presidential party organizations and the rules and procedures that regulate relations between the party leadership and lower-level branches are highly routinized,[18] and (b) the president's party has an electoral foothold in all subnational units. Conversely, it should be lower

---

[16] Coattails effects can also result in greater cooperation of subnational copartisans (Wibbels 2005; Rodden 2003). As Rodden (2003) notes, "copartisanship can encourage 'electoral externalities,' whereby subnational politicians aligned with the central government forego particularistic benefits in favor of policies [reforms] that benefit their party as a whole." If subnational officials fail to contribute to these policies, the argument goes, non-compliance may weaken the national party, thus reducing provincial incumbents' own chances of reelection. In this case, provincial rulers will give up their autonomy and follow the president's agenda/will out of concerns for what may happen in future elections if they do not (see Wibbels 2005).

[17] As Van Dyck (2013) notes, party activists can do campaign work, organize rallies, go "door to door," transport individuals to polling booths, while local party offices can provide financial, material, and logistical support for these campaign activities.

[18] According to Levitsky (2003) internal (formal or informal) routinization is one dimension of party's institutionalization. It can be defined as "a state in which the rules and procedures within an organization are widely known, accepted, and complied with" (2003: 18). Nonroutinization, by contrast, is a state in which (formal or informal) rules and procedures are fluid, contested, and routinely circumvented or ignored.

where (a) the presidential party's organization is weakly routinized and (b) it is electorally viable in just one district.

Routinization of Presidential Party's Rules and Procedures

To determine the level of presidential parties' routinization of rules and procedures, this subsection draws on secondary literature that has carried out in-depth studies on parties' internal structures. Specifically, it focuses on the centralized nature of the party bureaucracy, as this aspect critically shapes national party leaders' capacity to discipline subnational copartisans.

Building on the comprehensive work by Levitsky (2003) on the Argentine Peronist party (or PJ), the Peronist party of Néstor Kirchner and Cristina Fernández de Kirchner is classified here as a weakly routinized party. According to Levitsky (2003), the party's formal bodies of authority are weak and largely inoperative. The formal party structure is ignored, and power, resources, information, and even political careers pass through informal, self-organized subunits with only weak and intermittent links both to each other and to the party bureaucracy. The party, in Levitsky's (2003) account, can best be characterized as a decentralized and delinked organization, whereby subunits are not connected vertically into a central bureaucracy, simply because the latter is virtually nonexistent. As a result of this loosely vertical integration, national party leaders (Levitsky 2003) lack effective mechanisms with which to impose discipline on party subunits and their governors (Jones and Hwang 2005). In sum, Peronist subnational incumbents enjoy substantial autonomy form the party hierarchy.

In contrast, the Mexican PAN of Vicente Fox and Felipe Calderón is a highly bureaucratized party (Mizrahi 2003; Shirk 2000, 2005; Greene 2007; Wuhs 2008). Unlike the Peronist party, the PAN's formal bodies of authority—the National Assembly, the National Council, and the National Executive Committee—are operative and deeply involved in the party's functioning. The party is also highly centralized. The party's vertical integration, as well as its existing mechanisms to elicit cooperation from subnational PAN leaders, is also superior to that observed in the Argentine PJ. State-level party branches are well-connected to the national party's bureaucracy, and they participate actively in National Assembly decisions. Even though they are allowed to draft complementary state-level norms following the general party principles, state party organizations may not contravene decisions taken by the national bodies of the party (Mizrahi 2003: 52–3). This centralized and highly bureaucratized party structure exerts considerable leverage on PAN governors and PAN subnational leaders, preventing them from acting independently of the party hierarchy. Control over subnational PAN incumbents, which became stronger due in part to the National Executive

Committee's increasing intromission in the process of gubernatorial candidate selection (Wuhs 2006), resulted in even fewer possibilities for autonomy from the central party bodies.

In sum, a comparison of the internal functioning of the PJ in Argentina and the PAN in Mexico indicates that, up to 2009, Mexican PAN presidents enjoy greater presidential partisan power over copartisan governors than do their Argentine Peronist counterparts. As a result the former stood in a better position to discipline subnational copartisans and, in turn, to obtain their political cooperation and acquiescence.

Electoral Territorial Extension of Presidential Parties

To gauge the electoral territorial extension of presidential parties, this chapter uses the inverted Gini coefficient of the Party Nationalization Score (PNS) (Jones and Mainwaring 2003). A Gini coefficient of 1 means that the president's party received 100 percent of its vote in one subnational unit and 0 percent in all the rest. A Gini coefficient of 0 signifies that the president's party received the same share of the vote in every subnational unit. Jones and Mainwaring calculate the inverted Gini coefficient of the PNS by subtracting the Gini coefficient from 1 such that a high score indicates a territorially extended presidential party.[19]

Figure 4.4 plots Gini coefficients of presidential PNS for Argentina and Mexico. As demonstrated, until the mid-1990s, Argentine presidential parties obtained fairly homogeneous electoral support across all electoral districts, indicating that parties managed to have an effective electoral presence in all provinces. Indeed, the existence of party organizations across subnational districts was critical to the electoral presence of the Radical Party (UCR) during the 1980s and the PJ during the early 1990s across provinces. This trend, however, began to change during Menem's second administration (1995–9), as the PJ started to lose ground in some provincial districts. These losses became more pronounced in the late 1990s and early-mid 2000s, when presidential parties could only win elections in selected provinces (Calvo and Escolar 2005; Leiras 2006, 2007; Gibson and Suarez-Cao 2010). The late 2000s, however, saw a progressive expansion of the president's party, as the Front of Victory (or FpV) of Cristina Fernández Kirchner obtained a greater electoral presence in provinces that had previously been controlled by the opposition. This expansion, which peaked in 2007, began to recede in the subsequent years.

---

[19] Measured in this way, the PNS has two main advantages: it allows changes in a party's level of territorial extension to be traced over time, and it allows parties' level of nationalization across countries to be compared.

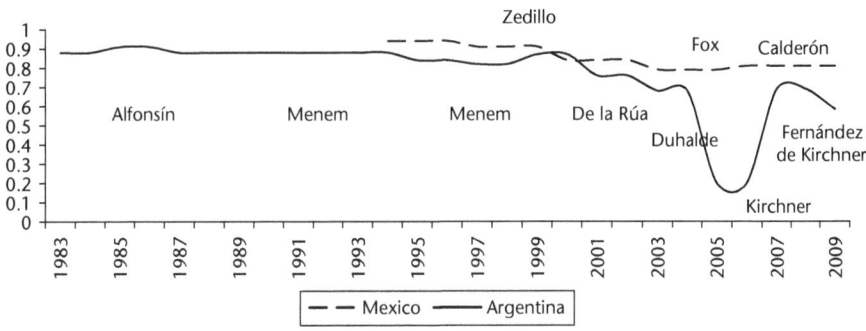

Figure 4.4. Gini coefficients of presidential PNS in Argentina and Mexico
Source: Argentina: 1994–2001: Jones and Mainwaring 2003; 2003–5: Leiras 2006; 2007: author's calculations; Mexico: 1994–2000: Jones and Mainwaring 2003; 2003–6: Olmeda and Suárez-Cao, n.d.

The existence of provincial parties in some Argentine provinces, which over time became more hegemonic and hence increasingly successful at winning provincial elections (Gibson and Suarez-Cao 2010; Gibson 2013), accounts in part for the increasing levels of party deterritorialization. Party splits in Argentina's main political parties also explain why presidential parties in Argentina became deterritorialized. Party splits, such as the one observed in the PJ since 2003, imply that presidents no longer wielded effective power and electoral control through their party organizations and networks of activists in every area of the country.[20] In fact, leaders of each of these newly created parties dominated and controlled different parts of the territory. In 2003, for instance, President Néstor Kirchner's party organization, the FpV, was strong and thus electorally powerful only in some Patagonian provinces and the province of Buenos Aires (Calvo and Escolar 2005). Beyond these districts, its party organization was limited and its electoral performance poor.

In Mexico, by contrast, presidential parties have generally been territorially extended. This was not surprising in the pre-2000 years, given the Institutional Revolutionary Party's (PRI's) hegemony and its concomitant ubiquitous territorial presence through a myriad of party-related organizations in every electoral district of the country. This presence was also not surprising during the administrations of Presidents Fox and Calderón.

---

[20] The 2003 split divided the PJ into three different parties: the Frente por la Lealtad (Front for Loyalty), led by former President Menem; the Frente Movimiento Popular—Unión y Libertad (Popular Movement—Unity and Liberty), headed by San Luis's former governor, Adolfo Rodríguez-Saá; and the Alianza FpV, led by Kirchner and his immediate predecessor, Eduardo Duhalde. In 2007 and 2011 the PJ continued to be divided into different parties. Two Peronist parties in 2007 competed for the presidency, i.e. the Alianza FpV, led by Cristina Fernández de Kirchner, and the Alianza Frente Justicia, Unión y Libertad (Front Justice, Union, and Liberty Front), led by Alberto Rodríguez-Saá. These two PJ parties competed against each other once in again in 2011.

Despite the fact that, until the 1980s, the PAN could not be considered as a nationally extended party, given that its core supporters and the party's branches were mostly located in the northern and central districts of Mexico (Mizrahi 2003), the post-1990 strategy of crafting alliances with non-PRI opposition parties, as well as the focus on winning control of local and state governments, propelled the party to strengthen its party organization and state-level branches in most Mexican districts (Shirk 2000). As a result of this progressive expansion, the party even managed to make political and electoral inroads in southern states (Shirk 2000, 2005; and the cluster of articles in the January 2007 issue of *Political Science and Politics*).

The fact that regional and state-level parties were not allowed to compete in national elections partly explains the existence of territorially expanded presidential parties in Mexico. Up to 2009, Mexican electoral rules require parties to become national political organizations and centralize their decision-making bodies before competing in national races (Loaeza 2003; Mizrahi 2003; Olmeda and Suárez-Cao n.d.). Additionally, in spite of internal partisan rifts, presidential parties in Mexico succeeded in avoiding party splits.[21]

A comparison between presidential PNS in Argentina and Mexico reveals that, up to 2009, presidential partisan power was consistently stronger in Mexico. Unlike their Argentine counterparts, Mexican presidents managed to extend their party organizations throughout the territory and, by so doing, obtained greater sway over both copartisan and opposition subnational incumbents. By contrast, Argentine presidents, who at the turn of the latest democratization period succeeded in exerting partisan power over most provinces, progressively lost the capacity to attract cooperation via partisan resources.

Assessing Sources of Presidential Power—Fiscal vs. Partisan Resources

In order to determine the primary resources or combination of resources available to each Argentine and Mexican president, this section compares and contrasts presidential access to the two instruments analyzed in the preceding sections. If fiscal powers are low, and party territorialization as well as the centralized nature of the party bureaucracy is high, a given president is classified as having partisan power. Conversely, a president is categorized as having fiscal power if (s)he has a low capacity to extend

---

[21] This is somehow different at the subnational level of government, where party elite defection, or *transfuguismo* as it is called in Mexico, is common.

her party throughout the territory, low capacity to discipline subnational copartisans, and good access to fiscal resources. It should be clear from the outset that this classification is not meant to indicate that presidents who are catalogued as having fiscal power lack partisan power (or vice versa). Rather, it is meant to denote that fiscal resources are considerably more accessible (and probably more effective) to induce the cooperation of subnational incumbents.

Table 4.3 displays information about the combination of fiscal and partisan resources at the disposal of both Argentine and Mexican presidents and provides information about the type of presidential fiscal and partisan power prevalent under different administrations. An assessment of the different resources available to presidents reveals that the type of resources available to the Argentine Presidents Néstor Kirchner and Cristina Fernández de Kirchner, and the Mexican Presidents Vicente Fox and Felipe Calderón, have been partisan and fiscal, respectively.

Table 4.3. Presidential power: fiscal and partisan instruments of cooptation

		Argentina		Mexico	
		Kirchner (2003–2007)	Fernandez de Kirchner (2008–2009)	Fox (2000–2006)	Calderón (2007–2009)
Fiscal resources	i. Stability of the revenue-sharing system's rules that determine the amount of and distribution of transfers that are sent to subnational units	moderate*	moderate*	high	high
	ii. Tax revenues not subject to sharing	very high	very high	moderate/low**	moderate/low**
Partisan resources	i. Routinization of presidential party's rules and procedures	low	low	high	High
	Electoral territorial extension of presidential party	Low	moderate	high	High
Predominant resource available to induce cooperation***		FISCAL	FISCAL	PARTISAN	PARTISAN

* Coparticipation percentages are reinstated but deductions of the provincial coparticipation remain in place
** Due to post-2003 introduction of provisions to earmark extraordinary revenues from oil
*** Based on resources most available to presidents

During the early and mid-2000s, when the level of presidential party nationalization in Argentina decreased, the country was ruled by a weakly routinized party (the PJ), and presidential fiscal power was nonetheless high—due in large part to the windfall gains of export/import duties—the Kirchners resorted to fiscal resources to discipline governors (see also Bonvecchi and Giraudy 2008). In Mexico, by contrast, the greater stability of the rules structuring the revenue-sharing arrangement, the lower availability of revenues not subject to sharing, and the provisions introduced to curtail the discretional allocation of these resources seriously limited Presidents Fox's and Calderón's capacity to discipline governors via fiscal instruments. However, the higher levels of presidential party territorialization, as well as the more bureaucratized nature of the PAN's internal organization, gave both presidents considerable partisan leeway to obtain the acquiescence of both copartisan and opposition governors.

Conclusion

This chapter has explored the instruments available to presidents to induce the cooperation and obtain the acquiescence of governors, and of subnational autocrats in particular. Drawing on the insights provided by the literature on fiscal federalism and political parties, the chapter showed that Argentine and Mexican presidents employed two major resources to subjugate autocrats: their party organizations and/or the federal funds that they could send to subnational jurisdictions. In emphasizing the availability of institutional and economic resources to induce cooperation of subnational incumbents, the chapter underscored the importance of assessing both resources in evaluating the actual power of presidents vis-à-vis subnational rulers. The focus on two, rather than one, types of instruments relevant to presidential power is advantageous, not only because it enables a more comprehensive assessment of intergovernmental interactions, but also because it demonstrates that power relations in multi-level polities are structured differently, and are highly contingent on the access of presidents to varied types of resources.

The chapter also revealed, but did not analyze in depth, the fact that presidential power can be exerted in ways that vary over time not only across but also *within* countries. The case of Argentina vividly illustrates this point, as not all resources were equally available and attainable to democratic presidents. While Peronist President Menem managed to resort to both partisan and fiscal instruments to obtain the acquiescence of governors, Peronist Presidents Duhalde and the Kirchners disciplined subnational rulers by employing fiscal resources. By acknowledging these differences, the chapter also demonstrated that power relations within multi-level polities and across presidential administrations (of the same party) are structured differently.

Finally, as noted earlier, this chapter measured and analyzed the absolute power that presidents have vis-à-vis subnational rulers, regardless of whether this power is neutralized by specific characteristics of subnational units and subnational incumbents. However, one of the central claims of this book is that there is significant variation between governors (and subnational units), and that this variation is key to preventing or neutralizing presidential encroachments over SURs, regardless of how much absolute fiscal and partisan power presidents actually possess. As noted in Chapter 2, the ability of presidents to obtain the acquiescence of subnational autocrats is shaped by a combination of national and subnational factors. To be able to exert leverage over subnational incumbents two conditions are necessary: (a) the president needs to have the means necessary to subjugate an undemocratic governor, and (b) the undemocratic governor's capacity to resist penetration from above must be minimal. Neither of these two conditions alone is sufficient for a president to gain leverage over provincial politics; rather the combination is necessary. With these insights in mind, the next chapters focus on cross-subnational differences and look at how these interact with presidential resources of territorial and political control, in turn determining trajectories of SUR continuity.

5

SUR Reproduction from Above in Argentina and Mexico: Quantitative Evidence

This chapter turns back to cross-subnational differences and explores how these affect the prospects of subnational undemocratic regime (SUR) continuity. In particular, it analyzes how variations in SUR's fiscal autonomy of the federal government and SUR's state structures neutralize or enhance the capacity of presidents to wield power over subnational undemocratic rulers/areas, and in turn, influence the possibilities for SUR reproduction from above. Analyzing the prospects of effective presidential power over SURs is crucial because, as argued in Chapter 2, presidents who can hold nondemocratic governors hostage stand in an excellent position to manipulate and make undemocratic incumbents meet their strategic needs. As a result, they are expected to contribute to SUR reproduction (from above) rather than to SUR weakening.

The chapter has three major goals. First, using quantitative techniques, it seeks to test the more general claims of the book, namely, that the power exercised by presidents over subnational autocrats (i.e. the independent variable) leads to SUR reproduction from above (i.e. the dependent variable), and that a lack of effective presidential power results in no reproduction from above at all. Second, the chapter aims to specify the scope conditions under which subnational autocratic support can be maximized. Finally, it seeks to test whether these theoretical claims have enough inferential leverage and are generalizable across the universe of SURs in contemporary Argentina and Mexico. To meet these goals, different cross-sectional time-series analyses are employed.

The first part of the chapter outlines the hypotheses and the conditions of subnational autocratic political support that will be quantitatively tested. The second section explores the actual forms through which presidents can promote the continuity of SURs, and provides a justification of the mechanisms of regime reproduction. The subsequent sections discuss the measures of the dependent and independent variables, as well as the analytic technique used to test the hypotheses. Statistical results and their discussion follow this section. The last section closes with some reflections about the generalizability of the findings.

SUR Reproduction from Above: Hypotheses and Conditions of Presidential Control

Conditions under which Presidents Maximize Power over SURs/Autocrats

As argued in Chapter 2, effective presidential power over subnational autocrats and SURs is more likely under two circumstances: (a) where SURs' fiscal autonomy from the central government is low, and (b) where non-patrimonial state structures prevail. SUR fiscal dependency on the central government enables presidents to wield effective fiscal power and, in turn, facilitates presidents' capacity to induce the cooperation of subnational undemocratic rulers. Indeed, as the literature on fiscal federalism highlights, highly indebted or financially profligate governors, who depend on the central government for their subsistence, can be expected to comply with the central government's political demands for fear of being deprived of funds (Wibbels 2005; Falleti 2005). By contrast, subnational rulers from fiscally responsible and low-indebted jurisdictions or those who rule provinces which amass abundant revenues, due, for instance, to efficient tax collection or to the existence of profitable natural resources, enjoy greater fiscal autonomy from the federal government, and thus more independence vis-à-vis national incumbents (Wibbels 2005). On these grounds, it can be hypothesized that presidents will help reproduce SURs that are in fiscal and financial dire straits, rather than SURs that are fiscally and financially sound, as the latter are more likely to refuse cooperation with the federal government than to meet presidents' strategic political needs.

Chapter 2 claimed that democratically elected presidents can maximize presidential partisan power where non-patrimonial state structures exist. In such institutional settings, state structures prevent subnational autocrats from (i) centralizing authority, and (ii) exercising tight control over state resources, territory, and opposition parties/groups. As a result, subnational autocrats are virtually powerless to circumvent local–national pro-democratic coalition-making, or in Gibson's (2013) words, to thwart boundary control situations. Accordingly, presidents in non-patrimonial SURs have greater ability to infiltrate these regimes. It is through coalition-building with local groups and subnational opposition leaders that presidents can penetrate SURs and, in turn, challenge and co-opt subnational autocrats from within. Hence, it is expected that presidents will help reproduce SURs in power where non-patrimonial state structures prevail.

Where these state structures exist, presidents' calculations regarding SUR reproduction should also be shaped by municipal factors. The existence of municipalities ruled by the party of the president, for instance, should play a decisive role in presidents' capacity to boost presidential partisan power over autocrats, as national–local alliances with copartisans may prove critical to put pressure on undemocratic governors to meet presidential political needs. On these grounds, it is expected that national democratic executives will have incentives to reproduce the SURs in which the share of municipalities that belongs to the president's party is higher, as the possibility of crafting local–national alliances to constrict autocrats from within is greater, as are the opportunities to increase president's likelihood of obtaining autocrats' political cooperation.

Conditions that Maximize Subnational Autocratic Political Support

As noted in Chapter 2, subnational undemocratic incumbents who can be disciplined from above can become key partners for coalition-making (Hagopian 1996; Snyder 1999; Gibson 1997, 2005; Hunter and Power 2007). With their tight control over local party machines, autocrats from SURs can help deliver votes that have decisive impact on general and mid-term national elections (Snyder 1999; Gibson 2005). Furthermore, subnational undemocratic rulers may provide invaluable legislative support for the passage of bills that are central to national incumbents' political projects.[1] Likewise, as argued in Chapter 2, these rulers can help maintain political stability and manage security threats, thus assisting presidents in areas that are strategic to national security and governability. For instance, recalcitrant autocrats, who usually control paramilitary forces, can be charged, as Snyder (1999) points out, with the presidential "mission" of managing security threats in key geographic areas.

From the literature on federalism and legislative politics we know that governors' ability to deliver legislative support stems from their capacity to discipline legislators' voting behavior. Several studies show that provincial/state-level executives in Argentina and Mexico can influence legislative

---

[1] Autocrats from SURs become attractive partners for legislative coalition-making because they usually rule small and underpopulated provinces/states, which are overrepresented in the national Congress, and whose legislative votes weigh far more heavily than those of larger and more democratic districts (Samuels and Snyder 2001; Gibson and Calvo 2001; Gibson 2004; Jones and Hwang 2005).

behavior simply because they control legislators' political careers (De Luca et al. 2002; Gordin 2004; Jones and Hwang 2005; Samuels 2003; Díaz-Cayeros 2006; Langston 2004, 2005; Langston and Aparicio 2008). This capacity to influence legislators' votes converts governors into legislative brokers and key partners for legislative coalition-making, as they can ensure the delivery of congressional support for presidents.

Yet autocrats differ considerably in their ability to deliver legislative votes. Because their capacity to ensure votes depends on their ability to control legislators' political careers, undemocratic governors can only exert leverage over deputies and senators who belong to their own political parties. They cannot, by contrast, influence the voting behavior of opposition legislators, simply because governors do not control their political careers. It thus follows that provincial executives' capacity to ensure and deliver legislative support is determined by the share of legislators that belong to his or her party. Autocrats who control the bulk of the legislative delegation (i.e. the largest share of copartisans), and who in turn can secure national incumbents more legislative votes, should be substantially more attractive to presidents than provincial autocrats who control small shares of legislators. For instance, Oaxaca's Governor Ulises Ruiz from the Institutional Revolutionary Party (PRI), who between 2006 and 2009 only controlled 21 percent of Oaxaca's PRI national deputies (i.e. four out of 19 deputies), and 33 percent of the senators (one PRI senator out of three), was less attractive than, for instance, PRI Governor Manuel Ángel Núñez from the state of Hidalgo, who controlled, and thus could secure the votes of five PRI deputies, that is, 50 percent of the state's legislative delegation.[2] On these grounds, it can be hypothesized that presidents will reproduce SURs where autocrats control a larger share of copartisan federal legislators, as these rulers are in a better position to ensure the delivery of legislative votes.

The disciplining capacity of autocrats over legislators is also mediated by electoral institutions and campaign financing rules that are specific to each country, which is why undemocratic rulers from some, but not all, countries can ensure the delivery of legislative support. The case of Mexico nicely illustrates how electoral rules can limit subnational autocrats' capacity to ensure legislative support. Mexico has a mixed electoral system, with 300 of the 500-member Chamber of Deputies filled through plurality races in single-member districts (SMDs) and 200 through closed proportional representation (PR) lists. Voters in Mexico cast only one ballot to choose SMD deputies and do not participate directly in selecting PR deputies. In this context, as noted by Langston and Aparicio, "PR deputy candidates do not run electoral

---

[2] Strictly speaking, Ulises Ruiz had control over three PRI federal legislators. The fourth deputy was his predecessor, José Murat, over whom Ruiz could not exert any leverage.

campaigns; if they are placed high enough on the closed list, they will enter the Chamber" (2008: 9). SMD legislators, by contrast, must win plurality races, and thus are interested in running successful campaigns. Given that successful campaigns entail access to resources, SMD candidates are dependent on the national party headquarters and, above all, on governors for a good deal of their campaign funds (Langston 2005). Subnational incumbents, then, become candidates' lenders of last resort, and consequently stand in a position to make SMD deputies far more beholden than PR deputies. These electoral and campaign rules considerably limit the capacity of Mexican subnational autocrats to guarantee the votes of both SMD and PR deputies. Hence, it is expected that presidents in Mexico will only contribute to the reproduction of those SURs where autocrats control the largest share of copartisan SMD deputies. Before exploring the validity of these hypotheses, a caveat about presidential strategies and the mechanisms they employ to promote SUR reproduction is in order.

Mechanisms of SUR Reproduction from Above

Democratically elected presidents can contribute to SUR reproduction in at least two different ways. First, they can stay neutral regarding SUR existence, in that they can maintain the status quo just by allowing SURs to survive. For instance, presidents who avoid sanctioning or weakening subnational autocrats and who, for instance, consent to subnational undemocratic incumbents staying in power until the next electoral cycle takes place, contribute to SUR reproduction. This type of reproduction can be referred to as "reproduction from above by omission." Alternatively, presidents can engage in what can be denoted as "passive reproduction from above" by deliberately engaging in activities to promote and reproduce SURs. For instance, they may veto legislation, such as a declaration of federal intervention seeking to overturn undemocratic regimes in specific subnational units. They can also discourage bills or veto laws intended to enhance subnational democratization in a given SUR, or prevent independent agencies of control such as the Supreme Court, the Constitutional Tribunals, or federal auditing agencies from sanctioning subnational autocrats. Finally, presidents can also actively sustain SURs in power by benefitting them economically. They can, for instance, reward SURs with additional subsidies or with special federal transfers and programs through which they help consolidate and maintain these regimes in power. This type of SUR reproduction, which entails active presidential involvement, can be referred to as "deliberate reproduction from above."

This book (and chapter) focuses on the latter type of presidential strategy of SUR reproduction. Instances of "reproduction by omission" are difficult to measure because they constitute non-events. Even though instances of "passive reproduction from above" are much easier to grasp, and their measurement is less controversial—events (such as vetoes) either happened or not—they can still be difficult to measure given that it is hard to find out the back room negotiations that, for instance, may have led presidents to discourage bills intended to hinder subnational democratization. For all these reasons, it seems more reasonable to focus on the type of reproduction that occurs via the transfer of federal funds, as this form is the easiest to assess (provided data is available).

Previous works have found that national politicians in both Argentina and Mexico do not distribute earmarked public money/programs following formal criteria, but rather on the basis of partisan and political criteria (Porto and Sanguinetti 2001; Gibson and Calvo 2000; Gibson et al. 2004; Díaz-Cayeros 2004b, 2006; Giraudy 2007; Magaloni 2006). This biased distribution suggests that federal incumbents may also use these programs and funds to reproduce SURs from above. Drawing on this evidence, the next section explores whether the allocation of two specific federal transfers—(1) funds for public works and (2) financial subsidies (PAFEF in Mexico and ATN in Argentina)—has also been used to sustain SURs that were easier to discipline and thus more likely to meet presidents' strategic political needs.

Measures of the Dependent and Independent Variables

The Aportaciones Program for the Enhancement of the Federal States (PAFEF), the National Treasury Funds (ATN), and funds for public works (i.e. the dependent variables) were selected because of their propensity to be distributed in a discretionary manner. Previous works show that each of these funds has been allocated on the basis of political rather than universal criteria (see Díaz-Cayeros 2006; Giraudy 2006; Cetrángolo and Jiménez 1997; Gibson and Calvo 2000; Bonvecchi and Lodola 2011). There are thus good reasons to suspect that these programs might have been used by presidents to reproduce SURs from above. All federal transfers are measured as a percentage of provincial/state-level total income (see Table 5.1 for a detailed description of each variable and its source).

Two indicators, *debt and surplus*, are used to identify a SUR's fiscal autonomy from the federal government. Both predictors were calculated as the yearly percentage of state/province's total revenues. High scores of debt indicate higher levels of indebtedness (i.e. SUR's lower fiscal autonomy from the federal government), whereas higher scores of surplus reveal greater fiscal autonomy. The second variable of theoretical relevance, *non-patrimonial state structure*, is measured using the index of patrimonialism described in Chapter 3

Democrats and Autocrats

Table 5.1. Variable description and data sources

Variables	Description	Source	
		Argentina	Mexico
Dependent variables			
Public works	Includes all funds for infrastructure projects	Cuenta Inversión (various yrs), Giraudy (2006)	Subdirección de Economía be
PAFEF	Subsidies destined for financial imbalance and infrastructural needs		Servicos de Inverstigactión y Analis (camara de Diptados)
ATN	Subsidies destined for emergencies and financial imbalances	CECE (1997), Ministerio de Economía	Informde gobierno 2007, based on SCHP data
Independent variables			
Main variables			
Governor's legislative support	% of deputies of governor's party†	Giraudy and Lodola (2008)	Cámara de Diputados
Non-patrimonial state structure	Patrimonial Index, Chapter 3	Book's Appendix	Appendix
Governor-president copartisanship	Dummy variable	Based on Andy Tow	Based on IFE
Fiscal autonomy (debt)	Debt as % of total revenues	Mecon-DNCFP	SHCP-UCEF
Fiscal autonomy (surplus)	Surplus as % of total revenues	Mecon-DNCFP	SHCP-UCEF
Municipalites belonging to presidential party	% of muncipalities belonging to presidential party	Micozzi (2009)	Based on CIDAC
Control variables			
Presidential election	Dummy variable	Ministerio del Interior	IFE
Gubernatorial election	Dummy variable	Ministerio del Interior	IFE
Legislative election	Dummy variable	Ministerio del Interior	IFE
Province of president	Dummy variable		
Population	Logged population	INDEC	CONAPO*
Poverty		Unsatisfied Basic Needs (INDEC)	
Index of infrastructure			A.regional**

* Projected, ** This index rank-orders states on the basis of their infrastructural coverage of: education, health, communications, and transport. The index is calculated every year.
†SMD deputies in the case of Mexico.

(see Appendix for a detailed explanation of how this index was built). High scores of this index denote a non-patrimonial state structure, whereas low scores indicate higher levels of patrimonialism. The third variable, *municipalities belonging to presidential party*, captures the president's electoral partisan presence at the local, municipal level. It is coded as the percentage of municipalities controlled by the president's party in any given year.

To measure the conditions under which autocratic support can be maximized, a fourth variable, *governor's legislative support*, was included in the regressions. The predictor is calculated as the yearly percentage of copartisan federal deputies who belong to subnational autocrats' congressional delegations.[3] For the reasons already outlined, this measure only includes federal SMD deputies in Mexico.

When appropriate, the models were run with additional control variables. The distribution of funds for public works should, in principle, be determined by infrastructural needs. Other things being equal, one would expect that undemocratic states and provinces which lag behind in terms of infrastructural development should receive a greater proportion of funds for public works than undemocratic subnational units whose infrastructure is more developed. Similarly, highly populated districts, where the demand for infrastructure (sewerage, housing, and paved roads) is higher, should also receive more funds for public works. To control for these effects, an *index of infrastructure* was employed in the Mexican models, and *necesidades básicas insatisfechas* (unsatisfied basic needs)—a proxy for poverty—was used in the Argentine regressions.

The argument about presidents' capacity to exert effective power over SURs/autocrats, which is hypothesized as a condition for SURs reproduction from above, should hold regardless of president–autocrat copartisanship and electoral cycles. In other words, autocrats belonging to any political party, provided they are subject to effective presidential power, should be strengthened from above. Likewise, SURs should be reproduced not only during electoral years, but on a constant basis (i.e. every year). Thus, either no effect or a negative effect of copartisanship and electoral processes is expected on presidents' decision to sustain SURs.

Several variables were included to control for the effects of copartisanship and electoral cycles. *Copartisanship* between presidents and subnational undemocratic rulers in Argentina is measured using a dummy variable that scores 1 when the presidential party equals a governor's party, and 0 otherwise. For the case of Mexico, where some governors of the National Action Party (PAN) have come to power through electoral coalitions with other national parties, two dummy variables were created. The first variable captures *Panista* autocrats who governed without a coalition (i.e. *governor–president copartisanship [non-coalition]*) and the other gauges *Panista* subnational undemocratic rulers who won elections, and thus governed in coalition

---

[3] The focus is on deputies, rather than senators, because senators are usually prominent political figures, who are less susceptible to following governors' orders. Senator Carlos Menem (ex-president), Senator Francisco Labastida (PRI 2006 presidential candidate and ex-governor of Sinaloa), and Manlio Fabio Beltrones (ex-governor of the state of Sonora) are examples of senators whose voting behavior was not influenced by the governors of the districts they represented.

(i.e. *governor-president copartisanship [coalition]*). Each of the dummies scores 1 for the years in which each of these two types of PAN autocrats ruled a given state, and 0 otherwise.

Three dummy variables—*gubernatorial, presidential*, and *legislative election*—were included in the models. Each variable was coded as 1 in the year in which presidential, legislative, or gubernatorial elections were held, and 0 otherwise. Given that electoral calendars across levels of government differ in each country (i.e. staggered versus concurrent electoral calendars in Mexico and Argentina, respectively), different combinations of these three electoral variables were included in each country model.[4]

Presidents who are native to SURs, such as Carlos Menem from La Rioja or Néstor Kirchner from Santa Cruz, may have a strong inclination to channel funds to their strongholds not only to sustain SURs but also for personal reasons. For instance, as former President Menem noted, "an outstandingly large amount of money was sent to La Rioja [one of Argentina's SURs] not so much to keep the regime alive but also to reward the loyalty of former staffers and to improve the wellbeing of my Riojanos" (interview by author, La Rioja, May 9, 2008). To control for these effects, a dummy variable, *province of President*, was included. Finally, the time span analyzed covers different presidencies. Dummy variables were included to control for political and partisan effects occurring during these various presidencies. Lastly, the variable *population* was included as an additional control.

Data and Analytic Technique

The balanced panel dataset used for the statistical analyses comprises all Argentine and Mexican SURs—i.e. the provinces and states that score between 0 and 0.5 in Argentina, and between 0.5 and 1 in Mexico (see Figures 3.2 and 3.3, Chapter 3).[5] This means that all Argentine provinces and Mexican states scoring below 0.5 and 1, respectively, are included in the dataset. Data span the period 1990–2006 (Model 1), 1996–2007 (Model 2), and 2000–8 (Models 3 and 4).[6]

---

[4] The existence of concurrent national and subnational elections in Argentina yields high correlations across the three electoral variables. Thus, one or two (at best) dummy variables were included in the models. By contrast, the staggered nature of electoral calendars in Mexico permits the inclusion of the three electoral variables.

[5] Data in each country are analyzed separately, not pooled. Cluster analyses were employed to set the cut-off points between states and provinces that rank zero or near zero from those ranking higher on the democracy scale.

[6] Time periods for Argentina (Models 1 and 2) differ because data for the dependent variable were available for varying time points.

When data are pooled across time and units, several of the ordinary least squares (OLS) standard assumptions are violated, and consequently the usual procedures for hypothesis testing are no longer appropriate (Long and Ervin 2000). Authors have provided alternative solutions to deal with these violations, including fixed-effects and random-effects models (FEM and REM, respectively), panel-corrected standard errors (PCSE), lagged dependent variable (LDV) models, and autoregressive (AR) models with corrections for first-order autoregression (AR1) (see Beck and Katz 1995; Achen 2000; Huber and Stephens 2001; Plümper et al. 2005; among others).

Some of these analytic techniques, such as PCSE and AR models, are inappropriate, because the data used in this study are not temporally dominated (i.e., $t > N$), but rather cross-sectionally dominated (i.e., $N > t$). Other techniques, such as FEMs or LDV models, are also inadequate given that several key independent variables have level effects and are relatively time invariant (i.e., they only change at a slow pace). In the presence of such variables, a FEM will improperly absorb the significance of these predictors (Plümper et al. 2005; Achen 2000).

For all these reasons, the problem of correlated errors in panel data is addressed using a combination of OLS estimation of the regression coefficients with a robust-cluster estimator of the standard errors. The robust-cluster variance estimator, as noted by Huber et al., "provides correct coverage in the presence of any pattern of correlations among errors within units, including serial correlation and correlation attributable to unit-specific components" (2006: 957).

Results and Discussion

The results of the quantitative analyses conducted in this chapter reveal that when the universe of Argentine and Mexican SURs is taken into consideration, presidents contribute to the reproduction of the regimes/autocrats that are susceptible to be disciplined from above, and that serve presidents politically well. Confirming the theoretical expectations advanced in Chapter 2, Table 5.2 shows that democratic presidents in Argentina and Mexico help sustain SURs where (a) autocrats are fiscally dependent on the national government, (b) non-patrimonial state structures exist, and (c) where copartisan mayors abound.

One of the most consistent findings of this chapter is that, ceteris paribus, presidents reward SURs that are in fiscal dire straits. In effect, increasing provincial surplus in Argentina by 1 percent leads to a decrease in ATN spending of 0.07 percent of the SURs' income (Model 1), and to a decrease in public works spending of 0.05 percent of the SURs' total revenues (Model 2).

Likewise, a 1 percent increase in the state-level surplus in Mexico results in a decrease in public works spending of 0.02 percent of the SURs' income (Model 4). The presidential decision to allocate more funds to SURs that have larger deficits and which are ruled by profligate subnational autocrats substantiates the theoretical claim that presidents opt to reward provincial undemocratic rulers who are more susceptible to being controlled, and thus more likely to be induced to meet presidents' strategic political needs. As noted earlier, financial dependency on the federal government not only seriously limits undemocratic governors' capacity to challenge and oppose the presidential agenda, but, more importantly, it places strong constraints on provincial incumbents to follow presidential orders.[7] This finding is consistent with qualitative and quantitative evidence of undemocratic profligate Argentine provinces (presented by Wibbels (2005), and in Chapter 6) that reveals that governors from these districts are forced to support most presidential initiatives for fear of being deprived of financial resources. The results presented in Table 5.2 reveal that this claim also holds true when a larger set of SURs is taken into consideration.

The inclination of Argentine and Mexican presidents to reproduce SURs where non-patrimonial state structures prevail is evidenced by both the positive sign and statistical significance of the *non-patrimonial state structure* variable in Models 2 and 3, and its statistical insignificance in Models 1 and 4.[8] Models 2 and 3 show that undemocratic regimes where autocrats (a) centralize power in their hands, (b) reduce followers' autonomy through the generational ties of loyalty and dependence, and (c) appropriate state resources for private economic or political gain, are rewarded with more federal transfers than regimes where autocrats exert power in a patrimonial way. This finding substantiates the argument that presidents' strategic calculations about SUR reproduction is conditioned upon the former's capacity to wield effective power over SURs and autocrats. Given that effective partisan presidential power is harder to attain where patrimonial state structures prevail, presidents opt to punish patrimonial SURs by not channeling federal funds and programs to these regimes.

Another possible interpretation of presidents' aversion to SURs/autocrats may have to do with the fact that national incumbents are reluctant to enhancing the position of already territorially and politically powerful bosses who could eventually challenge presidential authority. Actively sustaining clientelistic, illiberal, and patrimonial governors who plainly violate democratic and

---

[7] Another possible interpretation of the greater share of ATNs flowing to profligate SURs is the president's determination to ensure national macroeconomic stability.

[8] *Non-patrimonial state structure* in Model 3 has a strikingly powerful effect on the dependent variable: a unit increase in this independent variable results in an increase in PAFEF spending of 10.22% of the SUR's total income.

Table 5.2. Determinants of ATN, PAFEF, and funds for public works with robust cluster standard errors

	Argentina		Mexico	
	ATN	Funds for public works	PAFEF	Funds for public works
Independent variables	Model 1	Model 2	Model 3	Model 4
Governor's legislative support	0.049* (0.032)	−0.006 (0.015)	0.005 (0.006)	0.001 (0.009)
Non-partrimonial state structure	−4.02 (4.187)	3.579** (1.999)	10.22*** (1.189)	0.859 (1.626)
Governor–pres. copartisanship (coalition)			0.237 (0.334)	0.936** (0.455)
Governor–pres. copartisanship (non-coalition)	0.095 (0.708)	−0.192 (0.482)	−0.285 (1.191)	−1.299** (0.657)
Fiscal autonomy (surplus)	−0.071* (0.05)	0.056** (0.021)	−0003* (0.268)	0.024** (0.012)
Fiscal autonomy (debt)†			−0.024 (0.092)	−0.125 (0.078)
Municipalities belonging to presidential party	−0.007 (0.009)	0.022** (0.009)	2.422* (1.556)	1.781* (1.232)
Province of president	14.141*** (4.542)	3.701* (2.312)		
Presidential election†			−1.954*** (0.297)	0.602 (0.709)
Legislative election†	3.322** (1.3936)	−2.229** (0.833)	0.818** (0.292)	−0.121 (0.213)
Gubernatorial election†	−3.698* (1.763)	0.636 (0.521)	0.659* (0.383)	−0.490 (0.433)
Poverty†		−0.026 (0.028)		
Infrastructure index†				0.041 (0.034)
Popualation size (log)†			−0.391** (0.191)	−1.149*** (0.334)
De la Rúa	−2.765** (0.967)	−0.5 (0.836)		
Duhalde	0.109 (0.636)	−0.035 (0.469)		
Kirchner	−4.699** (2.119)	3.577** (1.363)		
Constant	0.299 (2.606)	4.993* (2.827)	−1.602 (0.871)	19.228*** (4.610)
R^2	0.37	0.20	0.54	0.34
N	193	118	119	106

* p ≤ .1, ** p ≤ .05, *** p ≤ .001.
† two-tailed test, otherwise one-tailed test. Standard errors in parentheses.

human rights standards, such as Governor Carlos A. Juárez in Santiago del Estero or Governor José Murat in Oaxaca (Gibson 2005), may also impose high political and reputational costs on presidents, as these governors are usually regarded as unpopular political actors. By contrast, while supporting undemocratic governors who exercise power in a comparatively less patrimonial manner may bring about fewer electoral benefits, it may also be less costly in terms of the reputational and political price that presidents are willing to pay.

In addition, the fact that non-patrimonial SURs get a lower share of transfers may also be explained by ideological factors. From studies conducted in Mexico we know that presidents who advanced technocratic and neoliberal agendas, such as Presidents Salinas (1988–94) and Zedillo (1994–2000), refrained from empowering and siding with entrenched, traditional, and anti-neoliberal governors, the so-called *dinosaurios* (dinosaurs), as they systematically opposed presidential initiatives and federal-led projects (Centeno 1994; Eisenstadt 2004; Hernández Rodríguez 2008).

The results presented in Model 3 indicate that similar ideological factors may have shaped presidential behavior vis-à-vis SURs during the years of the first *Panista* administration. Several studies show that Fox's political weakness, which largely stemmed from the fact that 21 (out of 32) governors belonged to the PRI, and from the lack of majorities in both chambers of Congress, led him to build legislative and electoral alliances with PRI undemocratic governors (Hernández Rodríguez 2008; Madrazo 2007). These alliances, however, were selective in that they were struck with PRI undemocratic governors who shared and upheld the PAN's business-oriented, neoliberal, and technocratic worldview, that is, governors who ruled states where political authority was exercised in a less patrimonial manner. In fact, as shown by Gibson (2005) and Durazo Herrmann (2010), and as confirmed in Chapter 7, Fox refrained from siding with traditional, patrimonial, and highly clientelistic undemocratic governors, such as the Governor of Oaxaca, as their behavior was largely incompatible with the PAN's ideological stance.

Models 2, 3, and 4 show that presidents channeled more funds to SURs where the share of municipalities belonging to the presidential party was larger. As displayed in Table 5.2, a 1 percent increase in the share of municipalities belonging to the president's party is associated with an increase in public works spending of 0.02 percent of the SURs' total income in Argentina (Model 2), and of 2.44 percent and 1.77 percent of the SURs' total revenues in Mexico (Model 3 and 4). The greater share of federal transfers flowing to SURs where the percentage of municipalities belonging to the presidential party is higher demonstrates presidents' inclinations to strengthen local copartisan bases of support. As noted in Chapter 2, local copartisan structures are "springboards" that enhance presidential power in subnational undemocratic districts, and thus serve as key vehicles to obtain the acquiescence and cooperation of subnational autocrats. As argued in Chapter 2, it is by applying pressure from within that presidents can induce provincial/state-level incumbents to deliver strategic political support to advance the presidential agenda. Evidence from Mexico presented in Chapter 7 indicates that President Fox rewarded SURs where the share of PAN-ruled municipalities was high because by strengthening and expanding the PAN local presence he could challenge opposition governors' territorial power and, eventually, constrain undemocratic governors' authority from within.

The statistical results reveal that democratically elected presidents have an ambiguous stance regarding the reproduction of SURs whose autocrats control a larger size of legislators. This is confirmed by the fact that the *governor's legislative support* variable only comes out positively signed and statistically significant in Model 1, where an increase of 1 percent in governor's legislative support, which equals a one point increase in the share of deputies belonging to the governor's partisan congressional delegation, is associated with an increase in ATN allocation of 0.04 percent of undemocratic provinces' total revenues. By contrast, both Mexican regressions, and Argentine Model 2 show that undemocratic governors who control the bulk of their legislative delegation, and who in turn stand in a better position to secure more legislative votes, are no more attractive to presidents than governors who control small shares of loyal deputies.

The fact that both Mexican models do not lend support to the importance of legislative assistance, and that Argentine Model 1 substantiates it, points to important cross-country differences regarding the capacity of Argentine and Mexican governors to discipline legislators. In Argentina, as numerous studies show, provincial executives are the main principals exerting influence over deputies (Jones and Hwang 2005; Gordin 2004). In Mexico, by contrast, a multiplicity of principals, including party leaders in Congress, the national party leadership, and governors, have control over deputies' behavior (Casar 1999; Langston 2005; Langston and Aparicio 2008). These cross-country differences may explain why presidents in Argentina (i.e. Model 1) favor SURs on the basis of the potential legislative support that may accrue from these districts and why Mexican presidents abstain from benefitting SURs on the basis of the potential legislative support which undemocratic governors can secure.

Casting doubt on previous theoretical expectations, and confirming this chapter's hypothesis as well as the argument advanced in Chapter 2, the negative sign and statistical insignificance of the *governor–president copartisanship* variable in both Argentine regressions (Models 1 and 2), and Model 3 in Mexico, shows that governor–president copartisanship does not necessarily determine presidents' strategies regarding cross-SUR federal funds allocation. Even though no conclusive (statistical) assertion about the role played by copartisanship on SUR reproduction can be made, qualitative evidence indicates that both Argentine and Mexican presidents have helped sustain, and thus reproduce, SURs from the opposition. Several works and reports conducted in Argentina show that presidents were eager to strike coalitions with opposition undemocratic governors who were controllable from above and thus willing to meet presidential strategic needs. President Menem's strategy of delivering selective benefits to SURs of the opposition in exchange of support to pass key pieces of legislation to implement his neoliberal agenda (Botto 1998; Gibson and Calvo 2001), as well as President Néstor Kirchner's multiparty coalition—the so-called Concertación Plural (Plural Agreement), which entailed alliances with opposition undemocratic governors in exchange for legislative and electoral support[9]—are some cases in point. A similar relationship between opposition undemocratic governors and presidents was observed in Mexico during the presidency of Vicente Fox, when the federal government rewarded undemocratic PRI governors, such as the rulers of Puebla, Veracruz, Hidalgo, Sinaloa, and Sonora, with subsidies and special transfers in exchange for electoral and legislative support (Madrazo 2007). In consonance with these findings, the statistical results presented in Model 4 show that SURs ruled by PAN governors who came to power in an electoral coalition are associated with an increase in public works transfers of 0.93 percent of state's revenues. By contrast, in SURs governed by non-coalitional PAN governors a decrease in public works funds of 1.29 percent of state total income was recorded.

Finally, the results presented in Table 5.2 show that presidents in both countries do not necessarily reward SURs during elections. This is confirmed by the statistically significant variables of Models 1, 2, and 3 that appear with different signs. Whereas some national incumbents seem to allocate more funds to SURs during elections, some others opt to send fewer resources to states and provinces ruled by autocrats during electoral races. These mixed results appear to indicate that no conclusive statement about presidents' inclinations to reward SURs beyond election day can be made.

Conclusion

This chapter has tested the more general claim of the book's argument, namely, that effective presidential power over autocrats leads to SUR reproduction from above. The cross-sectional, time series analyses performed revealed that neither Mexican nor Argentine presidents rewarded all SURs during their respective administrations. Instead, they selectively benefitted

---

[9] *Diario Río Negro* (Feb. 23, 24, 26, and Mar. 10, 2006).

those regimes and autocrats over whom they could wield effective power. Put differently, none of these presidents contributed to expanding the power of SURs upon which they could not exercise partisan or fiscal leverage.

The results of the quantitative analyses presented in this chapter, which are applicable to the universe of SURs in the post-transitional period in Argentina and Mexico, reveal that the theoretical claims raised in Chapter 2 can be generalized to all Argentine and Mexican SURs. In other words, the hypothesized causal relationship between the independent variable (effective presidential power over SURs) and one of the dependent variables (SUR reproduction from above) was demonstrated to hold true for all contemporary SURs in Argentina and Mexico. The findings of this chapter then contribute to increasing the inferential leverage of this book's argument.

The results of this chapter also reveal other important aspects of SUR continuity in the nationally democratic countries examined in this book (see Chapter 2). They show that, under certain circumstances, presidents are active promoters of SUR continuity. The fact that national actors shape the prospects of SUR sustainability underscores, on the one hand, like most works that assess SUR continuity from a center–periphery perspective (see Chapter 3), that subnational political processes are not impervious to the political dynamics that take place at the national level of government; quite to the contrary, they are greatly shaped by events occurring at higher levels of government (Snyder 2001a; Gibson 2005, 2013). On the other hand, the results reveal the potentially problematic role that central governments and the national democratic regime can play in the process of subnational democratization. As argued in Chapter 2, and as subsequent chapters will demonstrate, national incumbents' aspirations to build winning electoral and legislative coalitions at the national level, which are intrinsic to the game of democratic coalition-building, contribute to the obstruction of democratization at the subnational level.

Finally, confirming one of the central claims of this book, the statistical results presented in this chapter show that within-country interactions between presidents and subnational autocrats vary from SUR to SUR. Differences across these subnational regimes, as argued before, have important consequences for presidents' strategic calculations regarding regime reproduction. As noted in previous chapters, extant explanations about SUR continuity, tend to overlook these subnational differences, taking for granted that SURs within countries are homogeneous or uniform entities, to be analyzed and treated as equivalents—especially with regard to the relation they maintain with national rulers or national institutions. The results of this chapter highlight the importance of taking SUR differences seriously, as they critically shape intergovernmental relations and, in turn, presidents' calculations regarding SUR continuity.

6

Subnational Undemocratic Regime Continuity in Argentina: La Rioja and San Luis

The goal of this chapter is to present qualitative and comparative evidence to demonstrate that the potential to exert presidential power over subnational autocrats, as well as the prospects for obtaining their cooperation, strongly conditions pathways of subnational undemocratic regime (SUR) continuity. This chapter thus explores how presidential power during the years of the first two Kirchner administrations shaped pathways of SUR continuity in Argentina. As noted in Chapter 4, between 2003 and 2007, President Néstor Kirchner could neither count on a highly routinized party organization to exert sway over subnational autocrats, nor achieve an electoral foothold in all subnational units. This limited presidential partisan power contrasted sharply with the president's capacity to exert financial power and consequently discipline subnational autocrats. As discussed in Chapter 4, President Kirchner, and then his wife, Cristina Fernández de Kirchner (2008–present), not only benefitted from the greater fiscal discretion and power conferred by Argentina's fiscal federalism, but was also able to take advantage of a considerable amount of revenues not subject to sharing, most of which accrued from export duties. The access to abundant resources allowed the Kirchners to exercise the power of the purse over some provinces, and gave both of them the opportunity to obtain the acquiescence of some (non-democratic) provincial rulers who were in dire financial need.[1] On these occasions, both presidents opted to reproduce

---

[1] It should be noted that presidential partisan power increased after 2006, when the Front of Victory (FpV) managed to gain a significant electoral presence in most provinces. Still, due to the party's weak routinization, which yielded great strategic autonomy to lower-level subunits (see Levitsky 2003), the Kirchners were somehow prevented from disciplining subnational copartisans via their party organization.

SURs from above. In contrast, when presidential fiscal power was lacking, the Kirchners chose to oppose rather than support SURs in power. Despite strategies of SUR weakening, some autocrats reproduced their regimes by relying on sturdy coalitions of support.

This chapter conducts a paired subnational comparison of two SURs in Argentina to test the validity of the hypothesized causal chains leading to SUR reproduction from above and to SUR self-reproduction. These causal chains are examined following Van Evera's (1997) recommended method of breaking them down into their component parts. Accordingly, the chapter pays close attention to (a) the type and way in which presidential power was exercised, (b) how it helped or prevented presidents from obtaining the acquiescence and obedience of subnational autocrats, and (c) how it facilitated SUR presidential support and thus triggered a pathway of SUR reproduction from above. The chapter also examines the links of the alternative causal chain, in which the incapacity of presidents to exert power over subnational autocrats prevents the attainment of subnational undemocratic rulers' cooperation, and leads presidents to oppose, rather than support, SURs. Yet, in this chain SUR continuity still occurs through self-reproduction, given autocrats' capacity to ensure party cohesion and mass support.

To determine how the component parts of each causal chain affect the hypothesized outcome, this chapter relies on evidence collected from archival documents, newspaper articles, and official documents, as well as information gathered in 70 in-depth interviews with Argentine national and subnational top-ranking officials, journalists, and former politicians.[2]

The chapter is organized as follows. First there is a justification of the subnational cases selected to illustrate Argentine SURs' trajectories of continuity. Drawing on two case studies, La Rioja and San Luis, the following section illustrates with original evidence the two alternative pathways of SUR durability. The narrative and analysis of each case study proceeds as follows. First, a detailed description of the political regime and the state structure is provided. Second, the capacity of presidents to wield power over SURs is discussed. Special attention is devoted to the instruments of presidential power available to Presidents Néstor Kirchner and Cristina Fernández de Kirchner, as well as to autocrats' instruments of autonomy. Third, the prospects of obtaining autocrats' political cooperation are analyzed. Finally, the actions taken by presidents towards SURs and their reproduction are examined. The analysis of the case studies ends with an exploration of the type of SUR reproduction followed in each case.

---

[2] See the separate List of Interviews.

Subnational Case Selection

Following Gerring (2007), two "diverse cases" (e.g. La Rioja and San Luis) serve the purpose of testing the central hypotheses of the book.[3] Given that this chapter seeks to demonstrate that different SUR trajectories are triggered by the capacity (or lack thereof) of federal incumbents to exert effective power over subnational autocrats and their regimes, two cases that score very differently on the main variable facilitating or inhibiting effective presidential power are selected.

Chapter 4 showed that fiscal control was the main instrument of presidential control available to both President Kirchner (2003–7) and President Cristina Fernández de Kirchner during her first two years (2008–9).[4] Thus, in order to assess whether presidential fiscal power was conducive to obtaining the acquiescence of subnational autocrats and in turn triggering SUR reproduction from above, a case is needed where presidential fiscal control was exerted. By contrast, in order to assess whether a lack of presidential fiscal power led to the unwillingness of subnational undemocratic rulers to cooperate with the center, and, in turn, propelled opposition to SURs, a case is needed where presidential fiscal power did not exist or was neutralized. As explained in Chapter 2, one factor facilitating subnational rulers' capacity to neutralize presidential fiscal power is their fiscal autonomy vis-à-vis the central government. Profligate governors who engage in overspending and have high levels of indebtedness can easily become hostages of the federal government, and hence be forced to provide political support to federal incumbents. On the other hand, governors who are financially and economically responsible, and who, as a result, do not need to resort to the national government for financial aid, stand in a stronger position not only to preserve their autonomy and independence from federal politicians, but also to deny political support.

In light of these considerations, the key criterion for case selection was determined by the province's fiscal autonomy and not by the nature of the state structure, as occurs in the Mexican case.[5] Hence, one undemocratic fiscally dependent province (La Rioja), and one undemocratic fiscally autonomous province (San Luis) are selected (see Figure 6.1). The first

---

[3] According to Gerring (2007), this type of case study, "requires the selection of a set of cases that are intended to represent the full range of values characterizing independent variable of theoretical interest" (Gerring 2007: 98).

[4] As noted in Chapter 1, the focus of this book's analysis is up to 2009.

[5] In Mexico, because the main instrument of presidential power is partisan, the key criterion in selecting cases is the type of state structure present in each state, as patrimonial state structures, which prevent partisan power becoming effective, reduce the possibilities of autocrats' cooperation with the central government, and non-patrimonial state structures facilitate it.

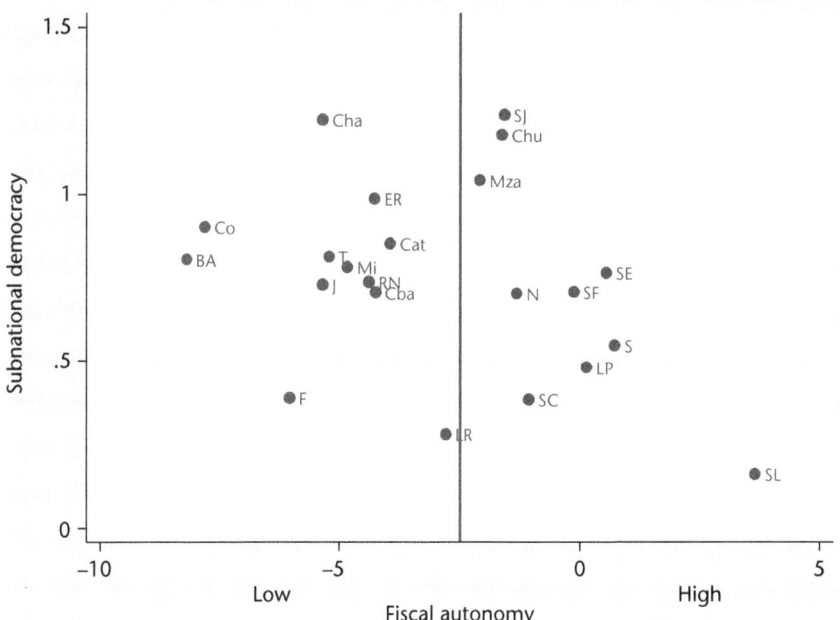

Figure 6.1. Levels of subnational democracy and fiscal autonomy in the Argentine provinces (average 2003–9)*

Notes: Fiscal autonomy values are averaged values for the 1996–2009 period. Y-axis: Higher values indicate higher levels of subnational democracy. Zero and near zero scores denote undemocratic regimes. X-axis: Higher values denote higher fiscal autonomy. BA (Buenos Aires), Cha (Chaco), Chu (Chubut), Co (Corrientes), Cba (Córdoba), ER (Entre Ríos), F (Formosa), J (Jujuy), LP (La Pampa), LR (La Rioja), Mza (Mendoza), Mi (Misiones), N (Neuquén), RN (Río Negro), S (Salta), SJ (San Juan), SL (San Luis), SC (Santa Cruz), SF (Santa Fe), SE (Santiago del Estero), TF (Tierra del Fuego), T (Tucumán).

* Financial dependency is measured using and additive index of deficit and debt as a share of total income.

case, La Rioja, is used to prove that, in the presence of effective presidential power, autocrats' cooperation is likely, and this cooperation results in SUR reproduction from above. By contrast, the second case is used to test whether the absence of effective presidential power, which deters autocrats' from cooperating with the federal government, leads to opposition to SURs. The case of San Luis also illustrates that, in the presence of mass support, autocrats can counterbalance presidential actions of regime weakening, and in turn contribute to the self-reproduction of political regimes.

In addition, these two provinces were selected out of the bulk of fiscally autonomous and fiscally dependent SURs (i.e. La Pampa, Formosa, Santa Cruz, La Rioja, San Luis) because they have several characteristics in common. Both provinces have been ruled by the Peronist Party (PJ) since 1983,

Democrats and Autocrats

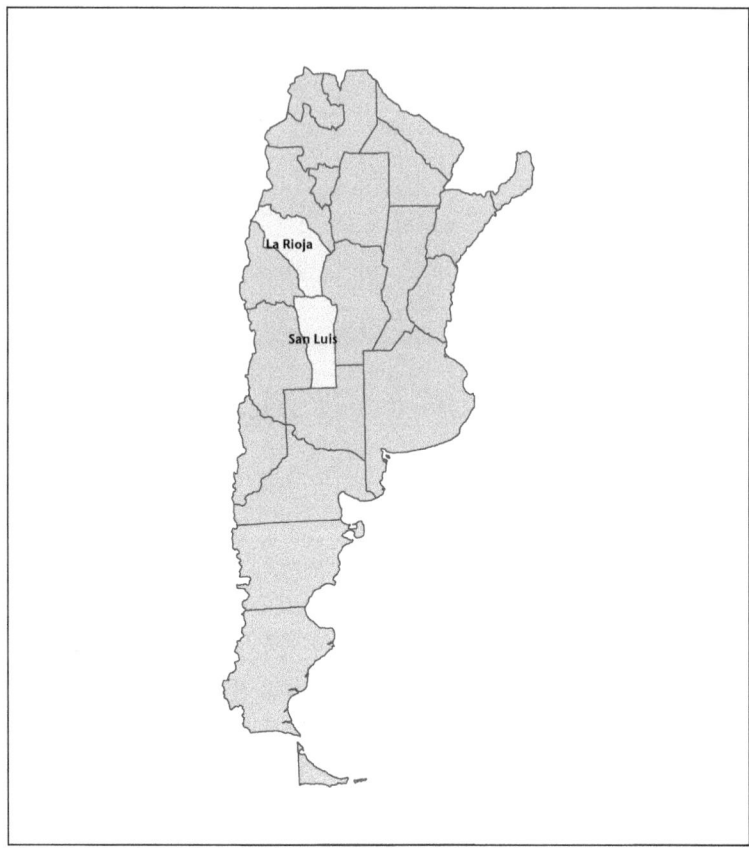

Figure 6.2. Geographic location of case studies

both are located in central-eastern Argentina (see Figure 6.2), which is why they share very similar geographical conditions, and even though their levels of socioeconomic development now differ substantially, they were similar in the early 1980s.[6] In addition, both are among the least-populated group of Argentine provinces, with a population of 333,642 in La Rioja, and 432,310 in San Luis (Census Data 2010). Despite these similarities, these two provinces differ on the main variable that facilitates or prevents effective presidential power, i.e. the level of provincial fiscal autonomy. La Rioja and San Luis then not only allow for a most similar case design, but also make a controlled comparison possible, facilitating in turn a more fine-tuned assessment of the main variable's effect on the hypothesized outcomes.

[6] San Luis and La Rioja, as discussed later in this chapter, benefitted equally from the industrial promotion regime (or RPI) instituted by the federal government in the early 1980s. RPI has been critical in shaping each province's economy.

96

La Rioja: A Case of SUR Reproduction from Above[7]

(a) *The Political Regime*

As detailed in Chapter 3 and in Figure 6.1, the province of La Rioja is (and has historically been) one of the least democratic provinces in Argentina. The province has been governed by the Peronist party (PJ) since the democratic transition in 1983, and only four governors, Carlos Menem (1983–91[8]), Bernabé Arnaudo (1991–5), Ángel Maza (1995–2007), and Luis Beder Herrera (2007–present), have ruled the province since then.

Table 6.1 presents disaggregated evidence showing La Rioja's low levels of democracy. Signs of sustained "undemocraticness" can be observed by comparing La Rioja's mean scores with those of the other provinces. In all of the indicators presented in Table 6.1, La Rioja scores well below the mean of the other Argentine provinces. A closer look at how each individual indicator has evolved over time reveals that gubernatorial elections in La Rioja have become less competitive, especially during the 1990s, as both the effective number of parties running for gubernatorial elections and the effective number of parties obtaining seats in the local legislature remained low. These two indicators, coupled with the party turnover indicator, which reports no party turnover over the entire period, highlight the sustained low levels of competitiveness of La Rioja's political regime. Additional information confirming this trend comes from the large gap observed between the winner and runner-up.

Table 6.1 shows that the two most competitive gubernatorial elections between 1983 and 2005 took place in 1983 and 2003. In 1983, the PJ won by a relatively low margin, obtaining 57.70 percent of the vote, against the 40.95 percent vote share garnered by the then electorally powerful UCR. Twenty years later, in 2003, the Peronist incumbent Ángel "Didí" Maza won by a margin of 15.10 points over the Frente con Todos (Front with Everyone), a new party formed in 2001 by Jorge Yoma, a splinter of the PJ. In between these two elections, electoral competition in La Rioja was very low, as were the other indicators of democracy, all of which experienced a pronounced decline in the 1990s. Finally, the low turnover of provincial executives, which have only rotated three times in the last 25 years, speaks to the PJ's dominance in La Rioja's political system.

The hegemony of the incumbent *Riojano* Peronist party, as well as the monopoly over the governorship by a few selected political figures in La Rioja, was possible due to the systematic and skillful manipulation of

---

[7] The main focus of this section will be on the administration of Peronist Eduardo Ángel Maza (1995–2007), and Luis Beder Herrera (2007–present) whose terms coincided with the presidencies of Néstor Kirchner and Cristina Fernández de Kirchner.

[8] In 1989 Menem assumed the presidency and was replaced by his vice-governor, Alberto Gregorio Cavero.

Democrats and Autocrats

Table 6.1. La Rioja's indicators of democracy

Year of election	ENP (governor's race)	Margin of victory in gubernatorial races* (between winner and runner up)	ENPL (legislative seats)	Strength of the opposition in the lower chamber (% of seats controlled by the opposition)	Turnover (party) (cumulated)	Turnover (head) (cumulated)
1983	2.00	16.75	1.36	16.00	0	1
1985			1.18	12.00		
1987	2.02	28.22	1.27	10.34	0	1
1989			1.34	6.90		
1991	1.52	60.19	1.13	10.00	0	2
1993			1.16	10.00		
1995	1.41	66.83	1.26	10.00	0	3
1997			1.35	13.33		
1999	1.92	37.63	1.28	16.67	0	3
2001			1.17	10.00		
2003	2.13	15.10	1.72	36.67	0	3
2005			1.34	36.67		
2007	3.30	14.31	2.61	n.d.	0	4
2009			2.61	n.d.		
La Rioja's mean	2.04	34.15	1.48	15.71	0.00	2.43
Provinces' mean	2.58	19.69	2.33	44.78	1.62	3.07
Min	1.23	0.29	1.13	6.9	1	1
Max	4.45	84.56	8.91	84.62	4	7

* Higher values indicate lower levels of democracy.
Source: Chapter 3.

provincial institutions and electoral rules, a pattern seen in other Argentine SURs (Calvo and Micozzi 2005; Gibson 2013). Among these manipulations were (a) the recurrent amendments to key provisions of the provincial constitution, including the executive's reelection clause or the size and the composition of the Supreme Court, which took place in 1986, 1998, 2002, and 2008; (b) the introduction of the *ley de lemas* (double simultaneous cumulative vote)[9] in 1991, its elimination in 1992, and its reintroduction in 2001; (b) the 1987 introduction of rules to overrepresent the rural districts of the province, where the PJ was stronger; and (c) the modification of the legislature's size, which entailed changing the number of seats from 54 in 1986, to 28 in 1991, then to 30 in 1998, 23 in 2002, and 36 in 2008 (see Leiras 2006, 2007).

---

[9] The "ley de lemas" allows parties to present different lists of candidates to compete in the same race. The vote obtained by each candidate is then added up and assigned *in toto* to the party label.

The strategic introduction of these reforms, as Calvo and Micozzi (2005) show, was critical for the local opposition's demise.[10] Electoral manipulation minimized the risk of electoral defeat, improved incumbents' control over local legislatures, and allowed them to escape the negative consequences of more competitive national-level races, thus enhancing the regime's capacity to survive despite national democratization.

In sum, periodic electoral and institutional engineering in La Rioja enabled autocrats to undermine the opposition's capacity to defeat incumbents. The use of the tactics discussed was critical for turning opponents into weak competitors, and preventing them from accessing governing positions and/or controlling majorities in legislative bodies. For many consecutive terms, the political regime in La Rioja was not democratic simply because, paraphrasing Przeworski (1991: 10), it was not a "system[s] in which parties lose in multi-party elections."

(b) *The State Structure and Autocrats' Exercise of Power*

Control over territory was further exacerbated by the nature of La Rioja's state structure. As noted in Chapter 3, La Rioja stood (and still stands) among the most patrimonial provinces of Argentina. A closer analysis of the three dimensions of patrimonialism (i.e. centralization of political authority, the appropriation of state resources for economic and political gain, and the generation of ties of loyalty and dependence among followers) reveals that levels of patrimonialism in La Rioja were notably high. In sum, La Rioja's indicators of patrimonialism not only reveal higher levels of patrimonialism than the other provinces, but they are also the highest among Argentine provinces.

The analysis of the stability of provincial Supreme Court justices, i.e. the indicator used to capture the extent to which autocrats centralized political authority,[11] reveals that *Riojano* justices' instability was relatively low during the early 1980s, increased during the 1990s, and became considerably higher after 2000. *Riojano* incumbents employed two different informal and formal strategies to undermine the watchdog powers of the province's supreme tribunal. First, using a variety of informal tactics, such as threats of impeachment—which not only entail losing one's job but also economic losses, as impeached justices are denied their pensions—and libel suits, governors succeeded in inducing the resignation of

---

[10] As one anonymous interviewee noted, "these reforms were introduced and rolled back depending on the relative power of the opposition forces; when the opposition became stronger, rules were modified, otherwise there was no need to alter them" (interview 4).

[11] It measures the yearly average tenure of provincial Supreme Court justices divided by the number of years of the political regime.

"autonomous" and disobedient justices (interviews Bruno, Mercado Luna, Porrás, Lanzilotto, Juárez, interview 5; see also Castagnola 2010).[12] Second, governors systematically modified the constitutional provision stipulating the size (i.e. number of justices) of the provincial Supreme Court. In 1986, Governor Menem, increased the size of the Court from three to five; in 2002, Maza reduced it from five to three; and Governor Beder Herrera, in 2008, augmented the size again to five. In every single case, incumbents replaced wholesale the sitting Court justices, who—despite the reforms—should have been kept in their posts.[13] In sum, either by changing the size of the Supreme Court or by inducing justices to retire, governors in La Rioja, most noticeably Governor Maza and Beder Herrera, managed to keep a subservient judiciary which, threatened by its own instability, was not able to check effectively the governor's exercise of political power. Quite the contrary, it validated (either by action or omission) most of the governors' actions (interview 5).

As argued in Chapter 3, one of the main traits of a patrimonial state structure is that public money and public goods are appropriated and distributed with particularistic and discretionary criteria rather than on the basis of universal standards. The rules regulating the distribution of public funds, then, constitute a good proxy for the level of patrimonialism prevalent in any political system.[14] Where these rules are permissive or where they simply do not exist, incumbents can distribute public monies virtually unchecked. La Rioja is one of the only three Argentine provinces (the others are San Juan and Jujuy), where a system to regulate the distribution of provincial transfers does not exist. *Riojano* autocrats have been (and still are) entirely free to determine the amount of money that each municipality receives, the intervals at which funds are distributed (i.e. on daily, monthly, quarterly, or yearly basis), and whether or not these transfers are channeled automatically. This fiscal discretion, in turn, has given *Riojano* autocrats a tremendous capacity to control and manipulate mayors. Moreover, municipal incumbents in La Rioja had virtually no administrative capacity to raise their own taxes (even though they legally could), which is why they depended heavily on provincial transfers to run their governments. The incapacity to collect revenues, coupled

---

[12] This strategy, as many interviewees reported, was even more frequent in provincial lower courts, where judges were induced to resign. As one top-rank official of La Rioja's Supreme Court noted, "here in La Rioja, it is easier to remove judges (who, in theory have life tenure) than a public employee" (interview 26).

[13] For instance, in 2002, when Governor Maza reduced the Court's size from five to three members, he removed all but one justices.

[14] The indicator used to measure rulers' fiscal discretion is the cumulative years of existence of a *ley de coparticipación municipal* (i.e. the law regulating the allocation of fiscal resources between the provincial government and the municipalities).

with the high level of autocrats' fiscal discretion, has transformed mayors into mere delegates of the governors (interviews Porras, Ortiz, Chamía).

Because none of them stood in a solid financial position to oppose the governor's policies, all mayors, with the sole exception of La Rioja City's mayor, abided by Governor Maza's and Governor Beder Herrera's decisions, agenda, rules, and policies. Mayors were systematically required to do as the governors requested, especially during local, provincial, and national political races, when autocrats asked them to deliver political support through mobilizing voters and the citizenry (interviews Maza, Ada Maza, Chamía). Refusal to do so, as occurred in 2003 when a group of mayors coalesced demanding approval of a municipal coparticipation law to regulate the distribution of transfers, stopped the flow of provincial money to the municipal coffers (interviews Bruno, Porrás, Chamía).

The lack of a provincial "coparticipation" law curtailed mayors' autonomy in two other important ways. Because mayors could not show they had a steady and regular income, they were banned from requesting loans from international development agencies and national or international banks. As a result, every time *Riojano* mayors wanted to apply for credit, they first needed to negotiate with Maza or Beder Herrera, who in turn would decide if the province would act as guarantor. "To get the governors' consent," as La Rioja City's mayor noted, "we needed to pledge yet more political allegiance" (interview Quintela, see also interviews Ortiz, De Leonardi). Additionally, the lack of a provincial coparticipation law further limited *Riojano* mayors' autonomy by preventing mayors from deciding where and how to spend provincial transfers, as it was the provincial government which made these decisions. By so doing, *Riojano* autocrats ensured that transfers would not be used to feed party machines that would enhance mayors' political bases of support (interviews Quintela, #4).

The final indicator of patrimonialism, the generation of ties of loyalty and dependence through employment patronage (measured as the number of inhabitants per 1,000 working in the provincial public administration), underscores that patronage in La Rioja has, on average, been very high throughout the period under study. In fact, La Rioja stands among the provinces with the highest rate of public employees per inhabitant, and has the city (Chilecito) with the highest rate of public employees per inhabitant of the country. Unlike other provinces, where patronage has been high but stable, the high level of patronage in La Rioja has also grown larger over the years. The fact that an average of 85 out of every 1,000 inhabitants work in the provincial public administration has conferred provincial autocrats with an impressive capacity to ensure the loyalty of a considerable portion of the local population, that, for fear of being removed from office, becomes easy to discipline and manipulate.

In addition to controlling agencies of horizontal accountability, distributing funds in a discretional way, and relying on employment patronage, governors in La Rioja turned to other patrimonial practices to further consolidate their territorial control over the province. For instance, to prevent mayors from becoming more autonomous, in 1998 Governor Maza passed a law that temporarily suspended the municipalities' constitutions (*Cartas Orgánicas*). This suspension, which later on became permanent, prevented mayors from managing their electoral calendars, and allowed Maza to: (a) take advantage of coattail effects, (b) prevent (intra-party) opposition forces from strengthening, (c) determine the election and appointment of candidates, and (d) control the electoral processes. Likewise, during his first administration (1995–8), Governor Maza centralized the municipal payroll with the goal of reducing mayors' capacity to exert control over public employees. As one top-ranked official of La Rioja's municipality put it, "public employees became aware that their patron, the one who paid their salaries, was the governor (and not the mayor), and that's why they became loyal to the governor and not the mayor" (interview Ortiz). According to different municipal leaders, this payroll centralization prevented mayors from building their own "troop of loyalists" to counterbalance the governors' power (interviews Ortiz, Quintela, Chamía, De Leonardi).

La Rioja's patrimonial state structure, which was central to facilitating *Riojano* autocrats' control over state bureaucracies, state resources, and lower (municipal) levels of government and territory, enhanced the capacity of provincial incumbents to control borders. Following Gibson (2005, 2013), *Riojano* autocrats should had been in a strong position to offset presidential power had it been exercised through national–local partisan-based alliances. Yet, given that presidential power during the years of the Kirchner administrations was mostly wielded through fiscal instruments, the existence of a patrimonial state structure was itself inadequate to neutralize the power of the national executive over *Riojano* autocrats.

Capacity of Presidents to Wield Power over Autocrats and La Rioja's SUR

As noted in Chapter 2, the ability of presidents to wield effective power over subnational autocrats is shaped by a combination of national and subnational variables. In order to exercise real and effective power over subnational undemocratic arenas/autocrats, subnational rulers' capacity to resist manipulation needs to be low relative to national incumbents' power of control. These two conditions are both necessary for a president to gain leverage over SURs and autocrats. This section explores how national and provincial variables combined to shape the capacity of presidents to exercise effective power over La Rioja's incumbents. It further examines how this capacity in turn affected the possibility of cooperation across levels of government and, eventually, the prospects of SUR reproduction.

(a) Instruments of Presidential Power

Chapter 4 shows that, since the late 1990s, and especially after 2003, political parties in Argentina have experienced a process of denationalization (Calvo and Escolar 2005; Leiras 2006, 2007; Gibson and Suarez-Cao 2010). This process resulted in, among other things, parties' inability to discipline (either from above or from within) subnational autocrats via partisan resources. Kirchner's party, the Front of Victory (FpV), a splinter of the Peronist party beginning in 2003, was not an exception. As discussed earlier, in the early years of his administration, the territorial reach of the Kirchners' party (FpV) was limited to the Patagonian provinces and to the province of Buenos Aires, where they indirectly exerted influence thanks to their alliance with the long-standing boss of Argentina's largest province, Eduardo Duhalde (Calvo and Escolar 2005).[15] Beyond these districts, the FpV lacked territorially extensive networks of offices, brokers, and members. Lack of party infrastructure in most of Argentine's SURs (and provinces) prevented Néstor Kirchner from crafting stable coalitions with provincial bosses, and in turn inhibited him from disciplining and controlling autocrats from within or above. Chapter 4 reports that while party denationalization was somehow offset during the first two years of Cristina Fernández de Kirchner's administration, the territorialization of political parties in Argentina, especially the Peronist party, remained high. In addition, the FpV's loosely vertical integration did not provide presidents with effective mechanisms with which to impose discipline on party subunits and their leaders (Levitsky 2003; Jones and Hwang 2005). As a result, autocrats in La Rioja were able to enjoy substantial autonomy from the party hierarchy.

The Kirchners' weakly routinized and territorially fragile party organization, which prevented both presidents from disciplining provincial autocrats via the party organization, contrasted sharply with their strong capacity to manipulate and influence governors with fiscal instruments. As detailed in Chapter 4, both President Kirchner and Fernández de Kirchner benefitted

---

[15] Recall that in 2003 the Peronists split into three different factions: the Frente por la Lealtad (Front for Loyalty), led by former President Menem; the Frente Movimiento Popular—Unión y Libertad (Popular Movement—Unity and Liberty), headed by San Luis's former governor, Adolfo Rodríguez-Saá; and the Alianza Frente para la Victoria (Front for Victory), led by Kirchner and his immediate predecessor, Eduardo Duhalde. Relying on their respective party (faction) organizations, each of these Peronist leaders controlled and wielded power over different parts of the country (Calvo and Escolar 2005).

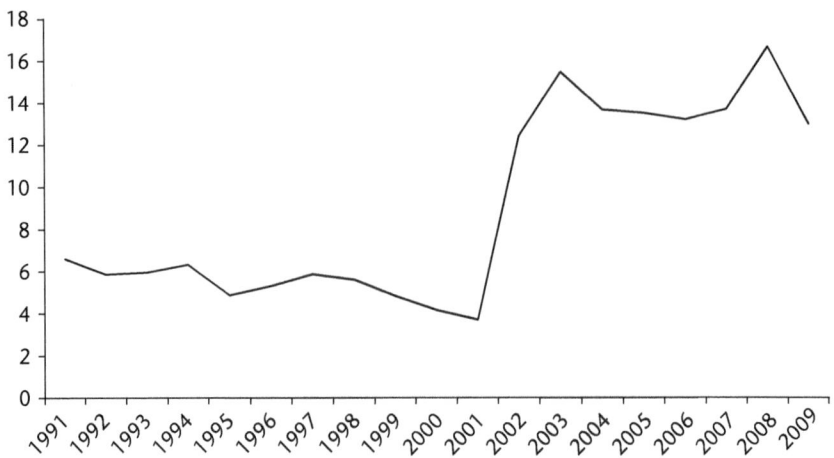

Figure 6.3. Percentage of export/import duties as a share of total central government's revenues
Source: Cuenta de Inversión, Mecon (1991–2009).

from the windfall gains of an economy that grew at an 8.83 percent average rate between 2003 and 2007, and 7.61 percent for the 2008–9 period (CEPAL, various years). This sustained growth, which increased the government's revenues to unprecedented levels, was accompanied by an extraordinary increase in export and import duties. Unlike any other president since the 1983 transition to democracy, the Kirchners were able to take advantage of a considerable amount of revenue, most of which stemmed from export/import duties that were not subject to sharing with the provinces (see Figure 6.3). The Kirchners were thus able to liberally exercise the power of the purse to induce the cooperation of several provincial autocrats and governors regardless of their party affiliation and/or ideology (see Bonvecchi and Giraudy 2008).

(b) Riojano *Autocrats' Instruments of Autonomy*

As Figures 6.1 and 6.6 illustrate, La Rioja is one of the most profligate provinces in Argentina. As a result, its rulers can easily be turned into vulnerable actors vis-à-vis national incumbents and, consequently, be induced to provide strategic benefits to presidents who stand in a strong position to discipline them via fiscal resources. The weakness of *Riojano* governors vis-à-vis national rulers stems from the fact that 90 percent of the province's total revenues comes from the federal government (MECON various years). As Figure 6.4 indicates, La Rioja's autonomous revenues (depicted by the solid white and solid grey rectangles) constituted only a negligible share of the province's total income. Reports from the federal Ministry of Economy indicate that an average of

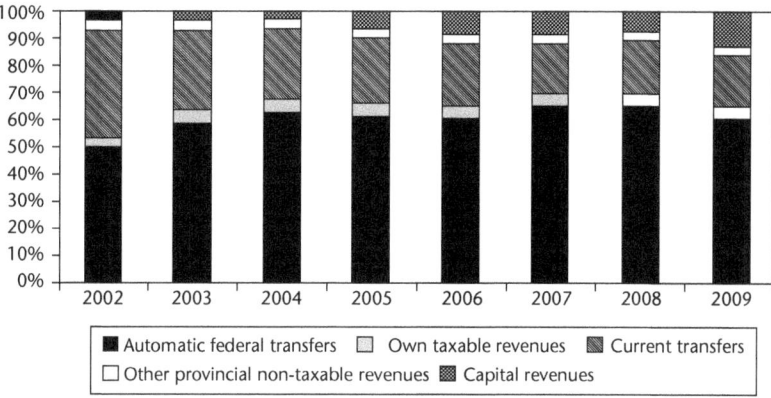

Figure 6.4. La Rioja: income sources (2002–9)
Source: Dirección Nacional de Coordinación Fiscal con las Provincias [Mecon—DNCFP].

60 percent of these transfers flowed automatically to the province, whereas the remaining 40 percent were comprised of funds that are contingent upon bargains between the national and provincial governments (see Figure 6.5).

Two additional factors prevented the province from becoming financially autonomous from the central government. First, the province's own revenues comprised an average of only 5.50 percent of its total income (Figure 6.4), showing that La Rioja had virtually no administrative capacity to raise its own taxes, and thus few alternative sources of financing. Second, La Rioja was one of the most indebted provinces in the country, with levels of indebtedness at an average of 77.83 percent of its GDP during the 2002–9 period (see Figure 6.7). Additionally, due to the province's low levels of economic development, *Riojano* rulers had limited capacity to issue debt or purchase

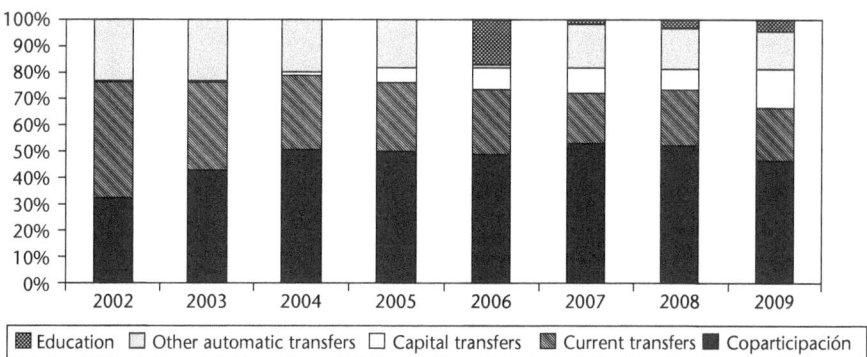

Figure 6.5. La Rioja: type of federal revenues as a share of total federal revenue (2002–9)
Source: Dirección Nacional de Coordinación Fiscal con las Provincias [Mecon—DNCFP].

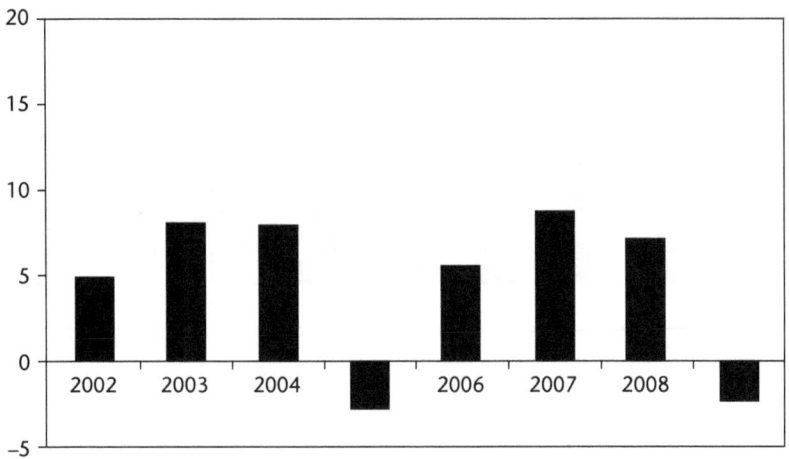

Figure 6.6. La Rioja: total income—total expenditures (1997–2009) (in millions of Argentine pesos)
Source: Dirección Nacional de Coordinación Fiscal con las Provincias [Mecon—DNCFP].

debt services beyond the federal government, making the national government the province's lender of last resort.

This financial dependence on the national government was one of the major factors allowing presidents to control provincial incumbents in La Rioja, and by extension, the area, resources, and persons that the provincial incumbents dominate. As two close advisors to Governor Maza put it, governors in La Rioja do not rule for their people, they rule for the president. They spend most of their time in Buenos Aires lobbying for money, subsidies, and programs (interviews Maza, #2). This financial dependence—which became more acute

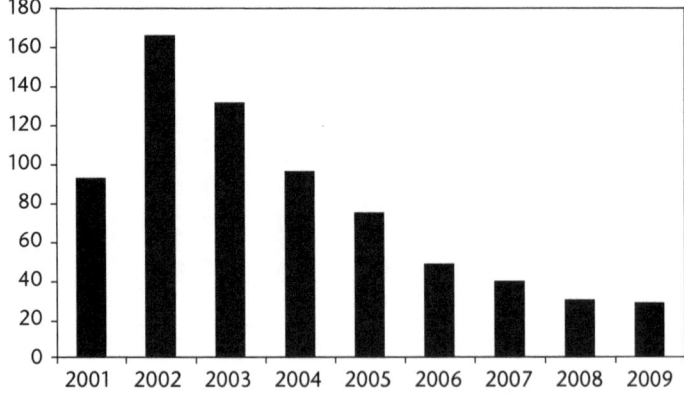

Figure 6.7. La Rioja: debt as percentage of provincial GDP (2001–9)
Source: Dirección Nacional de Coordinación Fiscal con las Provincias [Mecon—DNCFP].

after the 2001–2 economic crisis when the province's debt skyrocketed to unprecedented levels and when the federal government "nationalized" the provincial debt—increased the power of an already fiscally powerful president, as was the case with Néstor Kirchner.

Prospects for Obtaining Cooperation of La Rioja's Autocrats

La Rioja's lack of financial autonomy from the federal government was critical in shaping Governor Maza's positioning vis-à-vis President Kirchner. Soon after Kirchner took office in 2003, Governor Maza quickly closed ranks with the newly elected president. This move was highly symbolic for a governor who was a close ally of Carlos Menem, one of Kirchner's main political contenders.[16] Governor Maza, Menem's longest serving disciple, had been one of the main architects and operators of Carlos Menem's 2003 presidential campaign. His relationship with former President Menem, as well as his involvement in the 2003 election, put Maza in a very weak political position vis-à-vis Kirchner, since the newly elected president still viewed Governor Maza and Menem as political opponents. In Maza's words, "Kirchner was completely mad at me. Part of his anger came from the fact that I was Menem's ally, but also because I had encouraged Menem to step down from the runoff.[17] Kirchner seriously wanted a landslide over Menem, but once Menem stepped down, Kirchner had to assume the presidency as a weak president, with only 20 percent of the popular vote, and that is why he wanted me to pay dearly for my audacity" (interview Maza).[18]

According to many interviewees, that was precisely what Maza did after 2003. During the first year and a half of the Kirchner administration, the president and his federal ministers forced Maza and his provincial secretaries to show deference and respect. Between 2003 and 2005, as Maza himself and several of his closest advisors noted, the governor spent most of his time in Buenos Aires, holding weekly meetings with Kirchner and his ministers, and making both symbolic and substantial gestures of subordination, all of which were intended to prevent the financial isolation of La Rioja (interviews Ada Maza, Bengolea, Chamía, Fernández). "It was only by showing President

---

[16] Recall that in the 2003 presidential election Carlos Menem ran against the then victorious Néstor Kirchner.
[17] Maza reported that he convinced Menem to step down because "they [Menem's campaign team] had been informed that the Buenos Aires' election observers (*fiscales de mesa*) had surrendered to Duhalde [Kirchner's political mentor], and we no longer had money to buy them back" (interview Maza).
[18] These facts were further confirmed by Alberto Fernández, Kirchner's Chief of Cabinet, and one of his closest advisors and friends (author's interview, Buenos Aires, June 27, 2012).

Kirchner that I [Maza] could be counted on as one of his loyalists, that I could ensure that the president would keep on sending funds to the province, something that he did not do during his first year in office" (interview Maza).

La Rioja's chronic and dire dependence on non-automatic federal transfers helped to transform Governor Maza into one of Kirchner's most subservient allies, one upon whom the president could count when he needed political support. This acquiescence became especially profitable for a politician in a position like Néstor Kirchner's, with abundant economic resources at his disposal. Once it became apparent that La Rioja's autocrat could be considered as a loyalist, President Kirchner took full advantage of the political benefits that the governor could deliver. The cooperation and political support of this autocrat were desirable given Kirchner's initial weak political position.

In 2003, Kirchner won the presidency with a mere 22.24 percent of the votes, and only with the support of a single faction of the national Peronist party, the Alianza Frente para la Victoria (Alliance of the Front for Victory). To expand his electoral presence throughout the territory, as well as to strengthen his position vis-à-vis other Peronist leaders, Kirchner stood to gain much from crafting alliances with autocrats who were in a position to control their provincial domains, and who in turn could secure and deliver the much needed political support that the president was struggling to obtain. In this context, the capacity to wield effective presidential power over La Rioja's autocrat became extremely useful, as it could allow the newly elected and politically weak president to expand his base of support.

In addition, winning over La Rioja was symbolically important. The province was the home and stronghold of former president Menem, and "exerting power and controlling La Rioja," as one interviewee put it, "was not only valuable because it would allow Kirchner to expand his political influence through the FpV and hence consolidate the territorial extension of his party, but above all, because it enabled him to show the rest of the PJ that he could exert dominion even over Menem's own stronghold" (anonymous interview by author, La Rioja City, May 26, 2008).

Given Maza's vulnerability vis-à-vis the national government and due to Kirchner's capacity to threaten him effectively, Maza had few options for dismantling the president's political ambitions. In 2005, for instance, Governor Maza followed Kirchner's directives to bring Carlos Menem's political authority in La Rioja to an end. In the federal mid-term elections held that year, Maza campaigned for a seat in the national Senate against Menem, his own political mentor and close friend, who had decided to run. Maza, with his tight control over mayors, public employees, and the party machine, was the only candidate who could ensure a victory over the longstanding *Riojano* cacique Carlos Menem. As the governor himself put it, "we needed a very strong candidate to defeat Carlos [Menem], and I, as the governor, was the only candidate who could do that" (interview Maza). The decision to run against his former mentor was a difficult one but Maza knew well that the consequences of not doing so would be devastating. As the governor noted, "running against Menem was not an easy decision to make. I talked to Carlos [Menem] and told him that I could not support him, that I had to prioritize the province over his candidacy. By then I was reestablishing my relationship with Kirchner, and if I did not follow the president's orders, the province would not receive a single penny from the federal government. Carlos Menem understood it and said that I should care for the province" (interview Maza).

Governor Maza not only agreed to run against his own political mentor, but agreed to go to the polls leading the *Kirchnerista* FpV ticket instead of running as a PJ candidate. Maza's victory allowed Kirchner's FpV to get the first—and thus two—seats in the Senate, and just as importantly, it enabled Kirchner to extend his electoral and political presence in La Rioja and to damage Menem's political reputation in his own stronghold.[19] The 2005 legislative election marked the beginning of the partnership between the Kirchners and *Riojano* autocrats. In every single national and provincial election since 2005, La Rioja's incumbents went to the polls leading the FpV ticket, thus becoming key political cadres of the *Kirchnerista* Peronist faction.

The exercise of effective presidential power over La Rioja's autocrats was also important for securing support in the federal legislature. With his tight control over the *Riojano* congressional delegation, Governor Maza and Governor Beder Herrera could use "their" legislators in the federal congress to deliver legislative votes. Indeed, both governors became key allies for legislative coalition-building by making important contributions to the *Kirchnerista* cause. Unlike other undemocratic Peronist governors, Maza and, later on, Beder Herrera, systematically instructed their congressional delegation to back all *Kirchnerista* initiatives, even the most controversial ones—such as the set of laws passed in 2006 aimed at expanding presidential power, and the legislation introduced to nationalize previously privatized companies. *Riojano* federal legislators provided unanimous support for bills such as the alteration of the Consejo de la Magistratura's composition (i.e. the agency responsible for appointing lower court judges), which allowed Néstor Kirchner to control the greatest share of counselors. The legislators also voted in favor of the law regulating the use of presidential decrees, which further advanced presidential legislative authority. Likewise, *Riojano* legislators backed the *ley de Administración Financiera* (Financial Management Law), which granted the Chief of Cabinet, Alberto Fernández, prerogatives to reassign budget items

---

[19] In that election, the PJ-FpV also won two (out of five *Riojano*) seats in the House. Carlos Menem won the senate seat for the first minority.

without congressional consent and upheld the extension of the "economic emergency law," that granted extraordinary powers to Néstor Kirchner during the second term in office (Bonvecchi and Giraudy 2008). Likewise, years later, following Beder Herrera's orders, La Rioja's legislators backed the nationalization of companies and services, such as Aguas Argentinas, the country's water enterprise, Aerolíneas Argentinas, the country's flagship airline, and the pension system (Micozzi et al. 2009).

Presidential Action vis-à-vis La Rioja's SUR

In exchange for these political services, both President Kirchner and, later on, Fernández de Kirchner not only refrained from opposing and weakening La Rioja's SUR, but rewarded the province and its autocrats with non-automatic funds that were essential to run the provincial economy. As Figure 6.5 shows, after Néstor Kirchner took office in 2003, La Rioja saw a decrease in the non-automatic transfers sent by the federal government (depicted with the dashed and solid white rectangles) from 40 percent of the total federal revenues to about 20 percent. In fact, when compared to 2002, the amount of current transfers funneled to La Rioja was considerably lower. This trend was reversed in 2005, however, when Néstor Kirchner considered *Riojano* support as critical. As Figure 6.5 indicates, federal capital transfers increased in 2005, and continued to do so during the years of the Fernández de Kirchner administration, reaching a peak in 2009.

In addition, other non-automatic transfers, such as current transfers (depicted by the transversally dashed rectangle), also flowed constantly and smoothly into *Riojano* coffers, indicating that during the years of the Kirchners' administrations, presidents never stopped delivering funds for infrastructural development (i.e. capital transfers). Finally, and perhaps more importantly, Maza's and Beder Herrera's support was rewarded with the signing of ad hoc financial agreements with the federal government—the so-called Acuerdos Extra Coparticipables (agreements beyond coparticipation)—that were critical to mitigating the chronic provincial deficit.[20]

The case study of La Rioja's SUR demonstrates that the potential to exert effective presidential fiscal power over vulnerable autocrats is critical to altering national incumbents' incentives regarding the sustainability of SURs.

---

[20] These transfers, as many interviewees reported, are as important as the coparticipation funds. Without the "fondos extra-coparticipables," the province simply cannot cover its current and capital expenditures (interviews Chamía, Maza, Ada Maza, Mercado Luna, Quintela).

SUR Continuity in Argentina

After realizing that they could wield effective fiscal power to obtain key political benefits from La Rioja's autocrats, the Kirchners invested heavily in the continuity and stability of the province's undemocratic regime. This political decision delivered important political gains for the Kirchners, critical fiscal assistance to La Rioja's autocrats, and, most importantly, contributed to reproducing an established SUR in the Argentine periphery.

San Luis: A Case of SUR Self-Reproduction[21]

(a) *The Political Regime*

As shown in Chapter 3, San Luis, like La Rioja, ranks among the least democratic provinces of Argentina. A closer look at the province's indicators of democracy found in Table 6.2 reveals that, with the exceptions of 1983 and 1999 when the Civic Radical Union (or UCR) obtained a relatively high share of the vote, elections in San Luis have become less competitive over the years. Notably, the effective number of parties running for gubernatorial elections has decreased over time, and the margins of victory have become larger.

As in La Rioja, San Luis has been governed by the Peronist party since 1983. Yet unlike its neighboring province, which was ruled by four different PJ governors between 1983 and 2009, San Luis has been governed by only two governors, Adolfo and Alberto Rodríguez Saá.[22] Accordingly, levels of party and governor turnover in San Luis have been extremely low; in fact, they have been the lowest among Argentine provinces (see Table 6.2).

These indicators contrast somewhat with the legislative indicators. As displayed in Table 6.2, the effective number of parties competing for legislative seats in the house has fluctuated over time, reaching fairly high levels of competitiveness (for example, in 2003 the effective number of parties in the legislature (ENPL) decreased to 1.68, and in 2009, it grew to 3.06). The strength of the opposition in the provincial legislature has experienced radical fluctuations: the meager control of 25.58 percent of the seats by the opposition in 2003 contrasts sharply with the 55.81 percent control of the seats in 2001.[23]

---

[21] Even though this section provides a brief characterization of the administrations before 2003, the main focus is on the administration of Peronist Eduardo Alberto Rodríguez Saá (2003–11) whose terms coincided with the presidencies of Néstor Kirchner and Cristina Fernández de Kirchner.

[22] Adolfo Rodríguez governed from 1983 to 2001, when he stepped down to serve as Argentina's president for one week during the 2001–2 crisis. His younger brother, Alberto, assumed the governorship in 2003 (see Table 6.2).

[23] The legislative indicators displayed in Table 6.2 relate to the lower chamber. Still, because San Luis has a bicameral system, the legislative indicators only provide partial information about the strength and access of the opposition in the legislature. If one takes into consideration the composition of the Senate, the relative strength of the opposition becomes smaller, as the provincial Senate has been monopolized by the incumbent party. The only exception was in 2007, when the opposition managed to win one out of nine seats.

Democrats and Autocrats

Table 6.2. San Luis indicators of democracy

Year of election	ENP (governor's race)	Margin of victory in gubernatorial races* (runner up)	ENPL (legislative seats)	Strength of the opposition in the lower chamber (% of seats controlled) the opposition)	Turnover (party)	Turnover (head)
1983	2.81	3.26	2.07	43.33	0	0
1985			1.92	50.00	0	0
1987	2.58	19.20	1.93	44.19	0	0
1989			2.14	32.56	0	0
1991	2.46	12.32	2.27	48.84	0	0
1993			2.75	48.84	0	0
1995	1.82	55.03	1.97	41.86	0	0
1997			2.60	39.53	0	0
1999	2.00	10.44	n.d.	51.16	0	0
2001			1.72	55.81	0	0
2003	1.23	84.56	1.68	25.58	0	1
2005			2.57	32.56	0	1
2007	1.35	75.39	2.64	41.86	0	1
2009			3.06	46.51	0	1
San Luis's mean	2.03	37.17	2.26	43.05	0.00	0.17
Provinces' mean	2.58	19.69	2.33	44.78	0.29	0.84
Min	1.23	0.29	1.13	6.9	0	0
Max	4.45	84.56	8.91	84.62	1	1

Source: Chapter 3.
* Higher values indicate lower levels of democracy.

As in La Rioja and other SURs, autocrats in San Luis consolidated the regime by manipulating electoral rules and institutions. The regime's entrenchment was largely possible due to a one-time constitutional reform in 1986 that sought to undermine the opposition's (i.e. the UCR's) electoral power, and which many political observers saw as the key pillar upon which the Rodríguez Saás built their "dynasty" (interviews Laborda, Samper, Agúndez, interviews 6, 8, and 9; see also Samper 1993; Guiñazú 2003). This reform introduced indefinite reelection for governors, created a new chamber—the Senate (which overrepresented rural areas where the PJ was most powerful)—and provided the executive with new and expanded decree powers (Suárez-Cao 2001; Guiñazú 2003: 81–3; Samper 2006). Finally, the powers of the lower chamber were decreased and some key functions (the nomination of lower judges, the appointment of the General Attorney and the Accountant General, as well as the impeachment process) were transferred to the newly created Senate (see Guiñazú 2003: 82).

In addition to these institutional reforms, the Rodríguez Saás employed other tactics to curtail the power of the opposition and restrain the channels through which it could have access to ruling positions. Some examples were the 2000 law to redistrict the province's capital into four smaller districts, or the creation of new municipalities such as La Punta.[24] Nondemocratic and semi-illegal maneuvers were also employed to curtail the political power of opponents. In 2003, for instance, Alberto Rodríguez Saá, ignoring completely the right of San Luis city's mayor to call municipal elections, announced his own electoral calendar. Elections in the capital were held twice that year, as both the mayor and the governor followed their own calendars, fielded their own candidates, and elected their respective mayors. After the two elections were held, San Luis city was ruled by two mayors, had two seats of government, and required citizens to pay local taxes to two mayoralities and municipal employees to work for two different patrons. The conflict over the so-called "dual municipality," which lasted for more than one year, was finally resolved with a federal Supreme Court ruling against Alberto Rodríguez Saá that ordered "his" mayor, Angélica Torrontegui, to step down.

Finally, control over the mass media was another strategy employed by the Rodríguez Saá to undermine the electoral clout of the opposition. As Behrend (2007) reports, in 1984, shortly after Adolfo Rodríguez Saá became governor, the most popular provincial newspaper, *El Diario de San Luis* (later renamed *El Diario de la República*), was purchased by a corporation formed by close collaborators with the governor and directed by the Rodríguez Saás' sister, Zulema Rodríguez Saá de Divizia. A few years later, collaborators of the Rodríguez Saás purchased the province's second most popular newspaper, *La Opinión*, which was also managed by a family relative. In addition to controlling the major provincial newspapers, the Rodríguez Saás have also owned the province's most popular TV stations, Channel 13 and Carolina Cable Color (Behrend 2007). Monopoly over less popular news outlets has also been possible through generous advertising contracts signed with the provincial government.

In sum, for several consecutive terms, the actual opposition's capacity to defeat San Luis's incumbents (and/or their parties) in elections was

---

[24] La Punta, known in San Luis as "the first municipality of the XXI Century," was created from scratch in 2003, on the outskirts of San Luis city. Hospitals, schools, public housing, even a university, high tech centers, and soccer fields were built to attract San Luis city residents who, as the governor intended, shortly after moved to the newly created city, thus helping to lessen the electoral weight of the opposition-ruled capital city (interview Agúndez).

significantly handicapped. Periodic electoral and institutional engineering, which included gerrymandering and reforms to the provincial constitutions, enabled the Rodríguez Saás to restrict the entrance of competitors into the electoral race or simply underrepresent them in legislative bodies. This electoral engineering, coupled with a fierce control over the provincial media, allowed autocrats in San Luis to deny the opposition access to governing positions in the province, in turn allowing them to transform the regime into one of Argentina's most undemocratic provinces.

(b) *The State Structure and Autocrats' Exercise of Power*

Unlike the state structures prevailing in other Argentine SURs, San Luis's state organization can be characterized as fairly (and comparatively) non-patrimonial. A closer look at the evolution of the three individual indicators that make up the patrimonial index confirms this observation. Despite the fact that centralization of political authority was high—indicating that autocrats in San Luis succeeded in curtailing the power of watchdog agencies such as the judiciary—the appropriation of fiscal resources directed to municipalities, and the generation of ties of loyalty and dependence through employment patronage, were considerably lower than in other Argentine provinces. This phenomenon suggests that the Rodríguez Saás, compared to other subnational autocrats, exercised power in a less arbitrary manner.

As in La Rioja, the Rodríguez Saá brothers followed a tradition of centralizing political authority by manipulating the size and composition of the provincial Supreme Court. Wholesale changes in the size and composition of the provincial Supreme Tribunal occurred in 1991, 1994, 1996, and 2005. As in La Rioja, autocrats in San Luis resorted to illegal instruments to force the resignation of justices who acted autonomously (interviews Agúndez, Taurant, Samper). In 1996, for instance, three allegedly loyal justices who had been appointed in 1994, and who had sought to create a more autonomous Supreme Court by opposing several of Adolfo's initiatives, were libeled and accused of corrupt practices in the major provincial newspapers and TV stations (interviews Samper, Taurant). After months of undergoing these attacks, the three justices resigned, allowing the governor to appoint, once again, three new and subservient justices. The strategy of replacing justices by inducing their resignation, which continued to be implemented during the administration of the younger Rodríguez Saá, was used less frequently than in the past. The threat of judicial replacement was nonetheless sufficient to keep the judiciary subservient: threatened by its own instability, it was prevented from exercising an effective check on the arbitrary rule of the provincial executive.

The steady manipulation of the province's highest tribunal contrasted sharply with the other indicators of patrimonialism—the appropriation of fiscal funds directed to municipalities and the number of public employees working in the provincial state administration—which, as noted earlier, indicate that San Luis has a less patrimonial state structure than other SURs in Argentina. San Luis, unlike La Rioja, had a law regulating the distribution of provincial transfers among municipalities that was in place since the 1983 transition to democracy. This law, which in many aspects was similar to the federal coparticipation law (see Chapter 4), not only required that provincial funds be distributed on the basis of strict formulas, but also obliged the provincial government to allocate transfers to the municipalities on an automatic and daily basis.[25] In contrast to La Rioja, where the absence of such a law gave autocrats enormous leverage over mayors, the existence of and compliance with this law significantly constrained San Luis incumbents' fiscal discretion and prevented them from blatantly blackmailing mayors through manipulating the pace and amount of provincial transfers. As a result, and compared to La Rioja, autocrats in San Luis had less capacity to manipulate and control mayors, and hence fewer opportunities to exercise political power as arbitrarily as other Argentine subnational autocrats.

Despite the fact that the public administration in San Luis was not among the smallest in the country, no other province exhibited such stability in the size of its payroll (Mecon-DNCFP various years). In 1983, San Luis had 57 public employees for every 1,000 inhabitants. Ten years later, that number had diminished to 55, and it reached its lowest level in 2004, when only 46 inhabitants out of every 1,000 worked in the provincial administration (Mecon-DNCFP various years). The stable and comparatively smaller size of the public administration were the product of deliberate policies to optimize state bureaucratic efficiency. In 1987 and 1989, for instance, decrees were issued to freeze vacancies and suspend the overtime payment system (FUNIF 1999b). Likewise in 1990, in order to further reduce levels of patronage, the governor put off special pension regimes, and in 1993, he implemented meritocratic procedures for hiring civil servants (see FUNIF 1999b).[26] Anecdotal evidence also confirms the governors' determination to keep the public administration small. "Adolfo [Rodríguez Saá]," as one of his former Ministers of Economy put it, "would build new neighborhoods from scratch, with new houses, new schools, new police stations, new public libraries, and new hospitals. However, his obsession with keeping the size of the public

---

[25] Even though funds are channeled via strict formulas and automatically, the law establishes that only 8% of the federally coparticipated transfers be transferred to the municipalities. In addition, 16% of the property tax and the tax on cars must be channeled to mayors. It should be emphasized that these are low percentages when compared to the most developed provinces of the country, such as Mendoza and Córdoba.

[26] In addition, in 1988, the governor also passed several laws to establish wage caps for public employees, and in 1989, he suspended advanced payments for centralized and decentralized public personnel.

administration in check would lead him to the ridiculous point of not wanting to hire new public employees to work in the police stations, the schools, the libraries, and the hospitals" (interview Marín).

The Rodríguez Saás' commitment to building an efficient state bureaucracy that relied on qualified technocrats further reduced patronage levels. Unlike other Argentine subnational autocrats, who bloated provincial state bureaucracies with unskilled workers, friends, relatives, and followers, San Luis's autocrats aimed to hire the most qualified professionals (interviews Marín, Poggi, Samper, interviews 8 and 9; see also Guiñazú 2003). Highly competitive salaries and generous benefits not only attracted the province's most skilled technocrats, but also exerted a pull on prestigious professionals living in neighboring provinces. Altogether, the measures implemented during the Rodríguez Saás' administrations to keep the size of the provincial administration in check, as well as the decision to hire skilled technocrats, limited autocrats' capacity to rely on a "captive electorate" of public employees, who, fearful of losing their jobs and salaries, would remain loyal to the governor.

Low levels of patronage, coupled with low levels of fiscal discretion, created favorable conditions for restraining autocrats' political and territorial control over the province. A comparatively less patrimonial exercise of state power, in turn, put the Rodríguez Saás in a more vulnerable position to resist presidential encroachments should they have occurred through partisan means. However, as already noted, given that President Néstor Kirchner's and Cristina Fernández de Kirchner's major instrument to wield power over governors was fiscal, the existence of a non-patrimonial state structure did not necessarily enhance presidential leverage over San Luis's autocrats.

Capacity of Presidents to Wield Power over Autocrats and San Luis's SUR

As previously noted, the Kirchners were able to reap the benefits of a considerable amount of tax revenues, most of which stemmed from export/import duties that were not subject to sharing with the provinces (see Figure 6.7). Access to these resources was decisive in increasing both presidents' fiscal leverage over subnational governments, and in turn critical to obtaining the acquiescence of several provincial autocrats and governors regardless of their party affiliation and/or ideology (see Bonvecchi and Giraudy 2008).

Despite the Kirchners' access to vast fiscal resources, the presidents struggled to wield effective presidential fiscal power over San Luis's autocrats and to obtain their collaboration. The Rodríguez-Saás' austere and responsible fiscal and financial management not only granted autocrats high fiscal autonomy from the national government, but most importantly were

SUR Continuity in Argentina

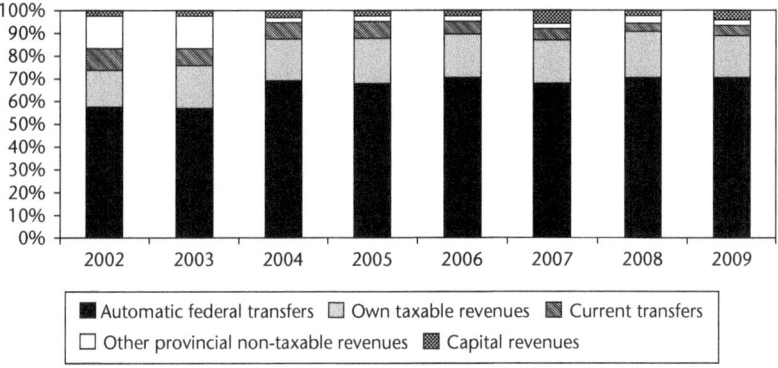

Figure 6.8. San Luis: income sources (2002–9)
Source: Dirección Nacional de Coordinación Fiscal con las Provincias [Mecon—DNCFP].

critical to neutralizing presidents' capacity to discipline provincial incumbents. The fiscal autonomy of San Luis's autocrats vis-à-vis the federal government stemmed from a series of policies carried out since 1983. Soon after swearing in, Adolfo Rodríguez Saá passed resolutions to attack inefficient government spending by penalizing ministers for unproductive and wasteful public spending, streamlined costly bureaucratic procedures, and implemented policies to improve provincial tax collection. Furthermore, during the 20 years of his uninterrupted administration, Adolfo Rodríguez Saá promoted and signed several bills that obliged the government to stick to a balanced budget that assigned half of its revenues to public infrastructure and investment. Equally important, the provincial government implemented a very tough policy with regard to public debt and savings, one which sought to maintain indebtedness at a minimum and savings at a maximum.[27]

Provincial statistics soon demonstrated the payoffs obtained from these measures. As Figure 6.8 shows, the provincial government was able to collect a considerable amount of revenue (an average of 20 percent) in the form of provincial taxation—a remarkable percentage given the generally low capacity of Argentine provincial governments to tax their populations. The province's fiscal autonomy has also been bolstered by the nature of the federal

---

[27] Probably the best example illustrating San Luis's commitment to saving occurred during the 2001–2 economic crisis. Due to its saving capacity, San Luis had a considerable amount of money in Argentina's National Bank. With the implementation of the so-called *corralito* in 2001, which froze bank accounts and assets, San Luis saw most of its savings confiscated. Interestingly, San Luis was the only province affected by such a measure.

Democrats and Autocrats

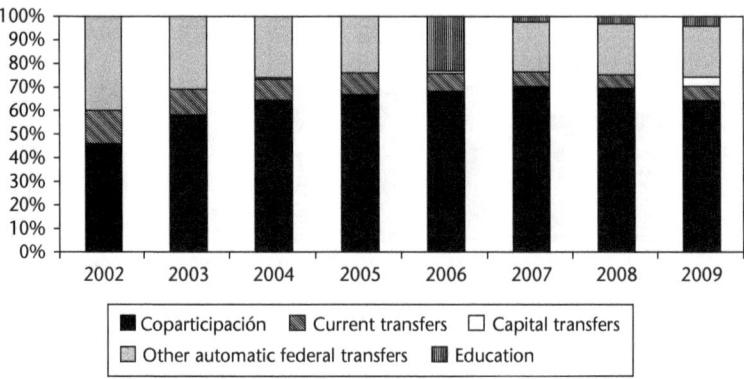

Figure 6.9. San Luis: type of federal revenues as a share of total federal revenue (2002–9)

Notes: Fiscal autonomy values are averaged values for the 1996–2009 period. Y-axis: Higher values indicate higher levels of subnational democracy. Zero and near zero scores denote undemocratic regimes. X-axis: Higher values denote higher fiscal autonomy. BA (Buenos Aires), Cha (Chaco), Chu (Chubut), Co (Corrientes), Cba (Córdoba), ER (Entre Ríos), F (Formosa), J (Jujuy), LP (La Pampa), LR (La Rioja), Mza (Mendoza), Mi (Misiones), N (Neuquén), RN (Río Negro), S (Salta), SJ (San Juan), SL (San Luis), SC (Santa Cruz), SF (Santa Fe), SE (Santiago del Estero), TF (Tierra del Fuego), T (Tucumán).

Source: Dirección Nacional de Coordinación Fiscal con las Provincias [Mecon—DNCFP].

transfers it receives. Even though San Luis relies on the federal government for its subsistence, as Figure 6.8 shows, the funds (i.e. coparticipation transfers) that have made the subsistence possible flow from Buenos Aires to San Luis on a formula-based and automatic basis (see Figure 6.9). This means that federal transfers, which in this case are not subject to presidential discretion, can protect autocrats from presidential encroachment.

San Luis has also had a record of sustained low levels of indebtedness. The province was not only able to maintain low levels of indebtedness, even in 2002 when the worst economic crisis in Argentine history hit the country, but above all became one of the Argentine provinces with the lowest levels of indebtedness (Cetrángolo et al. 2002; Cetrángolo and Jiménez 2004; MECON various years). As Figure 6.10 reports, throughout the period under study, debt made up 14.56 percent of the province's total revenues.

In addition to the austerity measures implemented throughout the 1980s and 1990s, as well as the policies carried out to increase tax revenues and the responsible management of the provincial debt, an aggressive and successful industrialist economic model further enhanced the province's fiscal autonomy. San Luis was one of four provinces which benefitted from one of the country's tax incentives programs for investment in underdeveloped provinces, the so-called Industrial Promotion Regime (RPI).[28]

---

[28] The other three provinces were La Rioja, San Juan, and Catamarca.

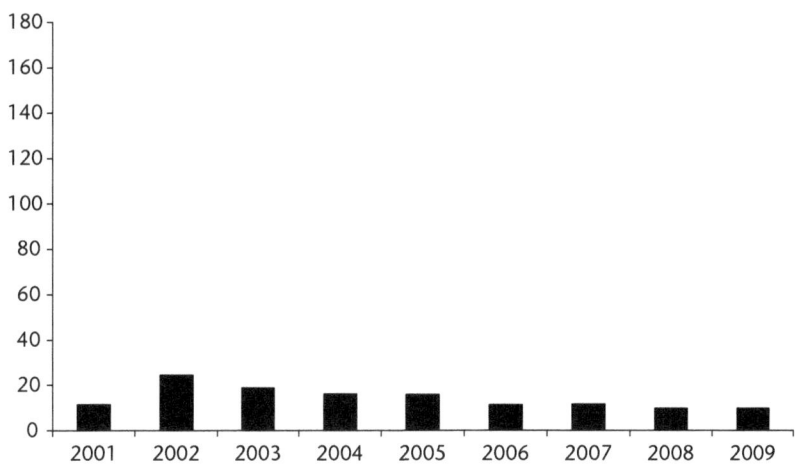

Figure 6.10. San Luis: debt as percentage of provincial GDP (2001–9)
Source: Dirección Nacional de Coordinación Fiscal con las Provincias [Mecon—DNCFP].

Reforms introduced by the federal government in 1979, 1982, and 1983 delegated the authority to grant federal tax breaks from the national government to provincial administrations and thereby conferred upon governors an enormous capacity for development (Eaton 2001; Guiñazú 2003). "By granting federal tax breaks," Eaton (2001) notes, "they could promote industries, provide jobs, and broaden locally generated tax revenues at the expense of other provinces" (2001: 101).

Unlike other provinces benefitting from the RPI, San Luis made industrial development the province's major economic activity. In 1980, before the RPI was implemented, industrial activity only comprised 14.70 percent of the provincial GDP; by 1991, it had reached 63.70 percent (DPEyC-San Luis). As a result of this rapid industrialization, the economically active population in the manufacturing sector grew by 245.50 percent between 1980 and 1991. The percentage of households living in poverty decreased from 27.70 percent in 1980 to 18.60 percent in 1991, and the percentage of households with no water and electricity dropped from 34.10 percent and 27.20 percent in 1980, respectively, to 19.90 percent and 12.10 percent in 1991 (Guiñazú 2003: 59–64). Additionally, Governor Rodríguez Saá worked to ensure that the process of industrialization was accompanied by a substantial investment in public works. Roads, highways, sewerage, housing for workers, and other public works were built at an impressive rate, enhancing the productivity of the newly installed industries and improving the living conditions of the local population (Guiñazú 2003).

In summary, the dynamism brought about by the RPI, which led to spectacular levels of economic growth, coupled with the Rodríguez Saás' austerity policies and efficient management of the provincial finances, helped to enhance San Luis' economy, and, in turn, its fiscal autonomy from the federal government. This autonomy, as shown next, diminished the effectiveness of presidential fiscal power and in turn reduced the prospects for political cooperation with national incumbents.

Prospects for Obtaining Cooperation of San Luis's Autocrats

High levels of fiscal autonomy gave San Luis's autocrats sufficient leeway to act independently from the center and to neutralize presidential attempts to control and penetrate the province. As two of the most prominent Ministers of Economy of San Luis explained, "since 1983, all Argentine presidents have found it difficult to discipline San Luis's rulers via fiscal instruments" (interviews Marín, Poggi). High levels of fiscal autonomy also bolstered the capacity of autocrats to confront national incumbents.

During the years of the two Kirchner administrations, Rodríguez Saá was among the few governors who dared to oppose presidential policies. He was, for instance, the only PJ governor who openly confronted one of the Kirchners' linchpin policies, the administration and (unconstitutional) appropriation of soy export duties, which diminished the portion of the tax proceeds that by law are sent to the provinces.[29] Rodríguez Saá not only denounced the president in the media for this violation of the law, but also filed claims with the federal Supreme Court demanding the complete refund of the income tax. Similarly, unlike other PJ (and even opposition) governors, Rodríguez-Saá did not hesitate to break ranks with Kirchner by unilaterally deserting several intergovernmental fora, such as the Consejo Federal de Inversiones (Federal Investment Board) and the Consejo Federal Vial (Federal Road Board). Also, on numerous occasions, San Luis's autocrat denounced the two Kirchner administrations for their discriminatory financial treatment, eventually filing claims with the federal Supreme Court against the federal government for its behavior (Escribanía de Gobierno 2006). Other claims were also filed with the federal Supreme Court to denounce the central government's refusal to allocate funds for federal housing programs (*Diario Perfil* 2008). Finally, perhaps the most notable example of Rodríguez-Saá's confrontational stance toward the president occurred in the 2007 presidential election, when he ran as the Peronist dissident candidate against Kirchner's wife, Cristina Fernández de Kirchner.

Rodríguez-Saá also confronted the Kirchners in Congress. Contrary to what occurred with other subnational autocrats, who instructed their congressional

---

[29] Rodríguez-Saá alleged that the soy export duties were unconstitutional because they reduced the producers' income, and, in turn, income tax. A reduction in this tax, which according to the coparticipation law is subject to provincial sharing, reduced the amount of money sent to the provinces (Escribanía de Gobierno 2006).

delegations to back the Kirchners' bills, San Luis's national deputies and senators—most of whom followed the governor's orders—opposed nearly all of the presidents' legislative initiatives. This opposition was vividly illustrated in 2006, when not a single San Luis deputy voted for Néstor Kirchner's most cherished initiatives, such as the law that enabled Kirchner to alter the composition of the Consejo de la Magistratura (the law regulating the use of presidential decrees, which further enlarged presidential legislative authority), or the *Ley de Administración Financiera*, which expanded Kirchner's budgetary powers. Likewise, this opposition was observed during the administration of Fernández de Kirchner, when the San Luis delegation in the national congress voted against key bills endorsed by the president, including the nationalization of the country's flagship airline Aerolíneas Argentinas, the Broadcasting Law, and the Resolución 125, aimed at increasing the amount of export duties retained by the federal government (Asociación por los Derechos Civiles. Área Poder Legislativo; Micozzi et al. 2009). Finally, Alberto Rodríguez Saá was the only governor to refuse to uphold Cristina Fernández de Kirchner's main anti-poverty program, the Asignación Universal por Hijo, alleging that it was discriminatory and not as truly universal as the president claimed.[30]

Similar confrontational behavior was seen during electoral campaigns and elections. Unlike what occurred in La Rioja in 2005 and 2007, Rodríguez Saá refused to go to the polls in alliance with the *Kirchnerista* faction, the FpV. As a result, in the 2005 mid-term elections, the FpV in San Luis was unable to obtain any seats in the lower chamber, and only managed to obtain one federal senatorial seat. The electoral gains of the FpV in San Luis were even smaller in the 2007 federal mid-term and presidential race, when apart from not winning a single seat in the House, the party only received 8.56 percent of the vote in the presidential race (DINE 2012). As a result of this refusal, the FpV in San Luis never attained the levels of penetration seen in other Argentine SURs.

Presidential Actions vis-à-vis San Luis's SUR

The capacity of Alberto Rodríguez-Saá to act as a successful "boundary closer" and, in turn, his ability to neutralize both presidential power and the Kirchners' attempts at manipulation, not only deterred Presidents Kirchner and Fernández de Kirchner from strengthening San Luis's SUR, but also led

---

[30] The governor argued that "the policy is not universal because it does not reach beneficiaries who are already getting benefits from other conditional cash transfers" (*Diario La Nación,* Dec. 11, 2009). Given that most low-income inhabitants in San Luis were already receiving some type of conditional cash transfer, the Asignación Universal por Hijo did not reach this segment of the provincial population.

them to implement strategies designed to weaken and destabilize the provincial regime. In contrast with their behavior towards other more malleable autocrats and SURs, such as *Riojano* autocrats and La Rioja's SUR, the Kirchners opted to punish Rodríguez Saá by refusing to assign additional federal programs and funds for the province. As Figure 6.9 shows, between 2003 and 2009, all federal funds flowing to San Luis were in the form of non-discretionary transfers, i.e. money that by law flows automatically and directly to the provinces.

Other measures taken by the Kirchners to weaken San Luis's SUR included the withholding of federal approval for a wide range of programs and policies that the governor sought to implement in order to increase his popularity and the regime's legitimacy. By refusing approval, the Kirchners delayed the implementation of different programs that were of utmost interest to the governor, such as the opening of new provincial radio stations, the building of new airports, the construction of new stretches of provincial highways, the approval of curricula for the newly created University of La Punta, and the authorization to produce new medicines in San Luis's laboratories, among others (Escribanía de Gobierno 2006). During the years of Néstor Kirchner's administration, many important federal programs that operated in San Luis, such as the Environmental Plan, various federally funded health programs (including the plan to eradicate Chagas disease and the plan to modernize several health care centers), federal subsidies for small landowners and small firms, and various federally funded housing programs were suspended (Escribanía de Gobierno 2006; Campos 2007).

In addition, and taking advantage of the comparatively non-patrimonial state structure of San Luis, in 2005 President Néstor Kirchner began to take steps toward penetrating the Rodríguez Saás' stronghold. To this end, he sided with the dissident Peronist mayor of San Luis city, Daniel Pérsico, who was a staunch opponent of the governor. During the second half of his administration, Kirchner directed abundant federal funds to the city, which were used to improve municipal infrastructure, launch new social programs, and boost expenditures (interviews 16, 17, 18). These resources helped consolidate the Kirchner–Pérsico alliance, empowered the opposition, and put increasing pressure on Rodríguez Saá's rule.[31]

These actions, while useful to discredit Rodríguez Saá, were not sufficient to threaten the governor's power or to destabilize San Luis's SUR. As noted in Chapter 2, a sturdy coalition of support can be a key factor in maintaining

---

[31] Due to Kirchner's weak party organization, the president was prevented from crafting stable coalitions with local leaders. National–local alliances in San Luis were opportunistic, unstable, and mostly based on exchanges of federal funds for political support. Hence, Kirchner's infiltration in the province, while momentarily disruptive, was not sufficient to allow the president to control the governor from within.

SUR stability. In particular, party elite unity (which results from party cohesion) and mass support, which creates vested interest in the continuation of the regime, help subnational autocrats to ensure the regime's long-term survival despite presidential strategies to weaken them.

Party elite unity was an important factor in establishing and sustaining one-party rule in San Luis. Efforts to exert tight control over the provincial Peronist party elite began early in the 1980s. With the twofold goal of preventing party elite fragmentation and ensuring party discipline, in 1988 Adolfo Rodríguez Saá reformed the party's *Carta Orgánica* (i.e. the party's charter). Among other changes, as Guiñazú (2003) notes, the new charter made significant changes to the organizational structure of the party's provincial council, the district councils, the PJ provincial Congress, and entrusted the governor with the capacity to exercise monopoly over nominations. Party reorganization facilitated control over the party elite and also served as an important tool to discourage internal opposition. The party could no longer be used as an arena to contest Rodríguez Saá's rule. By the late 1980s, the local PJ had closed ranks behind the new leader and dissidents had no option but to leave the party. As Guiñazú notes, "contending Peronist leaders opposed to Rodríguez Saá's all-powerful rule have since then recurrently confronted the 'Adolfist' strand 'from outside', forming extra-party electoral coalitions" (Guiñazú 2003: 95). These coalitions, however, never attracted many followers, as evidenced by their electoral performance, which has since 1986 never surpassed the 8 percent threshold of the total provincial vote (Guiñazú 2003).

The Rodríguez Saás also managed to elicit considerable mass support among San Luis's population. Despite the regime's undemocratic and hegemonic character, the Rodríguez Saás have had a longstanding reputation of implementing policies that greatly increased the well-being of the local population (Guiñazú 2003; Behrend 2007). This status, which was an important factor in boosting the brothers' popularity and legitimacy, not only allowed them to win elections by large margins, but has also helped to avoid political instability between electoral races. The implementation of two specific policies—the RPI in the 1980s and 1990s, and the Social Inclusion Plan (PIS) in the 2000s—was especially important to build mass support among San Luis's inhabitants.

The RPI, which in the 1980s expanded the manufacturing sector considerably, was critical to enlarging the size of the Peronist clientele in urban centers (Guiñazú 2003). Similarly, "transformations in the occupational structure of the rural *departamentos*, although quantitatively marginal in absolute terms, amplified the party's captive voting in the least populated and developed regions of the province. Raising living and consumption standards plausibly reinforced Peronist support among non-partisan fractions of the middle classes while state-led industrialization shaped electoral constituencies within the upper strata business-linked sectors as well" (Guiñazú 2003: 108). Industrialization and improved living and consumption standards, as Behrend (2007) underscores, were also central to sustaining the regime's legitimacy in the 1990s. The rising living standards associated with RPI "generate a feeling of belonging, exceptionalism, and affection, which made them [San Luis inhabitants] think, 'well, they [the provincial government] are serious people, they deliver, and we can trust them'" (cited in Behrend 2007: 204).

Like the RPI in the 1980s and 1990s, the Plan de Inclusión Social (Social Inclusion Plan (PIS)) in the 2000s helped Governor Alberto Rodríguez Saá to elicit mass political support and, in turn, legitimate the regime. The PIS, a popular conditional cash transfer program, was implemented in 2004 to offset citizens' discontent with the rising unemployment resulting from the increasing deindustrialization and the 2001 Argentine economic crisis.[32] The PIS benefitted 31 percent of the province's economically active population, and took up 25 percent of the provincial budget (Behrend 2007).[33] According to INDEC figures, shortly after its implementation, the PIS visibly lessened unemployment levels, reducing them to 1.2 percent. Due to its capacity to improve the living conditions of many families whose members had lost industrial jobs or suffered the effects of the country's 2001 economic crisis, the PIS came to be regarded by the beneficiaries as the equivalent of the RPI in the 1980s. The governor, for his part, was lauded for his capacity and effectiveness in responding to the population's growing unemployment and economic demands. The PIS's vast popular support was confirmed on August 22, 2004, in a plebiscite called by the provincial administration in which voters were asked about the continuity of the program. Overwhelmingly, the electorate voted 89.64 percent in favor of the plan. In sum, the capacity of the Rodríguez Saás to deliver effective and concrete benefits to core voters not only boosted their popularity among the electorate but also gave San Luis citizens a vested interest in the perpetuation of the regime. In spite of their undemocratic, hegemonic, and at times illegal rule, citizens in San Luis endorsed the Rodríguez Saás because they were regarded as the only political figures who could deliver tangible benefits (Guiñazú 2003; Behrend 2007).

The case of San Luis reveals that a sturdy coalition of support contributed to SUR durability. Party elite unity, which resulted from the cohesiveness of the local PJ, coupled with the mass support that resulted from the

---

[32] In 2003, the province's unemployment rate was 15.6%. This percentage was shocking for a province that had always been characterized by its low unemployment rates, which on average never surpassed 7% (see FUNIF 1999a; Suárez Godoy 2004).

[33] Like many other conditional cash transfers, the PIS distributed cash allowances conditional upon certain verifiable actions, such as providing communal services, or maintenance work in the public administration. Yet, unlike other employment programs implemented in Argentina, employees make contributions to the pension system and have healthcare coverage.

implementation of popular social and economic policies, were central to the durability of San Luis's SUR, even in the presence of presidential strategies to weaken the regime.

Conclusion

The in-depth, qualitative analyses of La Rioja and San Luis offer concrete and detailed evidence about SURs' modus operandi, and highlight that, despite important regime similarities, these two regimes differ considerably from each other. The comparison shows key differences across SURs—such as their fiscal autonomy from the central government—condition the extent to which these SURs are vulnerable to presidential power, and in turn the potential for presidents to obtain the acquiescence of subnational undemocratic rulers. The analyses of La Rioja and San Luis also demonstrate that SUR/autocrats' vulnerability vis-à-vis national incumbents and their cooperation with the central government figures prominently in presidents' calculations regarding the reproduction of SURs. Presidents who can exercise effective power over autocrats have strong incentives to contribute to the reproduction of the regimes that sustain them in power. By contrast, presidents who are prevented from wielding effective power over subnational autocrats oppose rather than support SURs in power.

The subnational comparisons confirmed that the hypothesized causal mechanisms leading to SUR reproduction from above and SUR self-reproduction were present in the case of La Rioja and the case of San Luis, respectively. In the case of La Rioja, where fiscal presidential power was effective and autocrats' cooptation and inducement were possible, SUR strengthening and SUR reproduction from above was also possible. The case of San Luis, which illustrates the alternative pathway of SUR continuity, demonstrates that a lack of effective presidential power prevented the Kirchners from obtaining the cooperation of the San Luis autocrat, and led in turn to SUR weakening. Yet, SUR continuity through self-reproduction was possible, given the governor's capacity to rely on a sturdy and durable coalition of support, which included the backing of the party elite and the general electorate. This support was critical to ensuring the regime's long-term survival.

7

Subnational Undemocratic Regime Continuity in Mexico: Puebla and Oaxaca

As in Chapter 6, this chapter explores how the possibility of exerting presidential power over subnational autocrats, as well as the prospects for obtaining their cooperation, conditions pathways of subnational undemocratic regime (SUR) continuity. Specifically, the chapter explores how presidential partisan power during the years of the two National Action Party (PAN) administrations shaped pathways of SUR continuity in Mexico. As shown in Chapter 4, President Vicente Fox (2000–6) and President Felipe Calderón (2006–12), unlike their counterparts in Argentina, were able to count on a territorially extended and routinized party organization to leverage power over subnational rulers from within. The existence of loyal and inducible copartisans at the local level of government was critical to foster national–local alliances that were decisive in challenging and curbing subnational autocrats' territorial and political power. The power exerted through these alliances was an important factor in obtaining autocrats' cooperation and was, in turn, central to encouraging presidents to reproduce SURs from above. Ineffective presidential partisan power over other subnational autocrats as well as the latter's lack of cooperation, however, propelled presidents to oppose some SURs. These regimes, nonetheless, continued to survive due to autocrats' ability to put together sturdy and durable coalitions of support.

In order to test the book's central hypothesis—that there are two different pathways of SUR continuity, which are triggered by the capacity (or lack thereof) of presidents to exert power over autocrats—this chapter performs a paired subnational comparison of two SURs in Mexico. Following Van Evera's (1997) recommended method of breaking down the causal chains into their component parts, the chapter pays close attention to (a) the type of presidential power that existed and the way in which it was exercised, (b) how the power helped or prevented presidents from obtaining the acquiescence and obedience of subnational autocrats, and (c) how it facilitated SUR presidential support and thus triggered a pathway of SUR reproduction from above. The chapter also examines the alternative causal chain, in which democratic presidents oppose SURs within which they cannot obtain subnational undemocratic rulers' cooperation and thus cannot exert power over these figures. Yet, in this chain it is still possible to observe SUR continuity through self-reproduction when subnational autocrats' are able to ensure party cohesion and mass support.

Using evidence collected from archival documents, newspaper articles, and official documents, as well as information gathered in 90 in-depth interviews with Mexican national and subnational top-ranked officials, journalists, and former politicians, the chapter demonstrates how the component parts of each causal chain affect the hypothesized outcome.

The chapter first provides a justification of the subnational cases selected to illustrate Mexican SURs' trajectories of continuity. Drawing on two cases, Oaxaca and Puebla, the two pathways of SUR durability are illustrated with original evidence. The narrative and analysis of each case study proceeds as follows. First, a detailed description of the political regime and the state structure is provided. Second, the capacity of presidents to wield power over the SUR is discussed. Special attention is devoted to the instruments of presidential power available to Presidents Fox (2000–6) and Calderón (2006–9),[1] as well as to autocrats' instruments of autonomy. Third, the prospects of obtaining autocrats' political cooperation are analyzed. Finally, the actions taken by presidents towards SURs and their reproduction are examined. The analysis of the case studies ends with an exploration of the type of SUR reproduction followed in each case.

Subnational Case Selection

Following Gerring (2007), two "diverse cases" serve the purpose of testing the central hypotheses of the book.[2] Given that this chapter seeks to demonstrate that different SUR trajectories are triggered by the capacity (or lack thereof) of federal incumbents to exert effective power over subnational autocrats and their regimes, two cases are selected that score very differently on the main variable facilitating or inhibiting effective presidential power. Chapter 4 showed that the party structure was the main instrument through which President Fox and President Calderón exerted power over subnational rulers. Thus, in order to assess whether presidential partisan power was effective and conducive to obtaining the acquiescence of subnational autocrats,

---

[1] As noted in Chapter 1, the focus of this book's analysis is up to 2009.
[2] According to Gerring, this type of case study, "requires the selection of a set of cases that are intended to represent the full range of values characterizing independent variable of theoretical interest" (Gerring 2007: 98).

and, in turn, to triggering SUR reproduction from above, a case is needed where presidential fiscal control was exerted effectively. By contrast, assessing whether the lack of presidential fiscal power led to the unwillingness of subnational undemocratic rulers to cooperate with the center, and in turn, generated opposition to SURs, a case is needed where presidential fiscal power did not exist or was neutralized.

As noted in Chapter 2, one important factor facilitating subnational rulers' capacity to control subnational autocrats via partisan resources is the existence of non-patrimonial state structures. Incumbents in these institutional settings have less capacity (1) to concentrate political authority, (2) to discipline the local population politically and economically, and (3) to control territory and municipalities. As a result, they are more susceptible to the infiltration of national-level political actors who forge alliances with provincial and local opposition forces. This local vulnerability to outside penetration becomes particularly acute when national incumbents can rely on territorially extended and highly routinized party organizations. Successful infiltration is important to disciplining and ultimately to obtaining the cooperation of subnational autocrats. As argued throughout this book, prospects for political cooperation are central to encouraging presidential approval and support of these rulers and their regimes.

By contrast, autocrats who rule in SURs where patrimonial state structures exist stand in a stronger position to neutralize presidential partisan power and to deny political cooperation to national incumbents. As already argued, patrimonial state structures play a decisive role in shaping the capacity of subnational autocrats to resist co-optation from the central government. In subnational jurisdictions where patrimonial state structures prevail, autocrats stand in a strong position to centralize authority in order to maximize political control over their domains. Consequently, they are better positioned to close subnational territorial borders and prevent presidential control from within. Where these state structures exist, to put it in Gibson's (2005, 2013) words, subnational autocrats can easily carry out strategies of boundary control, whereby they seek to maximize influence over local politics and deprive provincial oppositions of access to national allies and resources. The incapacity of presidents to discipline entrenched and recalcitrant subnational incumbents, and their subsequent failure to obtain routine political support (or gain it at a very high premium) raises the costs for national incumbents to support SURs, and their rulers, in power. The lower political returns yielded by uncontrollable SURs, coupled with subnational incumbents' capacity to threaten presidential authority, give presidents incentives to oppose these regimes. However, presidential opposition to SURs does not necessarily result in regime change. In contrast, it can result in a different trajectory of SUR continuity—SUR self-reproduction.

In light of these considerations, the key criterion for case selection was determined by the type of state structure prevalent in each state, and not by the

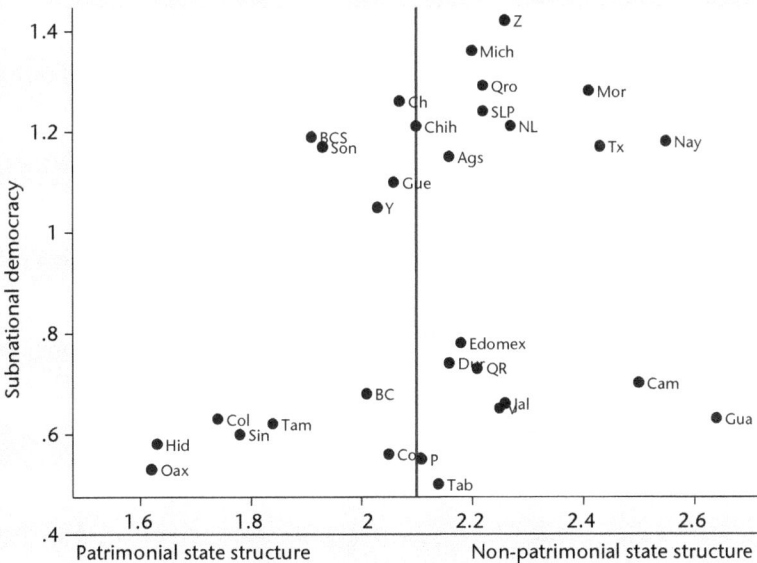

Figure 7.1. Levels of democracy and type of state structure in the Mexican states (average 2000–9)

Notes: Values are averaged values for the 1997–2009 period. Y-axis: Higher values indicate higher levels of subnational democracy. Zero and near-zero scores denote undemocratic regimes. X-axis: Lower values denote patrimonial state structures. Ags (Aguascalientes), BC (Baja California), BCS (Baja California Sur), Cam (Campeche), Ch (Chiapas), Chih (Chihuahua), Coa (Coahuila), Col (Colima), Dur (Durango), Edomex (Estado de México), Gua (Guanajuato), Gue (Guerrero), Hid (Hidalgo), Jal (Jalisco), Mich (Michoacán), Mor (Morelia), Nay (Nayarit), NL (Nuevo León), Oax (Oaxaca), P (Puebla), Qro (Querétaro), QR (Quintana Roo), SLP (San Luis Potosí), Sin (Sinaloa), Son (Sonora), Tab (Tabasco), Tam (Tamaulipas), Tx (Tlaxcala), V (Veracruz), Y (Yucatán), Z (Zacatecas).

Source: Secretaría de Hacienda y Crédito Público [SHCP –UCEF].

level of fiscal autonomy from the federal government as in the Argentine case. One non-patrimonial SUR (Puebla) and one patrimonial undemocratic state (Oaxaca) were selected (see Figure 7.1). This chapter uses the case of Puebla to demonstrate that in the presence of partisan presidential control, SUR reproduction from above ensues. By contrast, the second case, Oaxaca, tests whether the causal relationship between lack of partisan presidential control and opposition to SUR holds true. The case of Oaxaca also illustrates that, in the presence of party elite unity, autocrats can counterbalance presidential actions of regime weakening, and in turn reproduce the political regime.

In addition, these two states were selected out of the bulk of non-patrimonial and patrimonial SURs because they have several aspects in common. Both provinces have been ruled by the Institutional Revolutionary Party (PRI) since the 1930s, both are located in southern Mexico (see Figure 7.2), both

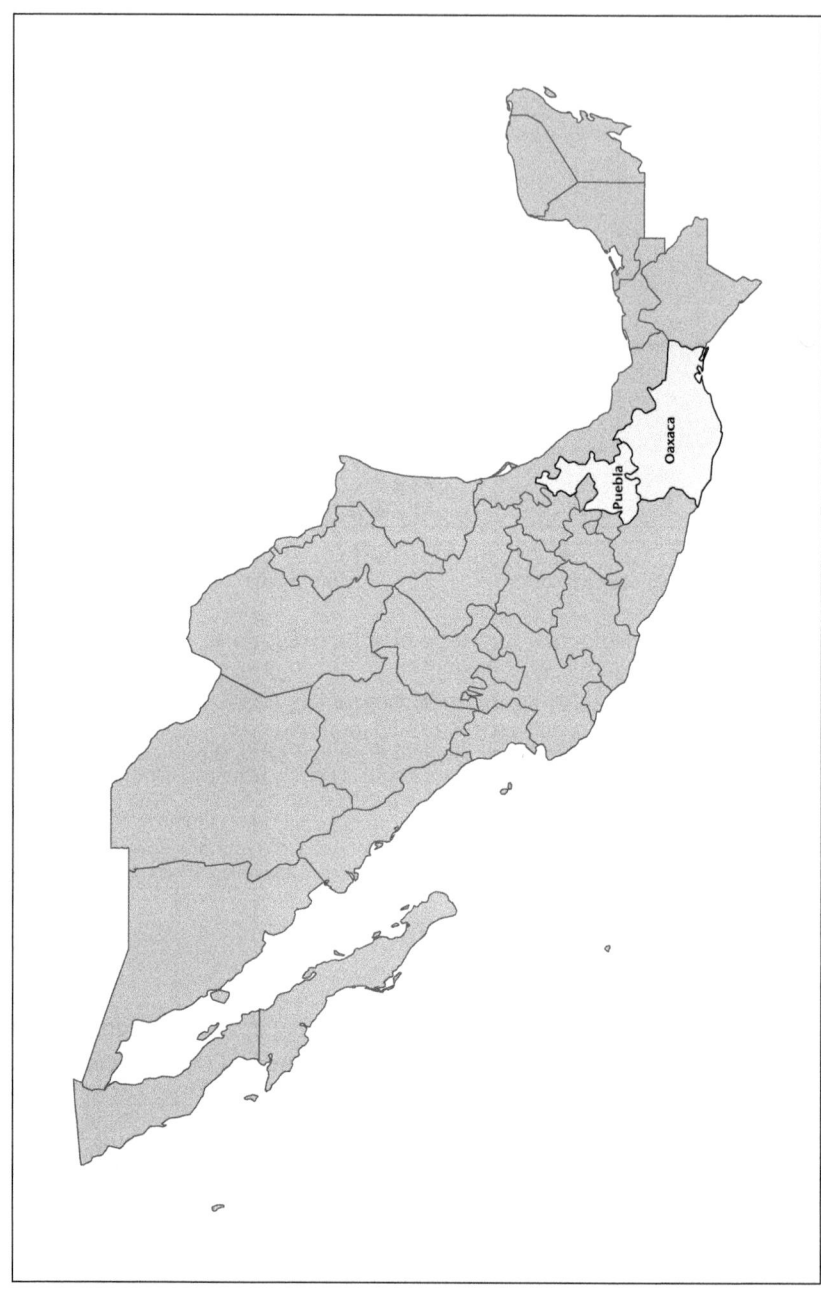

Figure 7.2. Geographic location of case studies

have similar levels of socioeconomic development,[3] and similar population sizes, i.e. 3.5 million in Oaxaca and 5.5 million in Puebla (Consejo Nacional de Población 2012). Despite these similarities, these two states differ on the main explanatory variable, the type of state structure. Puebla and Oaxaca then not only allow for a most similar case design, but also make a controlled comparison possible, facilitating in turn a more fine-tuned assessment of the main variable's effect on the hypothesized outcomes.

Puebla: A Case of SUR Reproduction from Above

(a) *The Political Regime*

As shown in Chapter 3, and as displayed in Table 7.1, the state of Puebla, ruled by the PRI, was one of the least democratic states in Mexico.[4] This was true despite the fact that Puebla's political regime experienced a precipitous liberalization in 1995 and 1998, when the PRI started to lose its grip on power both at the national and subnational levels of government (Ward and Rodríguez 1995, 1999; Beer 2003; Eisenstadt 2004, 2006; Ochoa-Reza 2004; Magaloni 2006).

Signs of political liberalization were seen at the gubernatorial level, where the vote share of the PRI declined from an average of 81 percent in the 1980s to 70.39 percent in 1992, 55.52 percent in 1998, and finally to 51.28 percent in 2004. As Table 7.1 outlines, this decline in the ruling party's vote share shrank the PRI's margin of victory while increasing the effective number of parties (ENP) competing in gubernatorial races. Whereas in 1980, only 1.53 parties competed in gubernatorial elections, this number jumped to 2.45 in 2004. Still, the higher levels of competitiveness were accompanied by increasing electoral fraud. As the indicator for clean elections in Table 7.1 shows, post-electoral conflict in 1998 decreased from 3 (i.e. absence of post-electoral conflict) to 1 (i.e. post-electoral conflict lasted between 8 and 30 days, and/or people were held in custody, and/or there were human/material casualties). Despite increasing levels of electoral fraud being ferociously claimed by the opposition, the PRI took advantage of the closer relationship between the governor's office and the state electoral commission (CEE) to legitimate its victories (Cleary and Stokes 2006).

---

[3] Literacy rates in 2000 were 78.5% in Oaxaca and 85.4% in Puebla; life expectancy at birth in 2000 was 72.5 in Oaxaca and 74.1 in Puebla, and per capita GDP in 2000 was US$3,489 in Oaxaca, and US$5,976 in Puebla (Consejo Nacional de Población 2012).
[4] Even though this section provides a brief description of the administrations that anteceded the transition to democracy, the main focus of this section will be on the administration of Melquíades Morales (1998–2004) and Mario Marín (2005–10) whose terms coincided with the presidencies of Vicente Fox and Felipe Calderón, the first two presidents of Mexico's democratic regime.

Table 7.1. Puebla's indicators of democracy

Year of election	ENP	Margin of victory in gubernatorial races	ENPL	Strength of the opposition in the legislature	Clean elections*	Turnover (head)**	Turnover (party)**
1984			1.59			s	
1986	1.53	69.11	1.59				
1987	1.53	69.11	1.67	24.14			
1989	1.53	69.11	1.67	24.14			
1990	1.53	69.11	1.7	24.14			
1992	1.88	53.27	1.7	24.14	3		
1993	1.88	53.27	1.67	24.14	3		
1995	1.88	53.27	1.67	24.14	3		
1996	1.88	53.27	2.22	43.59	3		
1998	2.44	25.84	2.22	43.59	1	1	0
1999	2.44	25.84	2.04	33.33	1	1	0
2001	2.44	25.84	2.28	39.02	1	1	0
2004	2.45	14.12	2.14	36.59	1	1	0
2007	2.45	14.12	2.19	36.59	1	1	0
Puebla's mean	1.99	45.79	1.88	31.46	1.66	1.00	0.00
States' mean	2.09	64.92	2.24	40.3	1.94	1.00	0.50
Min	1.08	4.01	1.19	8.7	0	0	0
Max	3.43	99.45	4.49	92.5	3	1	1

* The coding of this variable starts in the 1990s. Lower levels indicate higher levels of fraud.
** 1997 is the baseline, as it is the year that many Mexican scholars regard as the transitional year (see Magaloni 2005).
Source: Author's calculations (see Appendix).

Political liberalization also occurred in the state legislature, although here the trend was more erratic and less pronounced. The effective number of parties competing for state-legislative seats rose from 1.67 in 1993 to 2.22 in 1996. In the latter election, the opposition also managed to win almost a majority of the seats (43.59 percent). However, the opposition's initial gains in the 1990s were soon offset by the progressive legislative recovery of the PRI. The opposition only won 33.33 percent of the seats in 1999, 39.02 percent in 2001, and 36.59 percent in 2004 and 2007, never again attaining the remarkable results of 1995.

Apart from electoral fraud, SUR incumbents in Puebla resorted to other undemocratic practices to prevent dissident voices from gaining power and accessing office. For instance, under the administration of Governor Marín, severe violations of human, political, and civic rights were committed, especially in the small towns of the interior, and a fierce battle against local independent media and journalists was launched (interviews Mejía, Ehlinger, Mantilla, Aguilar, Ibañez, see also Rebolledo 2011). Under his administration,

Marín bought many newspapers and radio stations—or in some cases he simply forced them to close down—and incarcerated journalists who were vocal about their political opposition to the government (interviews Mejía, Rueda, see also Rebolledo 2011).

The most eloquent example of Marín's violations of civil liberties occurred in February 2006, after the breaking of the Lydia Cacho scandal. Cacho was an investigative journalist and director of a women's rights center in Cancún (state of Quintana Roo), who uncovered several networks of pedophiles and child pornographers operating in Cancún. These networks were headed by *Poblano* businessman Kamel Nacif, a close friend and campaign supporter of Governor Marín, and other local businessmen. Cacho was arrested in Cancún and transported for incarceration in Puebla in a questionable procedure carried out by Puebla's police outside their home state. Puebla's governor was implicated in the scandal through a tape of a conversation with businessman Nacif, in which the two men discussed plans to arrest and prosecute Cacho. The scandal, which sparked national outrage, also revealed Mario Marín's shady connections with a reprehensible business, his predisposition to participate in human rights violations, and his determination to curtail civil liberties.

In sum, despite the fact that opposition parties effectively competed in general and legislative elections, the PRI won systematically. It did so by employing a variety of undemocratic and illegal tactics, including the commission of electoral fraud, the exercise of tight control on electoral commissions in order to secure electoral victories by settling electoral and post-electoral conflicts in ways that favored incumbents, control over media outlets, and violations of civil and human rights. As a result, the political regime in Puebla remained undemocratic simply because, paraphrasing Przeworski (1991, 10), it was not a "system[s] in which parties lose in multi-party elections."

(b) *The State Structure and Autocrats' Exercise of Power*

Unlike the state structures prevailing in other Mexican SURs, Puebla's state structure could be characterized as comparatively non-patrimonial. A closer look at the evolution of the individual indicators that make up the patrimonial index confirms this observation. Despite the fact that centralization of political authority, measured as the per capita annual level of judicial spending, was low—indicating that autocrats in Puebla have checked the watchdog power of the judiciary—other agencies of control, such as the state-level comptroller, did not suffer encroachments from the executive power. Similarly, the appropriation of state resources for economic and political gain (the second indicator of patrimonialism) and the generation of ties of loyalty and dependence among followers (the third indicator of patrimonialism) remained low compared to other Mexican states. Altogether, the indicators demonstrate that Governors Morales and Marín (albeit the latter was clearly more patrimonial than the former), when compared to other subnational autocrats, acted and exercised power in a less arbitrary manner.

Depatrimonialization of state power in Puebla began during PRI Governor Manuel Bartlett's administration (1992–8) and was partly a consequence of the governor's resolution to modernize Puebla. Bartlett, as several interviewees put it, was determined to show the rest of Mexico what he would have done with the country had he become Mexico's new president (interviews Morales, Hernández y Génis, Ehlinger). His project was ambitious: he invested heavily in public works, engaged in important projects of urban development, and placed a strong emphasis on the construction of technological schools and universities. All of this investment contributed to the modernization of the state's physical and human infrastructure. Bartlett's project also sought to modernize the local PRI bureaucracy by neutralizing the power of the party's traditional and corporatist sectors, whose entrenched patrimonial practices gave the party a non-modern appearance to the outside world (interviews Hernández y Génis, Alcántara, Velázaquez). To this end, he removed many of the more traditional politicians of the local PRI regime and replaced them with out-of-state technocratic ministers. More importantly, Bartlett openly repudiated electoral coalition-making with the local PRI bosses who controlled the state's hinterlands (interviews Fraile, Hernández y Génis, Velázquez, Moreno Valle, Escobedo).

Bartlett's incipient depatrimonialization had an important unintended consequence: it made the PRI local bosses rebel against the governor. One of the strategies employed by local bosses to punish Bartlett's decision was to open up their strongholds to opposition parties, such as the PAN. As the former president of the PAN in Puebla noted:

> Before the 1990s, I had attempted, with little success, to campaign in the interior. Every time I visited these parishes and handed out fliers with information about the PAN, people would laugh at me and would return the fliers. My party's popularity changed abruptly in the mid-1990s, when the local bosses began to be ignored by Bartlett. José Esquitín, a powerful and well-known local boss from the Sierra in Puebla, for example, allowed me to colonize the Sierra and to open a PAN branch [there]. I began with 200 followers; little by little, and with the permission of Esquitín, I managed to entice new followers. (Interview Fraile)

As Table 7.2 shows, this penetration soon translated into PAN electoral victories. In the 1995 municipal elections, "the party's traditional bases, and the people in the interior," as Governor Bartlett himself noted, "repudiated us. They all turned to the PAN, which then began to gain considerable force"

Table 7.2. Percentage of municipalities under PAN, PRD, and PRI rule

Year of election	PAN	PRI	PRD	PRD Other parties
1997	10.14	86.18	3.23	0.46
1998	6.45	84.33	6.45	2.30
2001	21.20	65.44	8.76	4.61
2004	26.73	60.83	7.37	3.69
2007	23.50	67.28	5.53	3.69

Source: Author's calculations based on C1DAC database.

(interview Bartlett). The PRI's electoral debacle occurred not only in the interior but also in urban centers. For the first time since 1930, the party lost control of the state's capital, Puebla City, and other urban areas, such as Atlixco, to the PAN.

Threatened by the growing number of PAN-ruled municipalities, Bartlett resumed the former patrimonial practices and toughened his position toward PAN mayors.[5] During the last half of his administration (1995–8), Bartlett behaved like his counterparts of the patrimonial SURs of Oaxaca, Tabasco, and Chiapas. Reportedly, he commissioned thugs to generate conditions of ungovernability in PAN-ruled municipalities, thereby causing the political instability that would justify the (violent) apprehension of PAN municipal officials (interviews Mantilla, Hinojosa, see also Rebolledo 2011). It was in this context that the famous "ley Bartlett" (Bartlett law) was put in place. The Bartlett law allowed the governor to limit the amount of resources flowing to PAN municipalities, thus reducing the PAN mayors' capacity to deliver goods, and in turn their chances of increasing their popularity and political clout. In addition, the governor orchestrated state-led fraud in several PAN-ruled municipalities, including Huejotzingo, to undermine the electoral power of the PAN (Eisenstadt 2004).

The exercise of non-patrimonial state power, however, gradually resumed during Melquíades Morales's PRI administration. Morales reduced levels of patronage (or, what is the same, ties of loyalty and dependence) through cuts in public-sector employment, which decreased his capacity to rely on the allegiance of public employees who, for fear of being removed from office,

---

[5] Most scholars would see the patrimonial vs. non-patrimonial nature of state structures as a somewhat sticky variable, not subject to very rapid changes over time. The fact that levels of patrimonialism change rather quickly in Puebla is explained by the indicators selected to tap it. Such indicators capture rulers' actual actions, and as a result it is possible that they change quickly.

become subservient to incumbents (interviews Velázquez, Hernández y Génis, Moreno Valle, Ibáñez, Mantilla).

Morales was also averse to allocating public funds by partisan criteria. As noted in Chapter 3, Mexican governors are obliged by law to pass on 20 percent of the transfers they receive from the Law of Fiscal Coordination (LCF) to the municipalities. With the exceptions of 2001 and 2003, when only 12.23 percent and 5.31 percent of the funds, respectively, were sent to local governments, Governor Morales sustained a policy of ensuring the smooth flow of resources to the municipalities. In fact, he not only distributed the percentage required by law but allocated funds in amounts well above the 20 percent threshold. His commitment to the universalistic distribution of state resources went beyond the LCF. As many former opposition mayors indicated, the governor rewarded opposition municipalities based on their financial performance and their efficiency in the provision of public goods through a newly instituted program, the so-called FONCON.[6] The criteria by which program funds were distributed clearly benefitted PAN-ruled municipalities (over PRI and Party of the Democratic Revolution (PRD) municipalities), which, in general, were ruled by less corrupt, more managerial, and more efficient mayors.

Another factor reducing the patrimonial exercise of state power was Morales's commitment to refrain from implementing extreme tactics to crush, co-opt, or manipulate local opposition forces and local organized groups. As many *Poblano* opposition leaders noted, unlike what occurred during Bartlett's second half administration and in Mexico's other patrimonial SURs—such as Oaxaca, where governors blackmailed opposition mayors with the commission of state audits to investigate financial misdeeds (real or contrived) and with removals from office—opposition mayors in Puebla did not, for the most part, suffer these retaliations. "During Morales's term," as one former PAN mayor reported, "the governor ceased to threaten us, for instance, he would not commission state audits to extort us. During the years of his administration no single PAN mayor was removed from office" (interview Hinojosa). Quite to the contrary, opposition mayors were treated in a collegial manner despite the fact that the governor's territorial power was threatened by the growing electoral clout of the PAN in the state.

Finally, centralization of authority, measured as the independence of agencies of fiscal control, was relatively low during the years of the Morales

---

[6] The allocation of funds was done on the basis of a competitive process through which municipalities were assigned funds for public works. Municipalities offered to pay a given amount of money, and if that amount surpassed 50% of the total price, they were awarded the public work (in general, states in Mexico pay for 50% of public works, while the remaining part is paid by the municipality).

administration.[7] Unlike other SURs in Mexico, Morales did not have a policy of interfering with the central government's attempts to audit the management and allocation of state funds. Similarly, Morales was a precursor in the implementation of a modern law of fiscal administration. In 2000, one year before Mexico's national government passed the Law of Federal Fiscal Oversight (LSFF), Governor Morales was able to pass the first norm to modernize the state's accounting system, thus establishing the legal basis for the exercise of more efficient fiscal control.

The comparatively non-patrimonial exercise of state power could also be observed in the state legislature where Morales treated PAN and PRD legislators in a non-coercive, respectful, and institutionalized manner (interviews Velázquez, Mantilla). A similar relationship existed between the governor and the *delegados federales* (federal delegates).[8] Despite the fact that most of them had been appointed with Morales's consent and only a few belonged to the PAN properly speaking, and unlike other subnational autocrats of neighboring SURs (see discussion on Oaxaca below), Morales did not co-opt and coerce federal delegates affiliated with the PAN for the purpose of gaining control over federal programs and resources. Instead, he was respectful of their autonomy, and this respect enabled PAN delegates to mediate between the federal government and the local population (interview Mantilla).

The relatively non-patrimonial exercise of state power, which contributed to boosting the autonomy of opposition parties, opposition mayors, federal delegates, and the citizenry more broadly, deteriorated when Mario Marín assumed the governorship in February 2005. During his first year in office, and before the Lydia Cacho scandal broke in February 2006, Marín sought to centralize political authority by resuming the practices observed during the Bartlett administration. For example, as Rebolledo (2011) reports, he used the local Internal Revenue Service (IRS) to audit family members of anyone who was being vocal about their political opposition. The attorney general was used as a political arm, and both newspaper censorship and individual censorship were attempted. The governor also maintained patrimonial/patronizing relationships with PAN federal delegates, especially the Secretary of Social Development (Sedesol) delegate, who systematically refused to hand over Sedesol programs which the governor sought to use to favor the

---

[7] As explained in Chapter 3 (Appendix), one of the indicators that measures "centralization of authority" is "the independence of agencies of fiscal control," which is operationalized as follows. 1997–2003: Agreement between the state government and the Federal Superior Audit (AFS) to supervise budgetary items 28 and 33 (Ramos 28 and 33). Coded as 1 during the years in which the state led the AFS control the allocation of R 28 and R33, and 0 otherwise; 2004–8: Index of comptrollers office's independence (Figueroa Neri 2009).

[8] Most of Mexico's federal ministries and secretaries have *delegaciones federales* (federal delegations) in each of the 32 Mexican states. Among other things, the delegates appointed to these delegations are responsible for representing the federal government's interests, and for overseeing the allocation of federal programs specific to each ministry in the states.

campaign of the 2006 PRI presidential candidate Roberto Madrazo in Puebla (interview Mantilla). Similarly, during 2006, Marín made more discretional use of the *aportaciones*, with which he favored PRI mayors at the expense of PAN municipalities, and he also kept a closer eye on PAN mayors' expenditures, periodically threatening them with state audits (interview Contreras Coeto). However, this shift to patrimonial practices was only brief, becoming less pronounced after the 2006 Lydia Cacho scandal—when the governor, with the intention of offsetting his unpopularity, began to act in accordance with formal rules, and in a less confrontational, discretionary, and patronizing manner.

All in all, the comparatively less patrimonial exercise of state power, which was a result of the character of Puebla's state structure, prevented Governor Morales (and to a lesser extent Governor Marín) from exercising tight control over the state, its people, organized social groups and movements, and especially the political opposition. This type of state structure, as well as the less patrimonial practices promoted by Governor Morales contributed to dispersing political power, thus reducing governors' political clout and territorial control within Puebla's borders.

Capacity of Presidents to Wield Power over Autocrats and Puebla's SUR

The context of relatively low patrimonialism under Morales, and later on under the first half of Marín's term in office, which granted more political and economic autonomy to local opposition forces and local organized groups, helped, up to 2009, to expand the power and number of opposition municipal governments and local opposition groups within the state. In particular, and as noted in the preceding section, it was propitious for increasing the electoral presence of the PAN, which went from controlling 10.14 percent of municipalities in 1995 to 26.73 percent in 2004, including the most important and most populated city in the state (Puebla City) in 1998 and 2001. The election of new PAN federal deputies and senators in 2000 and 2006 was also critical for increasing the PAN's electoral clout in the state.[9]

The existence of loyal PAN-ruled municipalities and PAN federal deputies and senators, coupled with a more penetrable state structure, were important for increasing Fox's and Calderón's capacity to constrain *Poblano* autocrats from within. After PAN's 2000 presidential victory, PAN federal

---

[9] The PAN in Puebla went from holding 44.44% of Puebla's seats in the federal lower house in 2000, to 70% in 2006. Likewise, the percentage of PAN federal senators doubled within Fox's *sexenio*: it went from 33.33% in 2000 to 66.66 in 2006.

legislators began to have ready access to cash transfers and subsidies to expand the party's electoral clout in Puebla, and to more credibly challenge the territorial power of Puebla's autocrats. Local PAN brokers used these funds to reward adherents and attract new followers (interviews Moreno Valle, Ibáñez). For instance, PAN federal deputies and senators funneled additional federal resources to the local PAN branch, which, unlike its Oaxaca counterpart, was not co-opted by the governor. The distribution of these resources helped Fox sustain the PAN's base of support, win over opposition factions, and maintain a foothold in communities of the interior that had previously been under PRI control (interviews Moreno Valle, Germán).[10]

Puebla's non-patrimonial state structure under Morales also allowed President Fox and his party, and later on President Calderón, to penetrate the state via federal delegates. As already noted, and unlike other Mexican SURs, such as Oaxaca, where state authorities co-opted, threatened, and extorted federal delegates, federal delegates in Puebla had ample room for maneuver to act as representatives of the federal government's interests (interview Mantilla). As a result, various PAN federal officials managed to implement federal programs and distribute federal goods among the local population in ways that were beneficial for expanding the presence of the PAN and the federal government in the state.

Finally, and as importantly, the relatively less patrimonial nature of Puebla's state structure also enabled Fox and his successor (and the PAN) to side with local grassroots and local organized groups, which, unlike in the case of Oaxaca, maintained greater autonomy from the state government. By distributing a variety of state resources and handouts, such as bags of cement, food, medicines, and corrugated roofing, the PAN managed to attract the support of local indigenous organized groups of the interior, which were traditionally linked to the PRI corporatist structures (interviews Germán, Moreno Valle).

In sum, up to 2009, the electoral expansion of the PAN, as well as PAN mayors' greater financial and territorial autonomy, can partly be attributed to a less patrimonial exercise of state power. These factors, coupled with the PAN's extended territorial presence in Puebla, were all important variables in increasing presidential partisan power over *Poblano* autocrats, and, in turn, key to expanding the potential of obtaining autocrats' political cooperation.

---

[10] During fieldwork in Puebla, the author witnessed this type of exchange in visits to different Panista casas de campaña (local PAN offices) that were set up during the campaign for the 2008 local elections.

Prospects for Obtaining Cooperation of Puebla's Autocrats

Morales's policy of "de-patrimonialization without democratization" explains why effective partisan presidential power via electoral control of Puebla's local governments put the governor in a vulnerable, albeit not entirely weak, position vis-à-vis President Fox. As an undemocratic governor, Morales, and later on his successor, Marín, continued to exert tight control over the local PRI machine and the party's core supporters, as well as the local legislature and the PRI congressional delegation in Mexico City. Once it became apparent that, due to their limited territorial power, Puebla's autocrats could be induced to deliver political support, Presidents Fox and Calderón took full advantage of this possibility.

The cooperation and political support of autocrats from Puebla was desirable given Fox's initially weak political stance. When he took office in December 2000, 21 out of 32 states were ruled by PRI governors, and no single party held a majority either in the Chamber of Deputies or in the Senate (Shirk 2000, 2005; Mizrahi 2003). Under these circumstances, he was forced to strike political coalitions with opposition parties, and these coalitions also included alliances with subnational undemocratic rulers. The support of subnational autocrats, such as Marín, was also critical after 2006 and during the first years of the Calderón administration. The allegedly fraudulent 2006 presidential elections in which Andrés Manuel López Obrador from the PRD lost by a mere 0.58 percent of the vote against the PAN candidate, Felipe Calderón, which polarized the political elite, also pushed the PAN to entice the political support of the PRI. The PRI, as many interviewees noted, was the only party that could politically validate Calderón's victory, and provide legislative support in a Congress where the PRD could not be counted as an coalitional partner.

In this context, effective presidential partisan power over Puebla's autocrats became extremely useful, as it allowed both presidents to obtain the political support they needed to advance their political agendas. In federal legislative and presidential elections, for instance, PAN candidates in Puebla not only obtained the greatest share of the vote during both the 2000 and 2006 presidential contests,[11] but they also obtained a considerable share of federal senators and deputies (see n. 9). These results were quite remarkable in a nondemocratic state controlled by the PRI for more than 80 years, particularly because they were achieved under two governors whose control over the party machine was considerable, and who had sound expertise in ballot stuffing (Rebolledo 2011).[12] A major factor that contributed to these *Panista*

---

[11] In 2000, Vicente Fox obtained 42.53% of the vote, and Calderón 37.49% in 2006.

[12] See interview with one of Morales apprentices, who accounted for Morales expertise in committing electoral fraud <http://www.youtube.com/watch?v=clk1NWePEGU>.

victories, as several interviewees reported, was that PRI autocrats agreed not to engage in ballot stuffing and they guaranteed a lower turnout of PRI voters (interviews Ehlinger, Ibáñez, Velázquez).

At the legislative level, Morales and Marín also delivered critical support for Fox's and Calderón's initiatives. Morales, for instance, not only voted for Fox's less ambitious and politically less controversial pieces of legislation, such as the law of access to public information and the civil service law, but most notably he sided with Fox in those initiatives that were fiercely opposed by the national PRI leaders, such as the 2003 fiscal reform (interviews Alcántara, Ibáñez, and two anonymous interviews by author; see also Castañeda and Aguilar 2007).[13] On these occasions, unlike other undemocratic rulers (such as Murat from Oaxaca), Morales did not hesitate to break ranks with his party and vote for Fox's initiatives.[14] Marín exhibited similar legislative behavior during his first years in power, when he supported Fox's and Calderón's legislative initiatives—such as pension reform, the increase of the value-added tax to 16 percent, and the energy bill—despite the fact that the PRI instructed its legislators to vote against these bills (Castañeda and Aguilar 2007; Rebolledo 2011).

Governor Morales also played a key role as Fox's ally in one of the president's most ambitious projects, the so-called "Plan Puebla-Panamá" (a program of economic development and international integration). Morales was very influential among the governors of the southeast, and his role as a regional leader transformed him into the natural interlocutor between these states and the federal government. His brokerage was key to gaining the support of the PRI governors from the southeast (interview Ibáñez).

In summary, up to 2009 both governors, despite belonging to the party of the opposition, delivered important political support to Mexico's first PAN presidents. Unlike other PRI subnational autocrats who were less subject to co-optation and who in turn opted to confront Fox and Calderón, Morales and Marín's more vulnerable positions vis-à-vis the central government prompted them to maintain a collegial and cooperative relationship with the federal government.[15]

---

[13] The 2003 fiscal reform draft was so controversial that it split the PRI congressional delegation into two opposing bands: one favoring Fox's initiative, the other against it.

[14] The same occurred with other undemocratic (non-patrimonial) PRI governors, like the governors from Veracruz and Hidalgo, who also voted in favor of Fox's draft.

[15] Morales himself noted the detrimental consequences arising from a confrontation with the federal government: "It is not good to engage in a fight with the cook [referring to who has the power in the house], it is better to negotiate with her. That is why unlike other governors [referring to Governor Murat from Oaxaca], I preferred to avoid confrontations with the federal government. What was the purpose of filing a claim against Fox with the Supreme Court? You don't win anything if you confront the president" (interview Morales).

Presidential Action vis-à-vis Puebla's SUR

In exchange for these political services, President Fox refrained from opposing and weakening Puebla's SUR. For instance, as Rebolledo (2011) reports, during the 2004 gubernatorial election, President Fox and his party did not field a popular candidate, nor did he increase public spending to support the PAN candidate's media campaign. According to Rebolledo's (2011) figures, the spending by the federal government on media in the state of Puebla in 2004 decreased by 46 percent compared with the national average increase of 22 percent.

In addition, and far from weakening Puebla's SUR, President Fox rewarded the state with non-automatic funds that were essential to run the state's economy. As shown in Chapter 5 and as displayed in Figure 7.3 by the upper dotted rectangles, throughout the years of Fox's presidency, the flow of federal funds to Puebla was smooth and constant. Additional evidence gathered from Mexico's Treasury shows that Puebla, together with other undemocratic non-patrimonial states (such as Jalisco and Veracruz), was among the greatest beneficiaries of Mexico's Aportaciones Program for the Enhancement of the Federal States (PAFEF) and Convenios

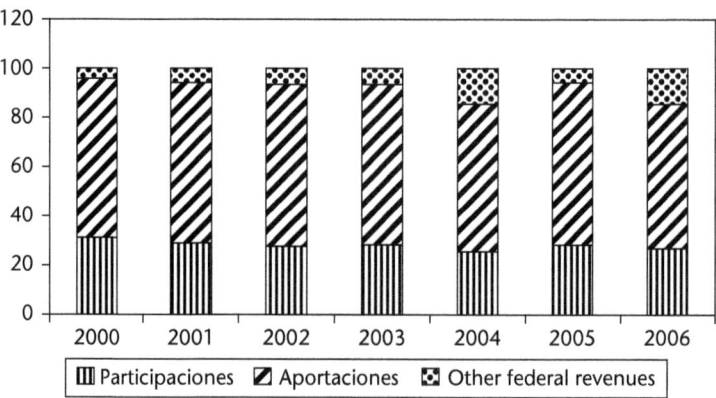

Figure 7.3. Puebla: *participaciones, aportaciones,* and other federal revenues as a share of total federal revenue

Notes: *Values are averaged values for the 1997–2009 period. Y-axis: Higher values indicate higher levels of subnational democracy. Zero and near zero scores denote undemocratic regimes. X-axis: Lower values denote patrimonial state structures. Ags (Aguascalientes), BC (Baja California), BCS (Baja California Sur), Cam (Campeche), Ch (Chiapas), Chih (Chihuahua), Coa (Coahuila), Col (Colima), Dur (Durango), Edomex (Estado de México), Gua (Guanajuato), Gue (Guerrero), Hid (Hidalgo), Jal (Jalisco), Mich (Michoacán), Mor (Morelia), Nay (Nayarit), NL (Nuevo León), Oax (Oaxaca), P (Puebla), Qro (Querétaro), QR (Quintana Roo), SLP (San Luis Potosí), Sin (Sinaloa), Son (Sonora), Tab (Tabasco), Tam (Tamaulipas), Tx (Tlaxcala), V (Veracruz), Y (Yucatán), Z (Zacatecas).

Source: Secretaría de Hacienda y Crédito Público [SHCP—UCEF].

de Descentralización (social development treaties by which the federation distributes earmarked transfers in specific areas like education, agriculture, and rural development) (SHCP 2008). Funds were also sent to the state after each of Fox's legislative initiatives earned the support of Puebla's governors. These included funds for the Puebla Children's Hospital (Hospital del Niño Poblano), as well as funds for diverse state projects, such as the construction of interstate highways, public works, and assistance for social development (interviews Morales, Ibañez). The financial concessions made by Fox to sustain Puebla's SUR led Morales to note that "Puebla had more financial problems with Zedillo than with Fox; Zedillo, who was from my own party, cut more funds and sent less money to Puebla than what Fox did" (interview Morales). A similar pattern of presidential rewards for the state was observed durthe first years of the Marín administration. As reported by Rebolledo (2011), between 2005 and 2008 the federal government increased automatic transfers by 34 percent (Ramo 28) and 40 percent (Ramo 33).

Another important backing Puebla's SUR and its autocrat occurred in November 2007 in the context of the Lydia Cacho scandal, when Mexico's Supreme Court, allegedly influenced by President Calderón and the leadership of his party, rejected a report by its own Commission that found that Marín and 29 of his officials had conspired to violate Cacho's rights. The Court's ten judges voted 6-4 that, although there was evidence of criminal acts, and some rights violations did take place, they did not meet the 'standards' for the court to recommend action to be taken. The Supreme Court, however, noted that local courts and prosecutors were welcome to use the facts and evidence to seek justice. This decision helped the governor to settle the issue of his potential impeachment in Puebla. By so doing, he ruled out the possibility that he would be charged by the state courts and/or impeached by the state legislature, both of which were controlled by the governor and his allies.

In conclusion, the analysis of Puebla underscores the importance of effective presidential partisan power over subnational autocrats for obtaining their cooperation and sustaining a SUR from above. Due to their limited territorial power, which was constrained by the existence of a less patrimonial state structure and the expansion of the PAN in the state, Morales and Marín were disciplined (via presidential control from within). Effective presidential power over these autocrats propelled gubernatorial cooperation, and in turn increased Fox's and Calderón's incentives to reproduce Puebla's undemocratic regime from above. Up to 2009, both presidents did so by channeling additional resources to the state, which contributed to the steadiness of the state's economy, and provided political and legal support for Puebla's autocrats. In so doing, both PAN Mexican presidents helped to enhance the political position of Governor Morales and

Marín and the political regime that kept them in power. As discussed in the conclusion, this political dynamic would change after 2009.

Oaxaca: A Case of SUR Self-Reproduction[16]

(a) *The Political Regime*

As shown in Chapter 3, Oaxaca, like Puebla, has historically ranked among the least democratic states of Mexico.[17] However, a closer look at the state's indicators of democracy found in Table 7.3 reveals that the Oaxacan regime had experienced political liberalization over the years. At the gubernatorial level, the vote share of the PRI declined from an average of 86 percent in the 1980s to 74.71 percent in 1992, 48.84 percent in 1998, and finally to 49.42 percent in 2004. As shown in Table 7.3, this precipitous decline in the ruling party's vote share shrank the PRI's margin of victory while increasing the effective number of parties (ENP) competing in gubernatorial races. Whereas in 1980 only 1.31 parties competed in gubernatorial elections, this number jumped to 2.56 in 1998 and, even though it declined a bit in 2004, it remained above 2 throughout the mid-2000s.

As occurred in Puebla, higher political competition in Oaxaca was accompanied by higher levels of fraud. Table 7.3 shows that the quality of elections during the 1990s gubernatorial races was low overall (Oaxaca scored 1 on a scale of 0 to 3, where 3 is no fraud at all) and very low during the 2004 elections (when the state got a score of 0). In that election, the PRI candidate Ulises Ruiz Ortiz won the governorship with slightly more than a 3 percent margin over the Gabino Cué, a former PRI politician who headed the PAN-PRD-Coalition "Todos Somos Oaxaca" (We All Are Oaxaca) (Gibson 2005; Martínez Vásquez 2006; Cué n.d.). The election, marred by charges of fraud and by large urban protests, none of which led to any official investigations, was a watershed in that it was the first truly competitive election in the state since the 1930s.

These signs of increasing competitiveness at the gubernatorial level were partially offset by the fact that the PRI continued to exercise tight control over the state's legislature. As Table 7.3 shows, until 1989 the opposition only controlled 25 percent of the seats of the local legislature. Consistent with the political opening observed in the 1990s, opposition parties increased their

---

[16] The main focus of this section will be on the administration of PRI Governors José Murat (1998–2004) and Ulises Ruiz Ortiz (2004–10), whose administrations coincided with the presidencies of Vicente Fox and Felipe Calderón.

[17] Other authors have also regarded the state as one of the least democratic of Mexico. See, for instance, Fox 1994; Snyder 1999, 2001a; Gibson 2005; Sorroza 2006; Martínez Vásquez 2007; Lakin 2008; Benton 2012.

Table 7.3. Oaxaca's indicators of democracy

Year of election	ENP (governor's race)	Margin of victory in gubernatorial races (between winner and runner up) in percentage terms	ENPL (legislative seats)	Strength of the opposition in the legislature (% of seats controlled by the opposition)	Clean elections* (Index Ch.3)	Turnover (head)**	Turnover (party)**
1980	1.31	82.60					
1983	1.31	82.60					
1986	1.32	82.51					
1989	1.32	82.51					
1992	1.72	65.29	1.70	25			
1995	1.72	65.29	1.72	25			
1998	2.56	11.39	1.73	25			
2001	2.56	11.39	2.04	32.25	1		
2004	2.18	3.33	2.40	40.47	1		
2007	2.18	3.33	2.17	40.47	1	1	0
			2.38	40.47	1	1	0
			2.38	38.09	0	1	0
			2.43	40.48	0	1	0
Oaxaca's mean	1.82	49.02	2.11	34.14	0.66	1.00	0.00
States' mean	2.03	64.92	2.24	40.3	1.94	1.00	0.50
Min	1.08	4.01	1.19	8.7	0	0	0
Max	3.43	99.45	4.49	92.5	3	1	1

* The coding of this variable starts in the 1990s. Lower levels indicate higher levels of fraud.
** 1997 is the baseline, as it is the year that many Mexican scholars regard as the transitional year (see Magaloni 2005).

Source: Chapter 3.

share of seats to 40.47 percent, only to lose ground in 2004, when they controlled 38.09 percent of the seats. This control over the legislature, as will be shown, was critical to ensuring the PRI control over other branches of power and lower levels of government, as well as to preserving the impunity of the state executive branch.

Systematic violations of human rights and both civic and civil liberties were common during the analyzed time period in Oaxaca. During the Murat administration, members of the business elite were systematically threatened and persecuted, eventually falling victim to state audits commissioned by the governor. As a strategy to monopolize media outlets, the governor harassed prominent members of the local media until they were found guilty and later incarcerated for crimes they probably had not committed (interview López Lena, Martínez Vásquez 2006). Similarly, in an attempt to silence dissident voices, the governor ordered the shut down or takeover of newspapers' printing facilities (interview Gómez, see also Martínez Vásquez 2006, 2009). Persecutions, killings, and incarcerations of political opponents (such as PRI dissidents[18]), indigenous groups, and political activists (including the head of the public employees union) were commonplace during the years of the Murat administration (Martínez Vásquez 2006). National and international human rights organizations, such as the National Commission of Human Rights (CNDH), the International Commission of Human Rights (CIDH), Human Rights Watch, and Amnesty International, have documented some of the wide range of human and political rights violations perpetuated by state officials that took place in both the small towns of the interior and the major urban centers.

The human and political rights violations in Oaxaca reached unprecedented levels during the administration of Ruiz. Governor Murat had implemented selective repression, but under Ruiz this was carried out on a massive scale. This political repression started the day after Ruiz assumed office, when he issued a gubernatorial order for the takeover of the major local newspaper (*Noticias*), and one of its journalists was killed, allegedly perpetrated by state officials (Martínez Vásquez 2006). Like Murat, Ruiz fiercely persecuted local dissidents and opponents. Perhaps the most vivid example of the governor's repression of the opposition was a December 2004 order to incarcerate one of Oaxaca's most popular opposition leaders—Ruiz's former opponent and the alleged winner of the 2004 gubernatorial race, Gabino Cué.[19]

---

[18] Aquiles López Sosa, a prominent local PRI dissident, who splintered the party in the 2004 gubernatorial election to from his own political organization and to compete against the PRI candidate, was killed in a strange car accident reportedly orchestrated by the governor and the local PRI (Martínez Vásquez).

[19] The order of incarceration soon backfired, when massive popular mobilizations were organized to prevent Gabino Cué from being jailed (interview: Cué, see also Martínez Vásquez 2006, 2007).

Governor Ruiz also initiated a fierce confrontation with local organized groups, such as the Regional Confederation of Workers and Peasants (CROC), the Popular Indigenous Council (Consejo Indígena Popular), and the Popular Oaxacan Magonist Coordinator (Coordinadora Oaxaaqueña Magonista Popular), which ended in kidnappings, incarcerations, and persecutions of local grassroots leaders (Martínez Vásquez 2006, 2007; interviews Gómez, Díaz Pimentel). The massive and systematic repression of local organized groups and social movements reached its peak in 2006, when 700 state police officers brutally confronted the local teachers' union, the so-called Section 22 of the National Teachers Union, as they went on strike in support of annual negotiations on pay and conditions. During this police operation there were widespread reports of the use of excessive force and several arbitrary detentions of union leaders. In response to the state-led repression, protests grew and a loose coalition of teachers, local social and political organizations, students, and others soon formed, calling themselves the Popular Assembly of the People of Oaxaca (APPO). The APPO conflict, which was active during 2006 and 2007, unleashed one of the most violent episodes of state-led repression in Mexico's post-democratic period.[20]

In sum, the opposition in Oaxaca was, for more than two consecutive terms, unable to defeat incumbents (and/or their parties) in gubernatorial and legislative elections. Despite the fact that opposition parties effectively competed in general and legislative elections, and at time obtained the support of their corresponding national party branches, the PRI won systematically. Murat and Ruiz resorted to electoral fraud, incarcerations of opponents, persecutions of dissidents, control over the media, and electoral commissions to prevent opponents from accessing the governorship. The use of these tactics as well as the sustained hegemony of the incumbent party transformed Oaxaca's political regime into one of the least democratic and most electorally violent regimes in Mexico.

(b) *The State Structure and Autocrats' Exercise of Power*

Chapter 3 presented evidence about the cross-provincial variation in Mexico's state structures, and showed that Oaxaca was among the most patrimonial states of Mexico. Oaxaca's indicators of patrimonialism not only ranked well above the other states' means, but they were also the highest among Mexican states. A closer analysis of some of the indicators of patrimonialism[21] explored in

---

[20] The conflict resulted in 23 persons being killed, hundreds being arrested and imprisoned, and in the filing of over 1,200 complaints with human rights commissions (see LASA 2007; Human Rights Watch 2007; Amnesty International 2007).

[21] These include: centralization of political authority, the appropriation of state resources for economic and political gain, and the generation of ties of loyalty and dependence among followers.

Chapter 3 reveals that Oaxaca's agencies of horizontal control, specifically the judiciary and the comptrollers' office, were weak, the appropriation of funds directed to municipalities was high, and levels of patronage were also high.

Governors Murat and Ruiz maintained a highly adversarial relationship with local agencies of control. As will be discussed in detail, both governors systematically rejected controls by state auditors, and made no attempts to endorse modern principles of fiscal control and administration. Unlike other SURs in Mexico, as of 2009, Murat and Ruiz had not implemented a modern law of fiscal administration, which would have presumably placed important checks on the discretional distribution of funds within the state.

As noted earlier, Mexican governors are obliged by law to distribute 20 percent of the transfers they receive from the Law of Fiscal Coordination (LCF) to the municipalities. Unlike the case of Puebla, where incumbents upheld this rule, Governors Murat and Ruiz generally allocated an average of 14 percent of the LCF to the municipalities. In 2001, 2005, and 2006, for instance, the percentages sent to the mayoralities never exceeded 8 percent, indicating that a sizeable amount of federal transfers sent to Oaxaca was illegally usurped by Oaxacan autocrats. In addition to the misappropriation of these funds, Governors Murat and Ruiz used a variety of state resources and programs to benefit those mayors who sided with them, and to penalize municipalities whose mayors refused to support them. As several opposition leaders and ex-mayors who denied political support to Murat and Ruiz reported, the governors would not give to opposition-ruled municipalities the *participaciones* and *aportaciones* which, by law, should have directly reached municipal coffers (interviews Esteva (a), Esteva (b), Altamirano, Cué).[22] In contrast, these funds flowed readily to those municipalities where opposition mayors were willing to side with Murat and Ruiz, and most notably to those opposition mayors who were eager to defect from their parties and join the PRI's ranks (Martínez Vásquez 2006). In sum, the particularistic allocation of state resources in Oaxaca was important to keeping mayors in check. Unlike the case of Puebla, where mayors were able to maintain a financially independent relationship with the state government, and thus enjoyed greater political autonomy, mayors in Oaxaca were forced to show respect and loyalty to autocrats who disciplined them financially.

The analysis of another indicator of patrimonialism, rulers' generation of ties of loyalty and dependence (measured as the number of inhabitants per 1,000 working in the provincial public administration), indicates that patronage levels in Oaxaca were, on average, high throughout the period under study. The fact that a sizeable portion of the economically active Oaxacan

---

[22] See also *Revista En Marcha*, Nov. 2002; del Collado 2003; Martínez-Vásquez 2007; Lakin 2008.

population worked in the state public administration conferred on governors an unusual ability to ensure their loyalty. Cué (n.d.), Martínez Vásquez (2006), and Díaz Montes (2009) present detailed accounts of the role played by Oaxacan top-ranked PRI officials working in the public sector. These officials harassed, threatened, and forced the rank and file (and their relatives) to participate in PRI-organized political rallies and mobilizations. Cué (n.d.) reports abundant and detailed evidence about the strategies employed by these PRI officials in the 2004 gubernatorial elections, in which thousands of public employees were mobilized and forced to vote for Ulises Ruiz (see Cué n.d.).

In addition to centralizing political authority, generating ties of loyalty and dependence by relying on employment patronage, and appropriating earmarked funds, autocrats in Oaxaca turned to other patrimonial practices to further consolidate their territorial control over state bureaucracies, state resources, lower (municipal) levels of government and civil society. A common patrimonial practice used by Governors Murat and Ruiz was the appropriation of state funds and programs for the purpose of co-opting and controlling voters and brokers (i.e. mayors, leaders of grassroots organizations, and organized groups). The governors employed two major strategies to this end. The first was to remove opposition mayors from office; the second was to control and influence the dealings of federal delegates in Oaxaca.

Using a state-level constitutional prerogative, the *desaparición de poderes* (literally "power disappearance"), which allows governors to remove mayors from office under conditions of civil disorder and threats to local governability, both autocrats managed to control municipalities and municipal coffers. Two different maneuvers were used to remove municipal executives from office. First, autocrats commissioned the state legislature to conduct state audits in those municipalities that did not comply with the governors' orders. Regardless of party affiliation and irrespective of whether municipalities had engaged in state resource mismanagement or not, state auditors would find evidence of state resource maladministration in opposition municipalities (interviews Esteva (a), Esteva (b), Altamirano). That evidence alone would suffice to remove mayors from office.[23] The second maneuver to remove municipal executives was to create civil unrest, thus generating local regime instability. With their skillful control over *organizaciones* (i.e. local organized groups which maintained close links with the PRI),[24] Murat and Ruiz sent thugs to take over municipal buildings. The purpose of these takeovers was to create the appearance of civil disorder and lack of

---

[23] State audits were generally not conducted in municipalities ruled by mayors loyal to the governor (see Martínez-Vásquez 2007).
[24] These include local branches of large confederations—such as the teacher's confederation, as well as medium and small unions, social movements, street vendors, and all PRI corporatist organizations.

governability needed to allow the Oaxaca Congress to declare the *desaparición de poderes* (interviews Esteva (a), Esteva (b), Altamirano; see also *Revista En Marcha* 2002; Lakin 2008).

Once mayors were removed from office, the state government appointed loyal PRI *administradores municipales*[25] (state administrators), who, after assuming office, diverted federal funds sent to the municipalities (i.e. *aportaciones*: funds originally destined for public works, education, and health programs) to the state government, thus helping to fill the Oaxacan government's coffers with additional resources (del Collado 2003, interview Esteva (b)).[26]

The removal of mayors reached unprecedented levels during the Murat administration. Del Collado reports that, between 1998 and 2003, Murat removed 25 percent of mayors (140 out of Oaxaca's 570 municipalities). According to del Collado (2003), after the 2001 local elections the PRD controlled 36 municipalities and, due to Murat's removals, that number dropped to 29 by mid-2003. Similarly, in 2001, the PAN controlled 29 mayoralities, and by mid-2003 all but 17 PAN mayors had been removed. Convergencia por la Democracia had won six municipalities in 2001, and by mid-2003 only one municipality, Oaxaca City, was ruled by this newly created party (see also Martínez Vásquez 2007; Bautista 2007). In sum, of the 140 removals, 48 were in opposition-controlled municipalities, while the remaining occurred in PRI-ruled mayoralities, suggesting that Murat not only attacked the opposition but also did not hesitate to punish PRI mayors.[27]

The second strategy used by Governors Murat and Ruiz to further appropriate state resources that should have reached municipalities was to control federal delegates. After taking office in 2000, President Fox appointed new federal delegates in the states. However, the president was prevented from recruiting delegates from his own party ranks by the lack of a strong *Panista* party organization in Oaxaca. As a result, Fox was unable to name his own delegates and was forced to negotiate the appointment of delegates with Murat.[28] The negotiated nomination of delegates enabled Murat to appoint

---

[25] By law, municipal administrators should serve as provisional mayors until new, "extraordinary" elections are called. In the case of Oaxaca, however, administrators stayed in office until the next electoral cycle came round (del Collado 2003).

[26] The gubernatorial practice of appropriating earmarked funds for municipalities was also common in PRI-ruled municipalities, where many mayors gave up money from *aportaciones*, and handed it over to the governor and his allies (del Collado 2003, interview Esteva (b)).

[27] Many interviewees reported that Murat exercised control over PRI mayors by way of threats and violence. Gabriel Esteva, a PAN federal delegate in the state of Oaxaca nicely illustrated how Murat disciplined his own copartisans: "before (the legislative) Election Day, Murat gathered PRI mayors and told them: 'I "appointed" you, and I have the power to remove you from office if I want to do so. I assign you the task of winning this election; if you don't win in your municipality, you are out'" (see also del Collado 2003).

[28] Interviews Gómez Nucamendi, Martínez, Varela Laguna, Altamirano, Esteva (a), Esteva (b), Aldaz, interviews 14 and 19. See also Gibson 2005; Martínez Vásquez 2006.

loyal officials in key agencies, such as the local branch of Sedesol or Segarpa. These nominations not only prevented the federal government from using delegates as brokers in Oaxaca, but also increased the governor's control over the distribution of key social programs such as Oportunidades, one of Mexico's flagship conditional cash transfer programs. The allocation of funds from Oportunidades—which was supervised by delegates in each state, and which in Oaxaca was overseen by two Muratista Sedesol delegates, Miguel Ángel Cuellar and Luis Martínez del Campo—would not necessarily follow formal eligibility standards. By contrast, during the first years of Fox's administration the distribution of Oportunidades in Oaxaca was done according to partisan criteria that benefitted the governor (interview Esteva (a)). In 2003 Fox managed to appoint *Panista* (who were allegedly loyal) delegates. However, Murat soon succeeded in undermining the delegates' loyalty to the PAN by blackmailing, threatening (through thugs he sent to the *delegaciones*), libeling, and buying off the newly appointed delegates—most of whom, scared by the governor's actions, ended up funneling federal program funds and federal subsidies to the governor's agencies, where they would be distributed in accordance to the governor's criteria (interview Esteva (a)).

In summary, Oaxaca's patrimonial state structure was central to facilitating Oaxacan autocrats' control over state bureaucracies, state resources, lower (municipal) levels of government, and territory. The existence of such a state structure, as well as the ubiquity of a patrimonial exercise of state power, was also fundamental to the successful obstruction of the exercise of presidential partisan power over Oaxaca's autocrats, and to thwarting Presidents Fox's and Calderón's capacity to discipline Murat and Ruiz.

Capacity of Presidents to Wield Power over Autocrats and Oaxaca's SUR

The context of high patrimonialism under the Murat and Ruiz administrations, which decreased the political and economic autonomy of opposition parties, opposition mayors, and dissidents, prevented the PAN from expanding its electoral presence in the state. As Table 7.4 shows, during the 1997–2009 period the PAN controlled an average of 9.12 percent of municipalities, never ruling in more than 14.67 percent of the municipal districts.

Presidents Fox and Calderón could not rely on such a negligible partisan structure at the municipal level to make inroads in Oaxaca. Murat's and Ruiz's capacity to co-opt and manipulate opposition mayors and federal delegates severely restricted President Fox's and Calderón's ability to work with the few *Panista* mayors and brokers who existed in the state and who could have

Table 7.4. Percentage of municipalities under PAN, PRI, and PRD control

Year of election	PAN	PRI	PRD	Other parties
1997	7.04	69.01	21.83	2.11
1998	5.92	73.68	19.74	0.66
2001	14.67	56.00	24.00	5.33
2004	13.33	49.33	31.33	6.00
2007	4.64	60.93	31.13	3.31

Percentages are calculated on the 152 municipalities (out of 570) where political parties *do* compete in local races. As noted in Ch. 2, since the 1990s, a system known in Spanish as *usos y costumbres* has allowed indigenous communities in Oaxaca to use customary laws in electoral processes. As Eisenstadt and Yelle (2012) note, customary law-observing communities use a mix of Western and traditional electoral means: citizens elect federal and state authorities according to standard liberal electoral processes of secret ballot and universal suffrage, and they elect municipal authorities via indigenous customs.

Source: Author's calculations based on CIDAC database.

become key allies to help restrict autocrats from within. As the president of the Oaxacan PAN put it, "all *Panista* and PRD mayors and delegates play for Murat. All local politicians end up switching party labels or siding with the governor. He succeeds at co-opting mayors from all stripes" (interview Esteva (b)). Local party leaders of the opposition were not in a position to stop this defection. This was in part because they did not have either selective or material incentives to sanction or induce copartisans' defection (interviews Esteva (b), 12, 15).[29]

At the local legislative level, the presence of the PAN was also limited. During the 1997–2009 period, the PAN never managed to possess more than 16.66 percent of the seats in the state legislature (CIDAC; Lujambio 2000).[30] This meager legislative presence in the state was an important obstacle to effective presidential power over Oaxaca's autocrats. One practice commonly used by Mexican presidents to wield power over and discipline governors is commissioning audits to examine the administration of federally funded programs, subsidies, and transfers (interviews Carrasco, 23). Federal audits,

---

[29] A vivid example showing opposition party leaders' incapacity to avoid party defection occurred during a meeting of the local PAN leader, PAN mayors, and Governor Murat. As the president of the PAN in Oaxaca put it, "in that meeting, [the PAN] mayor of Loma Bonita (Gustavo Zanatta) came to me and told me, in front of all the other mayors and the governor, that he was leaving the PAN and would join the PRI. Immediately after informing that he was becoming one of Murat's mayors, Zanatta stood up, shook Murat's hands, and handed him over a box of cigars. Not only did he break ranks with the PAN shamelessly, but he did so in front of all of us. Later on, the mayor would admit that Murat had offered him money and perks in exchange for his loyalty" (interview Esteva (b)).

[30] Neither did the PAN in alliance with other political parties obtain a simple majority.

which are conducted by the Federal Superior Audit (AFS), are in practice carried out with the assistance of the state-level audit, an agency that is responsible to the state's legislature.[31]

Given Murat's and Ruiz's misuse of federal funds, the state of Oaxaca was audited in 2002, 2003, and 2004 as well as during the first three years of the Calderón administration. These audits, however, proved disastrous for the purpose of disciplining Oaxacan autocrats' financial misdeeds, given the hegemony of the PRI in the state legislature. Both Murat and Ruiz were able to neutralize the potentially damaging effects of federal audits simply by instructing PRI legislators, who in turn controlled the state audit, to discredit any possible evidence about the autocrats' financial misuses (interviews Colmenares, 23).

In addition, the recurrent use of patrimonial tactics to co-opt and control other groups in civil society, such as the *organizaciones*, diminished Fox's and Calderón's capacity to side with or take control over local organized groups and grassroots movements, as they were all easily manipulated and disciplined by Oaxacan autocrats. Federal partisan penetration in Oaxaca was also hard to attain because PAN presidents could not side with or win over other local opposition forces, such as the PRD, Oaxaca's most powerful opposition party. The PAN and the PRD had long stood at opposite sides of the ideological spectrum (see Eisenstadt 2004, 2006; Díaz-Cayeros 2004a), and this ideological distance grew larger after the 2006 presidential election, when the PRD presidential candidate lost to President Calderón in an allegedly fraudulent election. Local PRD and PAN alliances were only possible in 2004, when Gabino Cué's campaign as the gubernatorial candidate of a multiparty alliance that included these two parties did not succeed. The existence of municipalities ruled by *usos y costumbres*—the system of indigenous customs—has historically helped maintain the PRI's control over indigenous-ruled municipalities (Benton 2012). Their existence also accentuated Fox's and Calderón's inability to side with or strike electoral alliances with non-PRI mayors, with whom they could have challenged the territorial power and control of Oaxacan autocrats.

The prevalence of a patrimonial administration, which seriously undermined the electoral clout of the PAN in Oaxaca, was an important factor in deterring Fox's and Calderón's attempts to breach provincial borders and to constrict recalcitrant rulers in Oaxaca from within. Until 2009, Oaxacan autocrats not only systematically denied political support for the central government, but more importantly, became strong challengers of *Panista* presidents.

---

[31] The AFS works in tandem with state-audits because of the lack of AFS personnel in the states (interviews Martínez, De los Santos).

Prospects for Obtaining Cooperation of Oaxaca's Autocrats

The autonomy enjoyed by Governors Murat and Ruiz during the years of the *Panista* presidential administrations had important implications for the prospects of political cooperation between the national and subnational governments. Oaxacan autocrats not only managed to neutralize presidential power, but also stood in a powerful position to oppose presidents on various fronts. For instance, Governor Murat played a leading role in the 2001 creation of the National Confederation of Governors (CONAGO), the organization that he sponsored with the then powerful PRD national leader, Andrés Manuel López Obrador. The CONAGO was created to counterbalance the power of the newly elected PAN president and to advance the collective interests of governors vis-à-vis the federal government. As Murat stated, "the CONAGO was created to limit Fox's authority, which it did, but it also turned the relationship between Fox and myself into a difficult and confrontational one" (interview Murat).

In 2001, following one of the audits commissioned by the federal government, which sought to investigate the misuse of *aportaciones* during the Murat administration, Governor Murat filed claims with the Federal Supreme Court (the so-called *controversias constitucionales*) to obstruct federal audits in the state. Contradicting Mexico's financial law, the LCF, Murat claimed that the *aportaciones* that had entered the state were not subject to federal oversight, arguing instead that "every peso that got into the state could be distributed according to state's laws and not federal rules. The federal audits on *aportaciones* were then a clear violation of the state's sovereignty" (interview Murat). The Supreme Court's decision, issued in 2005, eventually denied Murat's claim, but this did not serve the purpose of auditing Murat's financial mismanagement, as the governor had left office in 2004.

Other examples of Oaxacan autocrats' confrontational stances vis-à-vis the federal government include the violent episode reported in Chapter 1 (in which a group of Sedesol officials was kidnapped in the Oaxacan city of Mitla in August 2002), the 2001 sit-in in Mexico City's Zócalo during which Murat and his people demanded the release of federal funds withheld by the minister of Communications and Transport,[32] the mobilizations of thousands

---

[32] In 2001, Murat was able to mobilize a considerable number of Oaxacans, including members of his own cabinet, local deputies, mayors, and members of the opposition, to go to Mexico City. Once the protestors and Oaxacan politicians arrived in the country's capital, they were joined by the governor himself in their sit-in in the Mexican Zócalo, where they (including Murat) spent four days and nights demanding the ministerial funds that had been withheld (interviews Salinas, Díaz Pimentel, Pérez Audelo, Moreno Tello; see also Sorroza 2006). As a result of this mobilization, the funds, which had already been included in the federal budget and were earmarked for the construction an interstate highway, were eventually released.

SUR Continuity in Mexico

of *Oaxaqueños* organized by Murat in Mexico City to protest against Fox's policies, and the tense negotiations surrounding the appointment of federal delegates in Oaxaca already described.

Oaxacan autocrats also confronted Vicente Fox and Felipe Calderón in Congress. Contrary to what occurred with other undemocratic governors, who instructed their congressional delegations to back *Panista* bills, Oaxaca's national deputies and senators—most of whom followed the governors' orders—opposed several of the presidents' legislative initiatives, including the 2003 fiscal reform and the 2005 federal budget, evidencing, as Gibson (2005) reports, that Murat "had not turned out to be the 'interlocutor' among governors that Vicente Fox had hoped for" (2005: 119). Additional confrontational behaviors were apparent in federal elections. With their tight control over local actors, resources, and territory, Oaxacan governors could have become important mobilizing partners during elections. Yet, unlike autocrats in Puebla, who agreed not to engage in ballot stuffing and who guaranteed a lower turnout of PRI voters, Murat and Ruiz systematically instructed their party machine to vote against PAN presidential candidates. Not surprisingly, the electoral gains of the PAN in federal races were negligible.[33]

Presidential Action vis-à-vis Oaxaca's SUR

The capacity of Murat and Ruiz to act as successful territorial gatekeepers and to thwart encroachments from the center not only deterred Presidents Fox and Calderón from strengthening Oaxaca's SUR, but also led them to implement strategies designed to oppose and weaken the political regime. Contrary to their behavior toward other, more vulnerable SURs, such as Puebla, Veracruz, and Hidalgo, *Panista* presidents did not assign additional federal programs and funds to Oaxaca (interviews 1, Murat). As Figure 7.4 shows, only a tiny part of Oaxaca's revenue, i.e. "other federal funds," came from the voluntarily and discretionary contribution of PAN presidents.[34] Also, whenever possible, Fox and Calderón "punished" Oaxacan rulers by discouraging the signing of Convenios de Descentralización (treaties of social development transfers that are distributed by the federation for earmarked projects in specific areas such as education, agriculture, and rural development) (interview Lepine; SHCP 2008).

---

[33] Between 2000 and 2006, only 10.52% of Oaxaca's deputies belonged to the PAN. This number shrank to 5.26% in 2006. Until 2009, no single federal PAN senator had ever been elected in Oaxaca. The PAN vote share in the 2000 presidential election was 26.46% and 16.77% in 2006.

[34] For quantitative evidence, see Chapter 5.

Democrats and Autocrats

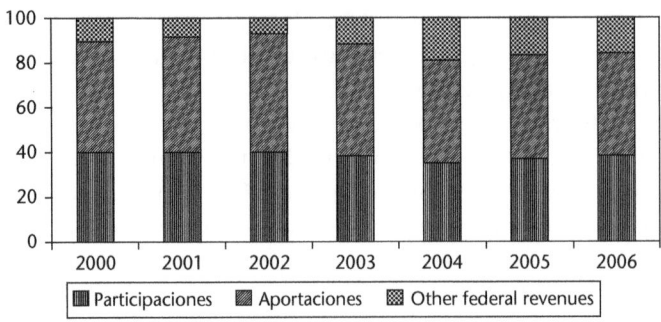

Figure 7.4. Oaxaca: *participaciones, aportaciones,* and other federal revenues as a share of total federal revenue
Source: Secretaría de Hacienda y Crédito Público [SHCP—UCEF].

In addition, *Panista* presidents commissioned several federal audits to investigate the financial mismanagement of Oaxaca's rulers and sought to limit the governors' exercise of arbitrary power by filing several claims with the federal Supreme Court against the state of Oaxaca, accusing incumbents of making unconstitutional use of *aportaciones*. Other measures taken by Fox and Calderón to oppose and weaken Oaxaca's SUR included the withholding of federal subsidies for a wide range of public works (mostly sewerage, housing, and roads) that Murat and Ruiz sought to implement in order to increase their popularity and the regime's legitimacy.

Finally, perhaps the clearest example of Fox's and Calderón's determination to bring Oaxaca's autocratic rule to an end occurred in the 2004 gubernatorial election and in the 2009 electoral campaigns, when the national PAN backed the opposition candidate, Gabino Cué. As Gibson reports, "the PAN had a strong interest in seeing Murat's candidate [Ulises Ruiz] defeated. Murat had become a major headache for the national PAN. . . . his rise as a major player in the PRI's national presidential strategies made him a target of the national leadership of the PAN" (2005: 119). Fox, Calderón, and their party saw great value in supporting Gabino Cué's multiparty alliance, which, among other parties, included the PAN. Figures reported by Rebolledo (2011) show that Fox increased federal spending on media in the state of Oaxaca by 55 percent to support the candidacy of Gabino Cué.

Despite Fox's and Calderón's strategies to oppose and weaken Oaxaca's SUR, up to 2009, Governors Murat and Ruiz managed to keep the regime alive. As already noted, in the 2004 gubernatorial election, Governor Murat followed dubious electoral procedures to ensure the election of the PRI candidate and thus the continuity of the electoral regime. Furthermore, he resorted to numerous undemocratic and patrimonial practices to crush and repress opposition leaders and regime dissidents, and incurred severe human, civil, and political rights violations. Still, the governor skillfully employed different methods to entice new followers and maintain the support of advocates, and succeeded in insuring party elite unity. As theorized in Chapter 2, mass support and, to a greater extent, party unity were critical to sustain Oaxaca's SURs despite national strategies to weaken the regime.

José Murat was a pragmatic governor, who ruled the state with a non-ideological agenda, and with an ad hoc ruling style. This ruling pattern had the advantage of giving the governor maneuvering room to court, without conflict and tensions, different bases of support. For instance, he maintained a cordial relationship with the leaders of medium and small unions, social movements, and street vendors, and most PRI corporatist organizations, sectors of the business community,[35] as well as with the leaders of the teachers' confederation—one of Oaxaca's most influential mobilizing social groups (interviews Gómez Nucamendi; Colmenares; Esteva (a); López Lena; see also Martínez Vásquez 2006, 2007; Sorroza 2006). To obtain their support, he deployed a wide variety of clientelistic strategies, such as the delivery of subsidies for housing, corrugated cardboard, food, medicines, and home appliances, as well as the provision of subsidies and perks. Still, as detailed in the preceding section, Murat also obtained political acquiescence by way of threatening, crushing, or even intimidating some of these organizations' leaders (Martínez-Vásquez 2006, 2007; Sorroza 2006).

This support, however, vanished under the Ruiz administration. Unlike Murat, who confronted but also courted local groups, Ruiz did not have an interest in obtaining the backing of local organized groups (interviews Diaz Pimentel, Murat, Trejo, Salinas). Rather, he alienated and crushed both local business elites and *organizaciones*. For instance, upon Ruiz's election as governor, he lost no time in ordering the takeover of the major local newspaper (*Noticias*), owned by one of the members of the Grupo Oaxaca (interview Gómez Nucamendi), and initiated a fierce confrontation with the local *organizaciones*, whose leaders and members were kidnapped, incarcerated, and persecuted (Martínez Vasquez 2006). Perhaps the most vivid example of the governor's lack of interest in courting local popular groups occurred in 2006 and 2007 during the teachers/APPO conflict, when leaders of the most prominent *organizaciones* and grassroots/indigenous groups were repressed, incarcerated, and even killed. Another example of Ruiz's disdain for enticing popular support was the relocation of several public and administrative offices to the outskirts of Oaxaca City to discourage local groups from

---

[35] Local contractors, for instance, were among the most benefitted sectors. Members of this sector reportedly allowed the governor to divert public monies with shady deals that were made for the construction of public works (interviews Gómez Nucamendi, Aldaz, Cué).

petitioning the government. With that goal, the governor moved the *palacio de gobierno*, i.e. the state's administrative office and the governor's residence, and the state legislature to the municipality of San Raymundo Jalpan, located several miles away from Oaxaca City.

Whereas mass support for Oaxaca's SUR changed from the Murat to the Ruiz administration, and decreased over time, both governors managed to build the necessary party elite unity that would ultimately contribute to maintaining Oaxaca's SUR in power despite national strategies of SUR weakening. Party elite unity in Oaxaca was possible due to a combination of local and national factors. At the state level, the unity of party elites during the years of the Murat and Ruiz administrations paradoxically resulted from Governor Murat's politics of party elite splitting. As Gibson (2005, 2013) notes, upon assuming office in 1998, Murat defied a long-standing norm of respect for *continuidad de equipo* (administrative continuity) by purging the state government of officers linked to his predecessor's administration. Murat not only fired PRI *Diodoristas*[36] who had served in the state executive branch but also replaced the leadership of the Oaxacan state congress with loyal *Muratistas*. *Muratistas*, who have high stakes in the continuation of Oaxaca's SUR, were allowed to remain in key party and bureaucratic positions upon arrival of Ulises Ruiz to the governorship. As Díaz Montes (2009) reports, Governor Ruiz appointed several *Muratistas* as secretaries of state, to the local legislature, and to the local PRI to insure the allegiance and support of PRI local politicians who had an interest in the perpetuation of Oaxaca's SUR.

Connections to key leaders of the national PRI also played an important role in ensuring party unity in Oaxaca. Murat and Ruiz were closely allied to the national PRI faction led by Roberto Madrazo, former governor of the state of Tabasco (1994–2000), president of the PRI (2002–6), PRI presidential candidate in 2006, and prominent and popular PRI politician.[37] Murat had played a key role in the ascendance of Madrazo as a PRI national leader, and was considered to be "one of the unquestioned leaders of the *cochinero* [pig pen] that took Roberto Madrazo to the presidency of the PRI" (quoted in Gibson 2005). Ulises Ruiz, for his part, had been one of Madrazo's protégés, who later on became one of his most influential political advisors, and eventually served as Madrazo's presidential campaign manager in the 2006 presidential

---

[36] Diódoro Carrasco, Murat's predecessor, was closely associated with President Ernesto Zedillo. He and his collaborators were regarded as more democratic and less repressive than the *Muratistas* who were appointed upon Murat's arrival.

[37] Under the party presidency of Madrazo, the PRI managed to win several municipalities, state-legislatures, governorships, and even seats in the federal congress. These victories, which helped compensate for the PRI's poor electoral performance in 2000, empowered Madrazo, as he was viewed as the main architect behind the PRI's post-2000 victories (interviews 12, 18, 20).

election.[38] Tight connections to the national PRI were important to ensure party elite unity in Oaxaca's PRI. The stakes for maintaining political loyalty and subservience to Murat and Ruiz were high, as career advancement in both the local and national PRI was highly contingent upon the influence of the Oaxacan autocrats (interviews Díaz Pimentel, Salinas, Trejo). Ambitious local PRI politicians who, by contrast, wanted to advance their political careers by opposing Murat and Ruiz had to do so by defecting to opposition parties. While some of them did so,[39] most PRI local politicians preferred to side with the governors, and back a regime that would, logically, help them advance their careers (interview Carrasco). Until 2009, party elites (and party cadres) supported the regime rather than sought to conspire against it. This was possible because, in exchange, both elites (and cadres) had possibilities of being promoted into rent-paying or ruling positions within the local and national PRI structure. Party elite unity, which resulted from the cohesiveness of the Muratista and Ruiz faction, was central to the continuity of Oaxaca's SUR, even in the presence of presidential strategies to weaken the regime.

Conclusion

This chapter has offered concrete and detailed evidence about the modus operandi of two of Mexico's most established SURs, Puebla and Oaxaca. The analysis of these case also revealed how key differences across these regimes, such as the type of state structure they possess, shape the prospects of wielding effective presidential power over autocrats, and in turn the possibilities of obtaining subnational undemocratic rulers' acquiescence. In so doing, the chapter underscored one of the central insights of this book, namely that, despite important regime similarities, SURs within countries can differ from each other, and so do the interactions they maintain with federal officials. These different SUR–national dynamics are critical to set SURs into alternate pathways of subnational undemocratic regime continuity. The analysis of the two case studies, then, underscores the importance of moving beyond the widely held assumption of within-country unity homogeneity in studies of SUR continuity. In particular, it highlights the value of acknowledging that SURs within countries maintain different, and at times opposed, relations with the federal government.

---

[38] Ruiz was deeply involved in the 2006 presidential campaign. As a matter of fact, during his first two years in office (2005–6) he spent very little time in the Oaxaca; instead, he was based in Mexico City, where he ran and coordinated Madrazo's presidential campaign (interviews Díaz Pimentel, Esteva (a)). Ruiz delegated his power to his secretary of state, Jorge Franco "Chucky" Vargas (Martínez Vasquez 2006).

[39] Prominent examples include former PRI Governor Diódoro Carrasco, and Gabino Cué, a former Diodorista politician.

The analyses of Puebla and Oaxaca also confirm another core idea advanced in this book, namely that SUR/autocrats' vulnerability vis-à-vis national incumbents and their cooperation with the central government figures prominently in presidents' calculations regarding the reproduction of SURs. Presidents who can effectively control subnational autocrats have logical reasons to contribute to the reproduction of these regimes that benefit their own political objectives. By contrast, the existence of autocrats over whom presidents cannot exercise effective power leads presidents to oppose, rather than support, existing SURs. In short, the study of Puebla and Oaxaca points to the importance of looking explicitly at presidents' actions and incentives vis-à-vis SUR reproduction, as national incumbents' aspirations to build winning electoral and legislative coalitions at the national level may act as important obstacles to advance subnational democratization.

Finally, the comparison of the two states demonstrates that the hypothesized causal mechanisms leading to SUR reproduction from above and SUR self-reproduction were found in the cases of Puebla and Oaxaca, respectively. In the case of Puebla, partisan presidential power was effective and autocrats' co-optation and inducement likely, making SUR strengthening and SUR reproduction from above possible. The case of Oaxaca exhibited the alternative pathway of SUR continuity. The experience of the Oaxacan SUR demonstrated that a lack of effective presidential power prevented Presidents Fox and Calderón from obtaining Oaxacan autocrats' cooperation, leading them in turn to implement strategies directed at opposing, and even weakening, the regime. SUR continuity through self-reproduction was possible, however, given the governors' capacity to ensure the party cohesion that was needed to guarantee the regime's present and future survival. As discussed in the conclusion, this situation, however, would change after 2009.

8
Conclusion

The argument advanced in this book fundamentally challenges the assumption that there is one single pathway to subnational undemocratic regime (SUR) continuity within countries. It shows instead the existence of multiple (within-country) pathways that lead to the same political outcome (i.e. regime continuity). The study is premised on the notion that SURs within countries not only differ among each other but that they maintain different relations with the federal government, which is why they are reproduced differently.

One of the main messages conveyed in this book is that alternative trajectories of SUR continuity within democratic countries result first and foremost from the capacity (or lack thereof) of national incumbents to wield power over SURs and autocrats. If presidents have the resources to induce cooperation from subnational autocrats and can thus secure credible and routine political support, the former have strong incentives to invest in the continuity and stability of undemocratic provincial regimes and autocrats. Under these circumstances, SUR reproduction from above, the first pathway of SUR continuity within a given country, takes place. Conversely, if presidents fail to exert effective power and are prevented from disciplining subnational undemocratic rulers via fiscal or partisan means, they will implement policies to oppose and weaken SURs and the autocrats who rule them. Presidential opposition to SURs and autocrats in general can occur as a result of presidents' aversion to autocrats who could eventually pose a serious challenge to a president's ambitions. This general opposition, however, does not necessarily lead to SUR breakdown. Local variables, such as subnational autocrats' capacity to ensure party elite unity and/or mass political support, shape the ability of autocrats to counterbalance presidential attempts at destabilizing SURs, and also allow autocrats to maintain the status quo and keep their regimes alive. Where this occurs, SUR self-reproduction, a second pathway of SUR continuity, takes place.

As the previous chapters reveal, presidential power figures prominently in this book. The possibility of exerting effective presidential power over subnational autocrats is not only important to turning autocrats—who due to their power can become real challengers—into allies, but is also critical to increasing the president's capacity to extract real and credible inter-temporal political concessions and support from subnational autocrats. In the absence of effective presidential power, it is possible for some subnational undemocratic incumbents to renege on their promises to provide political support.

Given the importance of presidential power for shaping pathways of SUR continuity, the book focuses extensively on the instruments through which presidents can exert leverage over subnational autocrats. The book also carefully analyzes the instruments through which autocrats can neutralize presidential power. This analysis is important because, as described in Chapter 2, presidential power is not absolute but relative (Mann 1986). Therefore, in order to wield power over subnational undemocratic arenas/autocrats, the capacity of subnational rulers to resist this pressure needs to be low relative to the power of democratic presidents.

Drawing on the insights provided by the literature on political parties and fiscal federalism, the book argues that presidents can, and usually do, resort to their party organizations and/or federal funds that are allocated to subnational jurisdictions to wield power over autocrats. Effective fiscal presidential power materializes when the main instrument available to presidents is fiscal (i.e. when they enjoy high levels of fiscal discretion), and when partisan power is low. In this scenario, effectively inducing the cooperation of subnational autocrats is only possible when subnational rulers are fiscally dependent on the central government. If such dependence does not exist, fiscally responsible and economically sound subnational incumbents are in a position to neutralize presidential power, no matter how much fiscal discretion presidents have.

Conversely, effective partisan presidential power materializes when presidents have low levels of fiscal discretion and, at the same time, (a) their party organizations, as well as the rules and procedures that regulate relations between the party leadership and lower-level branches, are highly routinized, and (b) their party has an electoral foothold in all of subnational units. For this to happen, one of the following two subnational variables must be present: (a) undemocratic incumbents' membership in the presidents' party, which enables presidents to exert direct partisan control from above, or (b) subnational autocrats' membership in an opposition party, whereby a non-patrimonial state structure must be in place—as this type of institution facilitates the subsistence of local opposition forces and subnational opposition groups, with which the center can ally in order to pressure and challenge subnational autocrats' authority from within.

Conclusion

In sum, the prevalence of fiscal or partisan presidential power, which is critical to allow presidents to control autocrats and induce their cooperation, determines whether the former support or weaken the latter, and helps to elucidate different pathways of SUR continuity within democratic countries. This argument, sketched in length in Chapter 2, was tested using different methodologies in Chapters 4, 5, 6, and 7. The first section of this chapter revisits the main findings of these empirical chapters. The second section analyzes the breakdown in 2010 of the two Mexican SURs, Puebla and Oaxaca, studied in this book. The purpose of this section is not only to account for the collapse of these two regimes, but also, and more importantly, to demonstrate that, in spite of this collapse, the argument advanced in this book is also well suited to explain SUR breakdown (not just SUR continuity). The chapter concludes with a discussion of the lessons learned from the analysis of Argentina and Mexico, emphasizing the contributions of the book to the literature on subnational undemocratic regimes and intergovernmental relations in multi-level polities.

Summary of Findings

Drawing on the insights provided by scholarship on fiscal federalism and political parties, Chapter 4 argues that presidents usually employ two major resources to wield power and subjugate subnational autocrats: their party organizations and/or federal funds that are allocated to subnational jurisdictions. The comparison between Argentina and Mexico reveals that, since the latest transition to democracy in each country, presidents in Argentina have enjoyed greater fiscal power than their Mexican counterparts.[1] This holds true despite the fact that the bulk of intergovernmental fiscal transfers in both countries is regulated by a well-established revenue-sharing system that operates along the principle of automaticity. Chapter 3 shows in detail that presidential fiscal power has been greater in Argentina than in Mexico because the rules of the Argentine revenue-sharing system that determine distribution of shareable revenues have been unstable and frequently altered to benefit presidents over governors. Indeed, as demonstrated in Chapter 3, with the exception of Alfonsín between 1988 and 1989, every Argentine president up to 2009 changed this fiscal arrangement. The suspension and

---

[1] Recall that presidential fiscal power was measured along three dimensions: (a) the existence of a revenue-sharing system that establishes the automatic allocation of transfers across levels of government, (b) the stability of the rules of the revenue-sharing system that determine the amount of and distribution of transfers that are sent to subnational jurisdictions, and (c) the percentage and distributional criteria of revenues that are not transferred to the provinces and which are administered by the federal level of government.

modification of the Argentine revenue-sharing system, as well as its detrimental effects on provincial fiscal autonomy, contrast sharply with the pattern observed in Mexico. After the transition to democracy in 2000, and up to 2009, presidents in Mexico did not engage in major legal alterations of the rules of the revenue-sharing system. When these alterations occurred, they curtailed, rather than expanded, presidential fiscal power. The greater share of non-transferable funds that were retained by Argentine presidents than their Mexican counterparts, as well as the absence of rules to decrease discretionary distribution, have been a second major cause of the greater fiscal power observed in Argentina. With the exception of the Argentine National Solidarity Fund instituted in 2009, which set clear criteria for distribution of 30 percent of the proceeds of soy exports, there were no attempts to earmark revenues not subject to sharing (i.e. export/import duties). By contrast, Mexican presidents saw a significant curtailment of presidential fiscal power after 2003, when revenues that were not subject to sharing, such as the extraordinary revenues from oil, began to be earmarked and distributed among the states.

Chapter 4 also demonstrates that, whereas fiscal resources available to presidents became increasingly constrained in Mexico, partisan resources remained strong. The assessment of presidential partisan power conducted in Chapter 4 confirms that Mexico's first two democratic presidents had greater capacity to induce the cooperation of subnational rulers via partisan resources than their Argentine counterparts. A comparison between presidential Party Nationalization Scores (PNS) in Argentina and Mexico shows that presidential partisan power was consistently stronger in Mexico. Unlike their Argentine counterparts, especially Fernando De la Rúa, Eduardo Duhalde, and the Kirchners, Mexican Presidents Fox and Calderón managed to extend their party organizations throughout the territory. By so doing, the latter obtained greater sway over both copartisan and opposition subnational incumbents. Conversely, Argentine presidents, who at the turn of the latest democratization period succeeded in exerting partisan power over most provinces, progressively lost the capacity to attract cooperation via partisan resources. Presidential partisan power was also greater in Mexico, thanks to the higher routinization of the National Action Party's (PAN's) rule and procedures. The comparison of the internal functioning of the Peronist party (PJ) in Argentina and the PAN in Mexico indicates that, due to the more centralized, hierarchical, and bureaucratized nature of the PAN, Mexican PAN presidents enjoyed greater presidential partisan power over copartisan governors than have their Peronist counterparts. Peronist presidents, in contrast, depended on decentralized and delinked organizations, without subunits connected vertically into a central bureaucracy. In short, Chapter 4's conclusion is that presidents in Argentina and Mexico resorted to different instruments to wield power over subnational autocrats. Whereas the former obtained autocrats' cooperation via fiscal inducements, the latter constrained the political authority of subnational undemocratic rulers by resorting to partisan resources.

As argued throughout the book, the capacity to obtain the collaboration of subnational autocrats decisively conditions presidents' incentives to reproduce SURs. An undemocratic governor who is subject to presidential manipulation can in fact be very beneficial for a president in need of political support. With their tight control over voters and national legislative delegations, subservient undemocratic governors can provide important benefits to national incumbents (Hagopian 1996; Snyder 1999; Moraski and Reisinger 2003; Gibson 2005; Hunter and Power 2007; Reisinger and Moraski 2010; Tudor and Ziegfeld forthcoming). If presidents can successfully induce governors to cooperate with the center, the latter might find it very convenient to reproduce SURs from above. This assertion was quantitatively demonstrated in Chapter 5. The cross-sectional time series analyses performed reveal that neither Argentine presidents nor Mexican national incumbents rewarded *all* SURs during their respective administrations. Instead, they selectively provided economic benefits to those regimes and autocrats over whom they could wield effective fiscal or partisan power. Put differently, none of these presidents contributed to expanding the power of SURs over which they could not exercise political leverage. In fact, as shown by all regressions models, the SURs/autocrats that were not controllable were punished, in that they received a lower proportion of federally funded programs/transfers.

Chapters 6 and 7 shift the research focus from quantitative comparisons to a qualitative, in-depth examination of two within-country comparisons in each country. Using evidence gathered from over 150 in-depth interviews with Argentine and Mexican national and subnational top-ranked officials, journalists, and former politicians, as well as from archival documents, the case studies of La Rioja, San Luis, Puebla, and Oaxaca show that different pathways of SUR reproduction occurred along the paths indicated by the theoretical framework outlined in Chapter 2. Moreover, Chapters 6 and 7 demonstrate that, despite differences in the way in which presidential power has been exerted in each country, the trajectories of SUR continuity in Argentina and Mexico have been identical. In cases where national incumbents have been able to wield effective power over autocrats, such as in La Rioja and Puebla, SUR reproduction from above has resulted in both countries. By contrast, when national incumbents were incapable of exercising authority over recalcitrant undemocratic governors, as occurred in San Luis and Oaxaca, they undertook actions of SUR weakening. In sum, the country analyses underscore that, in spite of dissimilar strategies of presidential encroachment upon subnational autocrats, the logic of the book's argument holds across countries, thus validating the generalization of the explanation.

The Argentine case studies conducted in Chapter 6 show that La Rioja's financial dependence on the central government created the conditions necessary for President Kirchner and President Fernández de Kirchner, who both had easy access to abundant fiscal resources, to wield power over Governors Maza and Beder Herrera. Interestingly, this power dynamic occurred despite the fact that La Rioja had a patrimonial state structure that would, in theory, have allowed *Riojano* governors to neutralize presidential control. Provincial fiscal dependency on Buenos Aires, and the central government's enormous fiscal leverage not only gave the Kirchners power to induce and obtain Maza and Beder Herrera's political cooperation, but also important reasons to reproduce La Rioja's SUR from above. The case of San Luis, which illustrates the alternative pathway of SUR continuity, i.e. SUR self-reproduction, demonstrates that a lack of effective presidential fiscal power prevented the Kirchners from obtaining Governor Rodríguez Saá's cooperation, and led in turn to SUR weakening. Indeed, contrary to the Kirchners' behavior towards other, more malleable subnational autocrats and SURs, both presidents opted to punish Rodríguez Saá and weaken his regime by refusing to assign additional federal programs and funds for the province. They took other measures as well to undermine the regime, including the withholding of federal approval for a wide range of programs and policies that the governor sought to implement in order to increase his popularity and the regime's legitimacy. Yet SUR continuity through self-reproduction was possible given the autocrat's capacity to rely on a sturdy and durable electoral coalition of core supporters that helped ensure the regime's long-term survival. The capacity of Governor Rodríguez Saá to deliver effective and concrete benefits to core voters not only boosted his popularity among the electorate but also gave San Luis's citizens a vested interest in the perpetuation of the regime. In spite of their undemocratic, hegemonic, and at times, illegal rule, citizens in San Luis endorsed Rodríguez Saá's government because he was regarded as the only political figure who could deliver tangible benefits (Guiñazú 2003; Behrend 2007). This mass support was central to self-reproduction of San Luis's SUR, even in the presence of presidential strategies to weaken the regime.

The Mexican case studies conducted in Chapter 7, for their part, also confirm that the capacity of presidents to wield power over subnational autocrats and SURs was critical to unleashing alternate pathways of SUR continuity. The case of Puebla showed that the existence of a comparatively non-patrimonial state structure, which rendered state borders more penetrable, coupled with a territorially extended presence of the presidents' party in Puebla, enabled Fox and Calderón to wield effective power (from within) over Puebla's autocrats. As a result of this leverage, political cooperation with the federal government followed suit, and so did the presidents' disposition to reproduce Puebla's SUR from above. By contrast, the existence of a patrimonial state structure, coupled with a low territorial PAN electoral presence in the state of Oaxaca, enabled autocrats Murat and Ruiz to neutralize presidential partisan power, and in turn gave both governors the authority they needed to confront and challenge presidential authority. Under these circumstances the federal government had few incentives to support Oaxaca's SUR. Indeed, contrary to how Fox and Calderón behaved with other more collaborative (and controllable) SURs (such as Puebla, Veracruz, or Hidalgo), both presidents took a series of measures to weaken the regime, among which were refusal to funnel additional programs and funds, the commissioning of several federal audits to investigate Oaxacan incumbents' financial misdoings, and the filing of several claims with the federal Supreme Court against the state of Oaxaca. Despite Fox's and Calderón's efforts to destabilize the regime, governors Murat and Ruiz managed to keep Oaxaca's SUR in place. Mass support, which oscillated between the administrations of Murat and Ruiz, never became a central pillar of the regime's stability. Party cohesion, by contrast, was a critical factor to insuring the regime's long-term survival.

Assessment of the Argument's Validity in Cases of SUR Breakdown

Chapters 5, 6, and 7 provide strong quantitative and qualitative evidence about the validity and generalizability of this book's argument. The results of the quantitative analyses conducted in Chapter 5, which are applicable to the universe of SURs in the post-transitional period in Argentina and Mexico, reveal that the main theoretical claims raised in Chapter 2 are generalized to all contemporary Argentine and Mexican SURs. Chapters 6 and 7, for their part, demonstrate qualitatively that the logic of the argument outlined in this book, as well as the hypothesized mechanisms that explain different within-country trajectories of SUR reproduction, operate almost identically in two different countries.

Yet, in order to further test the validity of this book's argument, the conditions hypothesized to be crucial for producing SUR continuity in the cases that have been analyzed must be absent, or not all present, in cases where SUR breakdown ensued. Hence, two conditions, ineffective presidential (fiscal or partisan) power in the first place, and the incapacity of autocrats to rely on party elite unity and/or mass support, in the second place, need to be present for SUR breakdown to take place. These two conditions, which were present in Oaxaca and Puebla after 2009, help to explain why these two

Puebla

The analysis of the case of Puebla conducted in Chapter 7 highlights that signs of increased patrimonialism were observed during the first two years of the Marín administration (2004–10). As described in Chapter 7, during his first year in office, and before the Lydia Cacho scandal broke out February 2006, Marín sought to centralize political authority, resuming the practices observed during the Bartlett administration (1992–8). For example, as Rebolledo (2011) reports, he used the local IRS to audit family members of anyone who was being vocal about their political opposition. The attorney general was used as a political arm, and both newspaper censorship and individual censorship were attempted. The governor also attempted to increase patrimonial/patronizing relationships with federal delegates, especially the Sedesol delegate, who systematically refused to hand over Sedesol (federal) programs which the governor sought to use to favor the campaign of the 2006 Institutional Revolutionary Party (PRI) presidential candidate Roberto Madrazo in Puebla (interview Mantilla). Similarly, during 2006 Marín made more discretional use of the *aportaciones*, with which he favored PRI mayors at the expense of PAN municipalities, and he kept a closer eye on the expenditure of PAN mayors, periodically threatening them with state audits (interview Contreras Coeto).

The patrimonial exercise of state power began to diminish in 2006 after the Lydia Cacho scandal broke and the governor's unpopularity reached unprecedented levels both locally and nationally. With the intention of offsetting this disapproval, Marín began to act in accordance with formal rules, and in a less confrontational, discretionary, and patronizing manner. However, after the federal Supreme Court chose not to rule on the Marín case and handed it over to the local courts and local legislature, thus making it clear that the governor's tenure would not end abruptly as a result of impeachment, Governor Marín gradually but steadily resumed patrimonial practices. Like his counterpart in Oaxaca's SUR, Marín implemented dubious tactics to control the opposition. As Rebolledo (2011) reports, when he was not able to buy opposition parties, Marín would finance dissident groups or factions within the opposition to obtain their allegiance.

---

[2] In 2010, Rafael Moreno Valle, a former PRIísta and Minister of Finance during the administration of Melquíades Morales, ran as the gubernatorial candidate of the multiparty alliance PAN-PRD-Convergencia-Panal. He won Puebla's governorship with 50.4% of the vote. That same year, Gabino Cué, also a former PRIísta, and candidate of a PAN-PRD-Convergencia alliance won the governorship of Oaxaca with 50.1% of the vote.

Conclusion

Higher levels of patrimonialism not only decreased the political and economic autonomy of minor opposition parties and regime dissidents, but also contributed to curtailing the PAN's capacity to keep its electoral presence in the state. Indeed, in the 2007 municipal elections the PAN, which in previous municipal contests had managed to obtain a considerable number of districts, only came out victorious in 51 mayoralities (CIDAC Database). In contrast, the PRI won in 145 municipalities, including the most populated ones, such as Puebla City and Atlixco. Similarly, in the local legislative elections held that same year the PRI also won by large margins, obtaining 25 of the 26 districts in the state despite the fact that the PAN had started ahead in the polls. The PRI practically swept the 2007 elections, an outcome that was referred to as *carro completo*. This pattern of PRI victories was repeated in the 2009 federal legislative elections, when the PRI won all districts in Puebla (15 out of 15), and almost completely reversed the composition of Puebla's congressional delegation, which in the previous two rounds had been dominated by the PAN.

In 2009 it became apparent that this decreasing PAN electoral presence in the state would be an important obstacle to effective presidential partisan power (interviews Moreno Valle, Ehlinger). The recurrent use of patrimonial tactics to co-opt members of minor opposition parties, coupled with the PAN's waning electoral clout, as several interviewees reported, clearly began to diminish Calderón's capacity to use his party organization or other political allies as ways of penetrating the state in order to exert control from within over Governor Marín (interviews Moreno Valle, Ehlinger, Contreras Coeto, Velázquez). This limited presidential power, in turn, began to hinder the capacity of Calderón to obtain the political acquiescence and cooperation of Puebla's autocrat. In line with the argument developed in this book, the fewer opportunities available to induce the collaboration of subnational autocrats with the federal government gradually changed Calderón's incentives to reproduce Puebla's SUR. Whereas during the first two years of his administration he actively endorsed Mario Marín's administration and regime, by mid-2009, particularly after the mid-term elections were held, Calderón began to act in a more reactionary manner vis-à-vis Puebla's SUR. By early 2010, Mexico's second democratic president actively employed strategies to weaken the regime over which he could no longer exert power.

The key strategy to undermining Puebla's SUR was to gain the cooperation of the PRD and other opposition to build state-level multiparty coalitions that could offset the power of the then-rising PRI (Sorroza 2011b). Fortunately for the PAN, as Gibson (2013) notes, "the PRD's national party leader, Jesús Ortega, shared its strategic vision. He broke with his party's de facto leader, Andrés Manuel López Obrador, and negotiated anti-PRI coalitions with the PAN in five states" (2013: 145), including Puebla.

The PAN and the PRD, in conjunction with other opposition parties, including Convergencia and Nueva Alianza (Panal), sponsored the candidacy of Rafael Moreno Valle, a former and disgruntled PRIísta who had left the PRI and joined the PAN ranks in 2006. Unlike previous PAN contenders for Puebla's governorship, who during the Fox administration had not obtained real support from their party or from the central government, the young PAN senator[3] received the full backing of President Calderón and the national PAN. As Rebolledo notes, "this time, the central government selected and supported a high-profile candidate . . . and made a massive effort to win the state" (2011: 33). Rebolledo (2011) also reports that the central government not only aided in getting the state election covered by the national media, where more objective information could be presented than in the co-opted local media, but it also sent emissaries and high-profile federal ministers to campaign for the PAN candidate, and instructed federal delegates to allocate various federal social programs according to electoral considerations (see *Quinta Columna*, July 14, 2010).[4] Despite exorbitant amounts of spending by the local PRI in 2010, and just one year after the PRI had swept the mid-term elections, the PAN won the governorship with 50.40 percent of the vote, obtaining more than a 10 percent vote differential over the PRI.

Throughout this book the cases have demonstrated that presidential maneuvers to weaken SURs do not necessarily translate into SUR destabilization, and much less into regime breakdown. As argued at length in the theoretical chapter, and as demonstrated in the case studies of San Luis (Argentina) and Oaxaca (Mexico), presidential strategies to oppose SURs can be neutralized, and SURs and their autocrats can stay in power if subnational undemocratic incumbents rely on a sturdy coalition of support. In particular, two variables endogenous to SURs, party elite unity (which is assured if cohesive political parties exist) and mass support, are critical to maintaining a robust and durable ruling coalition, and thus important to ensuring the regime's long-term survival. What accounts for Governor Marín's incapacity to rely on a sturdy coalition of support? Why did he fail to neutralize presidential strategies of SUR weakening?

Chapter 7 noted that Marín, like many other Mexican autocrats, resorted to various undemocratic practices to prevent dissident voices from gaining power. For instance, under his administration severe violations of human rights were committed—especially in the small towns of the interior—and a fierce battle against local independent media and journalists was launched not only to discourage independent investigative journalism, but also to

---

[3] Moreno Valle was elected federal PAN Senator in 2006.
[4] <http://www.quintacolumna.com.mx/columnas/tiempos/2010/julio/colum-tiempos-140710.php>.

prevent regime opponents from using media outlets to attract followers[5] (interviews Mejía, Ehlinger, Mantilla, Aguilar, Ibañez). While the curtailment of civil and human rights decreased the governor's popularity among the general population, it was not until the Lydia Cacho scandal broke that his base of support began to erode. After 2006, leaders of the main local business associations, who had supported autocrat Marín in the past, filed claims with the federal congress against Marín's human rights violations (Centro de Documentación 2006). Likewise, the private sector withdrew capital investments from the state, claiming that the lack of rule of law was not propitious for investment, and the middle class openly condemned the governor's shady deals and human rights violations in street mobilizations in Puebla City (interviews Ibañez, Mejía). By the end of his administration in 2010, Marín was still regarded as an unpopular governor. The human and civil rights violations committed throughout his tenure, coupled with Marín's incapacity to implement policies to improve the living conditions in one of Mexico's poorest states in spite of the large amount of funds he received from the federal government, and his failure to create a business-friendly environment, had turned Marín into one of the most unpopular autocrats of the last three *sexenios*.[6]

This lack of mass support could have been counterbalanced, and PRI continuity ensured, had the local PRI endorsed a popular, modern, technocratic, efficient gubernatorial candidate. In 2009, however, Governor Marín, resorting to an anachronistic PRI tradition, unilaterally handpicked and sponsored one of his closest collaborators—Javier López Zavala, an out-of-state politician and Chiapas native who had served as Secretary of Social Development—as the candidate for the governorship. This endorsement occurred despite public opinion polls indicating that Enrique Doger, Puebla City's former PRI mayor, was the most popular PRI candidate (Rebolledo 2011). The selection of Zavala, a politician who was viewed as no different from autocrat Marín, not only exacerbated within-party rifts among the PRI's local *camarillas*, but also failed to offset the PRI's unpopularity (Aguilar Balderas 2011). Quite the contrary, and according to public opinion experts, this selection was a major factor leading to the PRI's 2010 electoral debacle.[7] Zavala never managed to

---

[5] An illustrative example is quoted in Rebolledo (2011: 31): "Enrique Cardenas, head of the research institute *Espinosa Iglesias* attempted to buy some space in the *Milenio* newspaper to publish a program comparison between the PRI and the PAN. Even though it was a paid advertisement, the newspaper refused to accept the ad because it showed the PAN in a better light."

[6] Between 2004 and 2010, Puebla fell in several rankings, such as in those of transparency (Transparencia Mexicana), human development (UNDP), creation of new jobs, and foreign direct investment. Rueda provides a detailed analysis of these failures and a comparison between his and Bartlett's and Morales's administrations <http://www.quintacolumna.com.mx/columnas/tiempos/2011/enero/colum-tiempos-270111.php>.

[7] "La mala elección del candidato, el factor decisivo para que perdiera el PRI: demoscopistas," *La Jornada de Oriente*, July 21, 2010, <http://www.lajornadadeoriente.com.mx/2010/07/21/puebla/pol103.php>.

Democrats and Autocrats

attract urban and middle-class voters, who in July 2010 massively backed the multiparty coalition led by Moreno Valle.[8]

The analysis of Puebla's SUR's debacle indicates that ineffective presidential power altered Calderón's incentives vis-à-vis SUR reproduction. Whereas in the past the existence of a non-patrimonial state structure had facilitated effective presidential power, and in turn, the cooperation of Puebla's autocrats with the central government, Marín's turn to patrimonialism drastically changed the payoffs to sustaining Puebla's SUR in power. Faced with an autocrat who no longer delivered political benefits, in 2009 President Calderón and his party took steps to destabilize the regime. Marín's inability to rely on a sturdy local coalition of support (of copartisans or the general population) is the second factor which explains why Calderón's policies of SUR weakening ultimately led to party alternation and SUR breakdown in 2010.

Oaxaca

The analysis of the case of Oaxaca in Chapter 7 demonstrated that lack of effective presidential partisan power prevented Presidents Fox and Calderón from obtaining the cooperation of the Oaxaca autocrats, leading both presidents in turn to implement strategies directed at opposing, and even weakening, the regime. Yet, until 2009, SUR continuity through self-reproduction was possible, given the capacity of Murat and Ruiz to ensure the party cohesion that was needed to guarantee the regime's long-term survival. In 2010, however, the opposition candidate Gabino Cué led a multiparty coalition and ousted the PRI from power. What accounts for the failure of Oaxaca's autocratic rulers to prevent regime breakdown?

As noted in Chapter 7, Oaxaca's SUR could stay in power not so much due to the ability of autocrats to obtain the acquiescence of the electorate, but rather to their capacity to ensure party elite unity. Murat's and Ruiz's control over the local PRI as well as their tight connections with the national PRI faction led by Roberto Madrazo, gave Oaxacan rulers considerable leverage over the career advancement of local PRI party elites (and PRI party cadres). As a result, local PRI politicians who wanted to be promoted in the local and national PRI structure not only had strong incentives to please both autocrats, but also important reasons to support the regime that kept Murat and Ruiz in power.

This structure of incentives, however, began to change in 2007–8, when it became clear that Ruiz's connections to Madrazo and his faction, whose power within the PRI gradually waned after 2007, were not as decisive and

---

[8] The vote difference between Moreno Valle and Zavala was 200,000. Of those votes, around 150,000 were obtained in the capital city (see <http://www.quintacolumna.com.mx/columnas/tiempos/2010/julio/colum-tiempos-060710.php>).

Conclusion

important as in the past for the career advancement of ambitious local PRI politicians in the national PRI. Yet, in spite of this loss of influence at the national level, Ruiz still controlled the strings of local PRI politics, and thus had leverage to manipulate the careers of local copartisans (Martínez Vásquez 2007; Gibson 2013). As noted in Chapter 7, this control, coupled with the violent and illegal tactics he employed to obtain the acquiescence of local PRIístas, enabled him to ensure the collaboration of PRI mayors, PRI brokers, and *organizaciones* connected to the PRI.

Ruiz's capacity to prevent party defections, however, suffered an important setback in 2007 when teachers' unions, one of the PRI's historic core brokers and supporters, threw their support behind the PRD (Martínez Vásquez 2007; Durazo Herrmann 2010). This party schism not only affected the unity of the PRI's party elite but, more importantly, contributed to enhancing the PRD's (Party of the Democratic Revolution) statewide organization (Gibson 2013). In 2009, in the context of the PAN-PRD nationally coordinated strategy of subnational coalition-building, Gabino Cué announced his candidacy for governor as the head of a PRD-PAN-PT-Convergencia multiparty alliance. Unlike 2004, this time the prospects for winning Oaxaca's governorship were considerably higher. Not only had the PRD significantly expanded its electoral base, thus providing the opposition candidate with a larger number of followers and potential voters, but the PAN showed greater commitment to supporting Cué's candidacy by increasing the spending and coverage of Oaxaca's electoral race in the national media (Rebolledo 2011; Gibson 2013). In this new political scenario, local PRI elites, especially PRI mayors, saw greater guaranteed opportunities for political advancement in the opposition.[9] In the 2010 gubernatorial elections, only 265 out of 570 mayors, most of which belonged to the PRI, supported Eviel Pérez, the PRI candidate; by contrast, 305 mayors backed the opposition (Benton 2012).[10] Such party defection, as local observers noted, was a major cause for regime breakdown.[11]

The analysis of the Oaxacan SUR's demise reveals that in the absence of party elite unity, SUR self-reproduction was no longer possible. Unlike 2004,

---

[9] "La gubernatura se juega en las elecciones municipales," *Revista En Marcha*, June 1, 2010, <http://www.revistaenmarcha.com.mx/analisis/471-la-gubernatura-se-juega-en-las-elecciones-municipales.html>.

[10] The number of PRI defectors in 2010 rose significantly when compared to previous gubernatorial elections. In 1998 and 2004, when Oaxacan autocrats had greater capacity to prevent defections, the number of mayors who delivered PRI victories was 416 and 387, respectively (Benton 2012).

[11] "La gubernatura se juega en las elecciones municipales," *Revista En Marcha*, June 1, 2010, <http://www.revistaenmarcha.com.mx/analisis/471-la-gubernatura-se-juega-en-las-elecciones-municipales.html>; "Municipios de Oaxaca, ínsulas para el amigo o el cliente," *Revista En Marcha*, Dec. 29, 2010, <http://www.revistaenmarcha.com.mx/miscelanea/libros/611-municipios-de-oaxaca-insulas-para-el-cliente-o-el-amigo.html>.

when President Fox's strategies of SUR weakening could be counterbalanced by ensuring the support of local PRI elites (and cadres), Calderón's efforts at destabilizing and toppling Oaxaca's SUR proved effective given the incapacity of Ruiz to prevent party splits. Self-interested and ambitious PRI defectors, who eventually managed to advance their political careers by securing key positions in Gabino Cué's government,[12] contributed in large part to bringing Oaxaca's autocratic rule to an end.

The discussion of the events leading to the 2010 SUR breakdown in Puebla and Oaxaca confirms the validity of this book's argument. It shows that, in the absence of the two conditions that are hypothesized to be causally relevant—the capacity of presidents to wield effective (fiscal or partisan) power over SURs and autocrats, as well as subnational incumbents' reliance on a sturdy coalition of support to prevent SUR breakdown despite presidential strategies to weaken SUR—SUR continuity is not possible.

Lessons from Argentina and Mexico

This book makes several theoretical, empirical, and conceptual contributions to the study of subnational political regimes in nationally democratic countries, as well as to the analysis of intergovernmental relations in multi-level polities.

Contributions to the Study of SURs

CONCEPTS AND MEASUREMENT
At the conceptual and empirical level, this study moves past current works on subnational political regimes by offering a detailed and comprehensive discussion of how to conceptualize, operationalize, and measure subnational democracy. With few exceptions,[13] most works on subnational undemocratic regimes do not offer clear conceptual definitions of political regimes, much less a discussion of these regimes' dimensions, subdimensions, indicators, and their aggregation. Moreover, these works rarely provide rules for coding democratic versus undemocratic subnational units, and only some of them measure the degree of democracy across *all* subnational units *over time* of a given country. Complicating things further, analysts of regime juxtaposition use a variety of conceptual forms, such as hybrid, authoritarian,

---

[12] "Oaxaca, gobierno de cuotas," *Revista En Marcha*, Dec. 29, 2010, <http://www.revistaenmarcha.com.mx/reportaje/623-oaxaca-2010-gobierno-de-cuotas.html>.
[13] See, for instance, Solt 2003; McMann 2006; Gervasoni 2010b, 2010a; Saikkonen 2011; Rebolledo 2011.

neopatrimonial, or "closed-game" to refer to subnational political regimes that are not democratic. Each of these labels, in turn, is generally employed to denote a different set of empirical cases.

Some of the main contributions of this book are the careful conceptualization and operationalization of subnational undemocratic regimes, as well as the systematic and rigorous measurement of the level of subnational democracy in Argentine and Mexican provinces across time and space. The book thus expands our empirical knowledge about SURs in Latin America by generating new longitudinal, cross-provincial, and cross-country comparable databases on subnational democracy in two of the region's largest countries.[14] As a result, the book not only overcomes the problems of existing works of SURs, but also helps to fill the gap observed in the current data on democracy, which has until very recently overlooked subnational levels of government.

VARIETIES OF SURS

Chapter 3 presents empirical evidence demonstrating that, contrary to conventional wisdom, a significant number of SURs are characterized by having non-patrimonial state structures that thwart subnational autocrats' inclinations to exercise state power without necessarily abusing power. This finding, which has been generally overlooked in existing studies of SURs, suggests that states and provinces that have low levels of subnational democracy approximate two general types: patrimonial and non-patrimonial. Acknowledging the existence of different SUR types is critical for establishing well-defined and independent domains of cases within which analysts can identify causal (unit) homogeneity. This disaggregation, in turn, is essential for gaining a more thorough understanding of specific causal mechanisms that underpin regime continuity within each SUR type. The qualitative analyses of Puebla and San Luis, two SURs that have relatively non-patrimonial state structures, help illustrate these contributions.

The analyses of Puebla and San Luis revealed that mechanisms theorized to explain continuity in patrimonial SURs are insufficient to account for the reproduction of non-patrimonial SURs. As shown in Chapters 6 and 7, boundary control (Gibson 2005, 2013), one mechanism of SUR reproduction,

---

[14] Existing databases on subnational democracy in Latin America are not comparable across countries. Solt (2003), Gervasoni (2010b, 2011), and Rebolledo (2011) limit their measurement to just one country. Whereas Solt and Rebolledo measure subnational democracy in Mexico, Gervasoni gauges levels of subnational democracy in Argentina. In addition, authors employ different measurement strategies thus their measures cannot be compared with each other. Gervasoni conducts a Survey of Experts on Provincial Politics that assesses experts' subjective evaluations; Solt and Rebolledo employ objective indicators.

can only explain regime stability in patrimonial subnational units. Yet, as the case studies of Puebla and San Luis illustrate, regime continuity is possible even when SUR incumbents are unable to close subnational borders. The cases further revealed that, despite the existence of windows of opportunity for penetrating bureaucratic SURs, as shown in the province of San Luis, not all presidents are in a position to take advantage of such openings. National incumbents who lack a strong and territorially extended party organization at the local level, and hence lack a critical resource to win over municipal governments and the local opposition, are unable to wield power and discipline autocrats from within. Weak presidential disciplining power, in turn, enables subnational autocrats to maintain their regimes intact. In such cases, SUR self-reproduction is not the result of subnational rulers' capacity to close provincial borders and thereby prevent outside infiltration; rather, it is the result of low presidential capacity to wield power over autocrats/SURs.

Aside from helping to clarify the mechanisms of SUR reproduction, the distinction between patrimonial and non-patrimonial SURs is important for understanding the origins of these regimes and the possibilities for change. The evidence presented in Chapter 3 (Figures 3.5 and 3.6) suggests that levels of economic development and geographic location are good predictors of patrimonial state structures. These graphs demonstrate that provinces in Argentina with high levels of economic development, such as Mendoza, Santa Fe, Entre Ríos, and Buenos Aires, score high on the state structure axis—i.e. they are more bureaucratic. The same pattern can be observed in Mexico, where states with the highest levels of socioeconomic development, such as Jalisco, Nuevo León, and Morelos, obtain the highest scores on the state structure axis. In contrast, the provinces and states that present the highest levels of patrimonialism are those located in the least economically developed and poorest areas of Argentina and Mexico, such as the Argentine provinces of La Rioja, Formosa, Corrientes, and Jujuy, and the Mexican states of Oaxaca, Chiapas, and Hidalgo. These findings suggest that Max Weber's classic assertion about the "elective affinity" between capitalist development and non-patrimonial state structures applies to subnational levels of government. This correlation between SUR types and levels of economic development is a first step toward uncovering how each of these regimes came to exist in the first place.

Finally, as noted in Chapter 3, by taking SUR variation into account, researchers are also in a better position to assess the factors that explain regime change. Prominent scholarship on national political regimes has demonstrated that regime type—particularly whether a regime is patrimonial or not—affects the probability and nature of regime change (Linz and Stepan 1996), as well as transition patterns (Snyder 1992; Bratton and van de Walle 1994; Hartlyn 1998; Geddes 1999). There are good reasons to believe that different types of undemocratic regimes at the subnational level are also likely to follow distinct paths towards democratization.

In short, our understanding of SUR continuity, origins, and change can benefit enormously from the acknowledgment that SURs, while sharing certain attributes, are not of a single type. As a result, distinguishing among SUR types within countries has the potential to move the research agenda on subnational undemocratic regimes, and subnational political regimes more generally, in important and intriguing new directions.

Contributions to the Study of Intergovernmental Relations in Multi-Level Polities

More than a decade ago, Guillermo O'Donnell (1993) noted that the power of the central state was not homogeneous throughout the territory. He argued that in many countries of Latin America "blue areas" characterized by robust rule of law coexisted with "green areas" where the rule of law was partially attenuated, and "brown areas" where the rule of law was extremely attenuated. This book presents strong evidence to support this theoretical insight, offering numerous examples that show that the power of the central state (wielded by presidents either through partisan or fiscal means) varies subnationally, and is mediated by different characteristics of the peripheral units. However, contradicting conventional wisdom, this study reveals that the capacity of the central government to exert power homogeneously throughout the territory is not necessarily curtailed by the fact that subnational units are undemocratic. Indeed, the cases of La Rioja and Puebla show that presidents can wield power despite the absence of subnational democracy. Rather, the book underscores that what prevents the central government from exercising power in some subnational areas is the undemocratic nature of the political regime *in combination with* the patrimonial nature of state structures and/or the fiscal autonomy of subnational units, as exemplified by the state of Oaxaca and the province of San Luis. This finding, which has been largely overlooked by most studies of intergovernmental relations in the developing world, is central to understanding how power relations operate across levels of government, and under what conditions national politicians can expect to exert successful and effective power over subnational arenas.

Another important finding uncovered in this book is that presidential fiscal power in multi-level polities can be exerted in various ways, i.e. via partisan, fiscal, or partisan-fiscal means. By highlighting the multiple ways in which the central government seeks to dominate subnational actors/areas, this study further validates the fact that multi-level polities, and in particular federal systems, are not of one type, as the burgeoning literature on "varieties of federalism" has underscored (see, for instance, Stepan 2004; Obinger et al. 2005). This is an important finding because federal systems, frequently a key explanatory variable in studies of national democracy, welfare states, development, and political parties, are usually regarded as being of the same kind. In fact, countries are coded in a dichotomous way as being federal or non-federal. This oversimplification in the treatment of federal systems might come at the cost of overlooking key distinctive aspects of these countries that are central to elucidating the effects of multi-level structures on democratic, welfare, and developmental outcomes.

Finally, this book offers an important insight for scholars of multi-level government and intergovernmental relations. In general, the vast and growing literature on multi-level government and federalism has viewed intergovernmental politics as taking place between presidents and lower-tier incumbents as a whole. In this view, authority and power across levels of government within a given country are assumed to be zero-sum, i.e. power or authority are either located at upper or lower tiers of government. Moreover, this view assumes that all subnational units within countries are equally powerful or equally weak vis-à-vis the central government, and that all units and actors (a) act in the same way vis-à-vis the federal government, (b) are all constrained by the same subnational political structures, and (c) behave according to the same rank of preferences. However, one of the central contentions and findings of this book is that subnational units and subnational actors vary considerably from each other, and that these differences are consequential for shaping the central government's power and authority vis-à-vis subnational jurisdictions and actors. The acknowledgment of these subnational variations offers a fertile terrain for future studies of intergovernmental relations in multi-level polities.

Appendix

I. Subnational Democracy

As Goertz (2006) notes, the careful specification of a given concept's structure is central to achieving concept–measure consistency, that is, the use of the appropriate mathematical formalization to validly operationalize the concept into a quantitative measure.[1] This section operationalizes and aggregates subnational democracy's dimensions and indicators in a way that maximizes concept–measure consistency.

The definition of democracy adopted in this book utilizes one of the prototypical concept structures, i.e. the "necessary and sufficient condition" structure (Munck and Verkuilen 2002; Goertz 2006; Munck 2009). Accordingly, in order for a subnational political regime to be conceived of as democratic, a number of conditions must be present (i.e. they are necessary), and these conditions, in turn, are jointly sufficient to classify a given polity as democratic. If any of these conditions is absent, the subnational polity cannot be considered democratic.

To translate a necessary and sufficient concept structure into mathematical terms without violating concept–measure consistency, this study follows Goertz's (2006) suggested aggregation procedure of multiplying (rather than adding) individual conditions (or democracy's dimensions). Accordingly, as Figure A1 shows, contestation (for both executive and legislative posts), and clean elections (two of the necessary and sufficient conditions) are "connected" via the logical AND, a first cousin of multiplication (denoted with the * symbol) (for the addition operation regarding the turnover dimension see discussion later in this appendix).

Description and Aggregation of Indicators

As Figure A1 shows, democracy is made up of seven indicators: Head, Party, Effective Number of Parties (ENP), Margin of Victory, Effective Number of Parties in the Legislature (ENPL), Governor's Seats, and Post-Electoral Conflict. At the indicator level, addition (rather than multiplication) is a desirable option because indicators are substitutable. Substitutability is normally associated with the logical OR, which in turn is closely connected with arithmetic addition (Goertz 2006). Since individual indicators that make up each of the secondary levels weigh the same, they are averaged. For example, the dimension Contestation (Executive) is calculated as follows:

---

[1] For a discussion of the negative consequences that might arise when measurement strategies/techniques do not capture the underlying concept that is sought to be measured, see Adcock and Collier 2001; Lieberman 2002; Goertz 2006; Soifer 2008.

Appendix

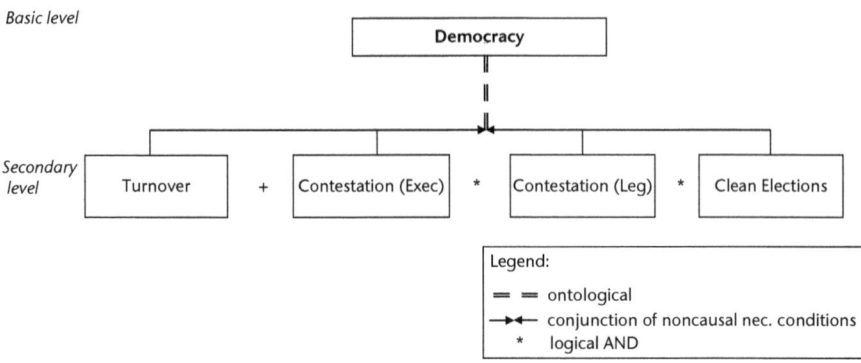

Figure A1. A necessary and sufficient concept structure of subnational democracy

(ENP + Margin of Victory)/2.[2] Each of these indicators, as well as their sources, is described in detail in Table A1.

Turnover and Clean Elections

As Mainwaring et al. note, considering turnover (or alternation) as one of the constitutive elements of democracy might lead to the misclassification of cases (2007: 130–1). An example of this potential misclassification is the case of countries/provinces where citizens are satisfied with the party and governor who governs, and decide to reelect both. Two major reasons justify the inclusion of turnover as a constitutive dimension of subnational democracy in the study of SURs in Argentina and Mexico. As Calvo and Micozzi (2005) show for the Argentine case, between 1983 and 2003, provincial incumbents implemented 32 constitutional reforms and 34 electoral reforms in order to reshape the subnational electoral map of Argentina. These reforms, as the authors convincingly demonstrate, aimed at both securing control of provincial incumbents over local legislatures, and at entrenching incumbents' position in power. The lack of turnover indicator captures the manipulation of electoral rules that enabled incumbents to make provincial electoral systems less competitive and more hegemonic. As Gibson (2013) notes, this hegemony is one of the defining traits of subnational undemocratic regimes.

For the Mexican case, the inclusion of turnover as one of the constitutive dimensions of subnational democracy is of paramount importance given the country's tradition of partisan hegemony and lack of alternation. In a country where the same party (i.e. the Institutional Revolutionary Party, or PRI) has ruled for over 70 years

---

[2] The remainder indicators are calculated as follows: Contestation (Legislature) = (ENPL + Governor's Seats)/2; Turnover (Argentina) = (Governor in office for less than 3 consecutive terms + Party in office for less than 3 consecutive terms)/2; Turnover (Mexico) = (Governor in office for less than 12 consecutive years + Party in office for less than 12 consecutive years)/2.

Table A1. Indicators of subnational democracy

Indicator	Description	Calculation*	Source Argentina	Source Mexico
HEAD	Measures governor's tenure	Governors who were in office for less than 3 consecutive terms or 12 consecutive years. This rule follows Levitsky and Way (2010) criterion	Author's calculations based on Base de Datos Provinciales del Centro de Investigaciones en Administración Pública (Base CIAP), Facultad de Ciencias Económicas, UBA	Author's calculations based on *Rulers* Database
PARTY	Measures the incumbent party's tenure	Parties that were in office for less than 3 consecutive terms or 12 consecutive years are coded as 1, and 0 if otherwise. The rule of 3 consecutive terms or 12 consecutive years. This rule follows Levitsky and Way (2010) criterion	Author's calculations based on Base de Datos CIAP	Author's calculations based on CIDAC's Electoral Database
ENP	Measures the effective number of parties competing in gubernatorial elections	Following Laakso and Taagepera Index (1979): $1/\Sigma si2$, with si representing the number of votes cast for party i during gubernatorial elections	Calvo and Escolar (2005) and author's calculations based on Andy Tow's Atlas Electoral	Author's calculations based on CIDAC's Electoral Database
Competitiveness	Measures the margin of victory between winner and runner up in gubernatorial elections	Measured as vl − v2, where vl is the vote share of the winning gubernatorial candidate, and v2 the vote share of the second-place candidate**†	Author's calculations based on Andy Tow's Atlas Electoral	Author's calculations based on CIDAC's Electoral Database
ENPL	Measures the effective number of parties competing in legislative elections	$1/\Sigma si2$ with si representing the number of seats held by party i	Calvo and Escolar (2005) and author's calculations based on Andy Tow's Atlas Electoral w	Author's calculations based on CIDAC's Electoral Database

(continued)

Appendix

Table A1. Continued

Indicator	Description	Calculation*	Source	
			Argentina	Mexico
Strength of legislative opposition	Measures the % of legislative seats controlled by the opposition	100 – % of governor's party (or party coalition) legislative seats	Author's calculations based on Giraudy and Lodola (2008) Database; 2007–2009: Andy Tow's Atlas Electoral and DINE, Ministerio del Interior	Lujambio (2000) and CIDAC's Electoral Database
Clean elections	Index that measures the existence, durability, and intensity of post-electoral conflicts	Post-electoral conflict ranges from 0 to 3, where 3 = absence of post-electoral conflict, 2 = post-electoral conflict lasted less than a week (7 days), and there were no dead and/or human/ material casualties, 1 = post-electoral conflict lasted more than one week (from 8 to 30 days), and/or people were held in custody, and/or there were human/ material casualties, 0 = post-electoral conflict lasted more than one month and/or there were deaths	N/A***	Author's calculation based on a review of major local (state-level) newspapers (1991–2009)

(and in some states, over 80 years), and where the permanence of the same party in power has not been exclusively related to the satisfaction of the electorate with the ruling party's performance (Magaloni 2006), it seems reasonable to take into account the incidence of the lack of turnover in state-level democracy.

These considerations justify the inclusion of turnover as a necessary albeit not sufficient dimension of (subnational) democracy, and give reason for its aggregation through addition (instead of multiplication). Various other empirical tests were run in order to confirm that the inclusion of this dimension did not misclassify cases. When subnational democracy was measured with and without the turnover dimension, the correlation between the two measures yielded a score of 0.83 in the case of Mexico, and 0.62 in the case of Argentina. The results thus indicate that the measure of subnational democracy employed in this study is not significantly altered when turnover is included.

A final clarification on the "clean elections" measure is in order. The concept of "clean elections" is perhaps one of the most difficult to operationalize and measure at the subnational level, as it demands a retrospective review of every gubernatorial election held in 32 states and 24 provinces over a period of 25 years. This indicator is only measured in Mexico, where electoral fraud has been ubiquitous. In Argentina, in contrast, little fraud or manipulation of the vote-counting processes has occurred since 1983 (Levitsky and Murillo 2005; Gervasoni 2010b, 2011), which is why it was not measured.

A good way to grasp the cleanness of elections is to measure the occurrence *and* intensity of post-electoral conflicts. The presence of post-electoral conflicts and their intensity reflect the extent to which official electoral results fail to correspond to reality as perceived by opposition parties. Following one of the leading works on post-electoral conflicts in Mexico, this study assumes that post-electoral mobilizations were provoked by high perceptions of electoral fraud (Eisenstadt 2004: 135–40). Thus, the *occurrence* of post-electoral conflicts is considered to be a proxy for electoral fraud, while the *intensity* (duration and severity) of post-electoral conflicts is considered a proxy for how "damaging and detrimental" the rigging was for the "defeated" party.

To code the existence and intensity of post-electoral conflicts in gubernatorial races, state-level newspapers were reviewed for a period of four consecutive weeks beginning the day after the election. Post-electoral conflicts are defined as instances of social mobilization following gubernatorial elections in which protestors demand a vote recount. The intensity of post-electoral conflicts was coded as reported in Table A1.[3] A list of the newspapers used to code clean elections is displayed in Table A2.

II. SURs' Patrimonial State Structures

Underlying the definition of a patrimonial state structure is a family resemblance concept structure. Unlike the necessary and sufficient concept structure, the family resemblance structure "is a rule about sufficiency with no necessary condition requirements" (Goertz 2006: 36). Concepts within the family resemblance structure can be assessed by identifying attributes that are present to varying degrees, rather

---

[3] It should be noted that many gubernatorial elections in Mexico are held concurrently with legislative and presidential elections. Concurrent elections are difficult to code because it is not always easy to determine whether post-electoral conflicts were driven by fraud in (either or both) state-level and/or national elections. In the cases where concurrent elections were held and there was evidence of post-electoral conflict, the coding rule was to make sure that the post-electoral conflict revolved around gubernatorial elections. To do so, more than one state-level newspaper and two major national newspapers (*Reforma* and *El Universal*) were reviewed. When it was not possible to discern whether post-electoral conflicts were driven by the occurrence of fraud in gubernatorial elections, the state was coded with 1.

Table A2. State newspapers used to code clean elections

State	Newspaper
Aguascalientes	*Hidrocálido*
Baja California	*Semanario Zeta*
	El Mexicano
Baja California Sur	*Sudcaliforniano*
Campeche	*Novedades de Campeche*
Coahuila	*El Sol del Norte*
	El Siglo de Torreón
Colima	*Diario de Colima*
Chiapas	*Cuarto Poder*
Chihuahua	*El Heraldo de Chihuahua*
Distrito Federal	*La Jornada*
Durango	*El Sol de Durango*
Guanajuato	*El Heraldo de León*
	El Sol del Bajío
	El Universal
Guerrero	*El Sol de Chilpancingo*
	El Sol de Acapulco
Hidalgo	*El Sol de Hidalgo*
Jalisco	*El Occidente*
	Ocho Columnas
Estado de México	*El Demócrata*
	El Sol de Toluca
Michoacán	*El Sol de Morelia*
	El Diario de Michoacán
	El Sol de Michoacán
Morelos	*El Diario de Morelos*
Nayarit	*Meridiano de Nayarit*
	El Heraldo de Nayarit
Nuevo León	*El Norte*
Oaxaca	*El Imparcial*
Puebla	*El Sol de Puebla*
	El Heraldo de Puebla
	Novedades de Puebla
Querétaro	*Diario de Querétaro*
Quintana Roo	*Novedades de Quintana Roo*
San Luis Potosí	*El Sol de San Luis*
Sinaloa	*El Sol de Sinaloa*
Sonora	*Nuevo Día*
	El Independiente
	El Imparcial
Tabasco	*Avance*
	Milenio Tabasco
	El Heraldo
Tamaulipas	*El Sol de Tampico*
Tlaxcala	*El Sol de Tlaxcala*
	ABC Noticias
Veracruz	*El Sol de Veracruz*
	El Liberal del Sur
Yucatán	*Diario de Yucatán*
	Diario del Sureste
	El Mundo al Día
Zacatecas	*Novedades de Zacatecas*

Appendix

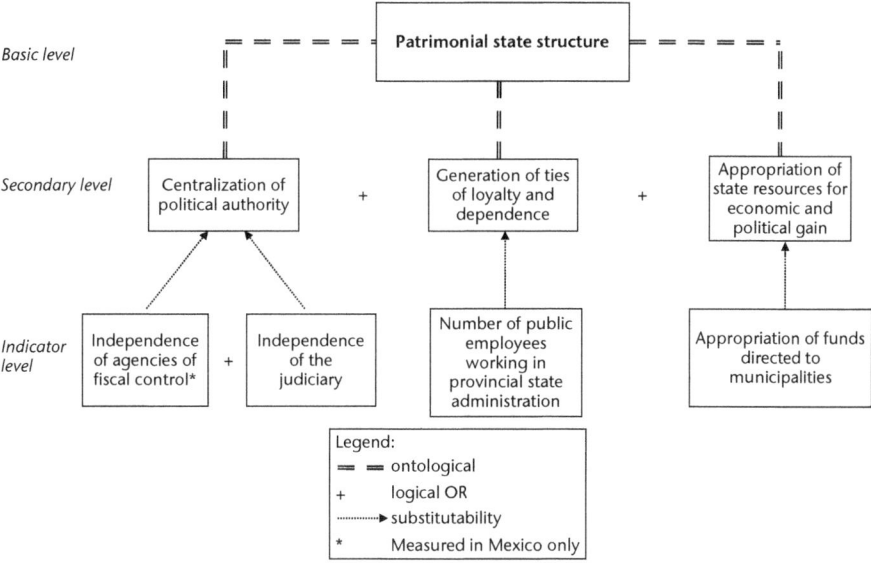

Figure A2. A family resemblance concept structure of patrimonial state structure

than simply being present or absent (Collier and Mahon 1993). Moreover, the family resemblance concept structure allows the absence of any given characteristic to be compensated for by the presence of another characteristic. Accordingly, the secondary dimensions (see Figure A2) are "connected" via the logical OR, and aggregated through addition (rather than multiplication)[4] (Goertz 2006: 39–44).

Description and Aggregation of Indicators

As Figure A2 shows, patrimonial state structures are measured using four indicators: independence of agencies of control, independence of the judiciary, number of public employees working in the provincial state structure, and appropriation of funds directed to municipalities. With the exception of the number of public employees working in provincial state administrations, identical indicators are not used because each country has different rules to appoint justices or to distribute funds across subnational levels of government. In order to ensure measurement equivalence, system-specific indicators were used to operationalize the two remaining secondary-level dimensions of patrimonial state structures. In Argentina, "appropriation of state resources for economic and political gain" is operationalized by assessing the cumulative years of existence (or lack thereof) of a law that regulates the transfer of funds from

---

[4] This only applies to the indicators that measure the centralization of political authority, which only correspond to the Mexican states. Data to measure the independence of agencies of fiscal control for the Argentine provinces were extremely difficult to obtain.

Table A3. Indicators of patrimonial state structure

Indicator	Description	Calculation* Argentina	Calculation* Mexico	Source Argentina	Source Mexico
Independence of agencies of fiscal control	Measures state-level comptrollers offices'	N/A**	1997–2003: Agreement between the state government and the Auditoría Superior de la Federación (AFS) to supervise budgetary items 28 and 33 (Ramos 28 and 33). Coded as 1 during the years in which the state led the AFS control of the allocation of R28 and R33, and 0 otherwise; 2004–8: Index of comptrollers office's independence	N/A**	1997–2003: Giraudy (2009); 2004–8: Figueroa Neri (2009)
Independence of the judiciary	Measures the autonomy of the judicial institutions vis-à-vis the provincial executive power	Yearly average tenure of provincial Supreme Court justices divided by the number of years of the political regime	Annual state-level judicial spending per capita	Base de Tribunales Superiores de Justicia Provinciales (Leiras et al. 2012)	Ingram (2009, 2014)
Number of public employees working in provincial state administration	Measures the number of public employees working in provincial state administration	Number of employees/1,000 inhabitants working in public administration.† Scale reversion was done with the following formula: 1,000 – [# of public employees/1,000 inhabitants]	Number of public sector employees/1,000 inhabitants of the economically active population. Public sector employees = administrative personnel (teachers and doctors are not included)	Base de Datos Provinciales del Centro de Investigaciones en Administración Pública (Base CLAP), Facultad de Ciencias Económicas, UBA	INEGI publication: Sistema de Cuentas Nacionales de México. Gobiernos Estatales. Cuentas Corrientes y de Acumulación, various editions
Appropriation of funds directed to municipalities	Measures the capacity of provincial incumbents to appropriate funds and transfers that should be sent to municipalities, as well as their capacity to distribute these resources in a discretionary manner	Cumulative years of existence of a municipal coparticipation law (i.e. the law regulating the allocation of fiscal resources between the provincial government and the municipalities)	% of Fondo General de Participaciones that governors did not transfer to the municipalities	Fundación CECE (1996, 1997), Ministerio de Economía, and various laws provincial	INEGI publication: Finanzas Públicas Estatales y Municipales de México, Anexo A, various years

* All individual indicators were standardized between 0 and 1 to make their scales comparable.
** No data available.
† Reversed scale.

Appendix

provincial to municipal levels of government. By contrast, in Mexico, this secondary-level dimension is measured using an indicator that reflects the percentage of fiscal funds that governors did not transfer to the municipalities.[5]

To operationalize the centralization of political authority, an indicator that captures the level of judicial independence (from the executive) was selected. In the case of Argentina, the chosen indicator measures the stability of provincial Supreme Court justices, i.e. the tenure of each sitting justice. This indicator was appropriate because (a) a vast body of literature shows that more stable courts are said to ensure greater judiciary autonomy, thus increasing justices' ability to limit rulers' centralization of authority (Iaryczower et al. 2002; Bill Chavez 2004; Helmke 2005), and (b) the selection, appointment, and number of provincial Supreme Court justices varies considerably across provinces.[6] In Mexico, by contrast, the rules that regulate justices' selection and appointments do not vary across states. Hence, an indicator that captures cross-state variance, such as the per capita judicial spending in each state, seemed more appropriate to measure the independence of Mexican state-level courts, as "punitive cuts" in judicial budgets can result in serious "assaults on judicial independence" (Bermant and Wheeler 1995; Kaufman 1999; Douglas and Hartley 2003; Ingram 2014).

Table A3 presents a description of the indicators that make up each of the three secondary-level dimensions of patrimonial state structures.

---

[5] By law, Mexican states are obliged to pass 20% of the transfers that they receive from the Law of Fiscal Coordination (LCF) to the municipalities.

[6] There are some provincial constitutions that establish a fixed number of justices, thus limiting to a great extent the capacity of rulers to engage in court packing. Other provincial constitutions, by contrast, establish a fixed number of justices in the constitution but stipulate that the size of provincial Supreme Courts can be either augmented or diminished by statutory law. These laws, in turn, differ regarding the type of majority (i.e. 1/2 or a 2/3 majority) needed for passage. Finally, there are some other provinces where the number of justices is determined by statutory law (see Leiras et al. 2012).

References

Achen, Christopher H. 2000. "Why Lagged Dependent Variables Can Suppress the Explanatory Power of Other Independent Variables." Annual Meeting of the Political Methodology Section of the American Political Science Association. UCLA.

Adcock, Robert, and David Collier. 2001. "Measurement Validity: A Shared Standard for Quantitative and Qualitative Research." *American Political Science Review*, 95(3): 529–46.

Aguilar Balderas, Lidia. 2011. *La pugna por el poder politico, 1973–2010*. Puebla: Nuestro Siglo XX: Ediciones de Educación y Cultura.

Amnesty International. 2007. *Oaxaca: Clamour for Justice*. Mexico City: AI.

Área Poder Legislativo. Asociación por los Derechos Civiles [cited Feb. 13, 2007]. Available from <http://www.adclegislativo.org.ar>.

Bates, R. H. 1981. "Food Policy in Africa: Political Origins and Social Consequences Food Policy." *Food Policy*, 3 (Aug.): 147–57.

Bates, R. H. 2008. *When Things Fell Apart: State Failure in Late-Century Africa*. Cambridge: Cambridge University Press.

Bautista, Eduardo. 2007. *Procesos locales de dominación y resistencia en el régimen político mexicano. Una interpretación de rupturas, ajustes y discontinuidades del poder político en las ciudades de Juchitán y Oaxaca*. Mexico City: UAM-Xochimilco.

Beck, Nathaniel, and Jonathan Katz. 1995. "What to Do (and Not to Do) with Time-Series Cross-Section Data." *American Political Science Review*, 89(3): 634–47.

Beer, Caroline. 2003. *Electoral Competition and Institutional Change in Mexico*. Notre Dame, IN: University of Notre Dame Press.

Behrend, Jacqueline. 2007. "Democratic Argentina and the 'Closed Game' of Provincial Politics: Protest and Persistence." D.Phil., University of Oxford.

Behrend, Jacqueline. 2011. "The Unevenness of Democracy at the Subnational Level. Provincial Closed Games in Argentina." *Latin American Research Review*, 46(1): 150–76.

Benton, Allyson. 2011. "Subnational Regime Dynamics After National Authoritarian Breakdown: When Political Competition and Turnover Don't Indicate Democratization." Workshop on Elections, Electoral Behavior and the Economy in Latin America. Hotel Clarendon, Quebec City.

Benton, Allyson. 2012. "Bottom-Up Challenges to National Democracy: Latin Americas (Legal) Subnational Authoritarian Enclaves, the Case of Mexico." *Comparative Politics*, 44(3): 253–71.

References

Bermant, Gordon, and Russell Wheeler. 1995. "Federal Judges and the Judicial Branch: Their Independence and Accountability." *Mercer Law Review,* 46(2): 835–62.

Bill Chavez, Rebecca. 2004. *The Rule of Law in Nascent Democracies: Judicial Politics in Argentina.* Stanford, CA: Stanford University Press.

Bollen, Kenneth, and Richard Lennox. 1991. "Conventional Wisdom on Measurement: A Structural Equation Perspective." *Psychological Bulletin,* 110(2): 305–14.

Bonvecchi, Alejandro, and Germán Lodola. 2011. "The Dual Logic of Intergovernmental Transfers: Presidents, Governors, and the Politics of Coalition-Building in Argentina." *Publius: The Journal of Federalism,* 41(2): 179–206.

Bonvecchi, Alejandro, and Agustina Giraudy. 2008. "Argentina. Victoria presidencial oficialista y tensiones en el esquema macroeconómico." *Revista de Ciencia Política,* 28(1): 35–59.

Boone, Catherine. 2003. *Political Topographies of the African State: Territorial Authority and Institutional Choice.* Cambridge: Cambridge University Press.

Borges, André. 2007. "Rethinking State Politics: The Withering of State Dominant Machines in Brazil." *Brazilian Political Science Review,* 1(2): 108–36.

Botto, Mercedes. 1998. *La relación partido/gobierno en Argentina post-dictatorial. Estudio comparativo de las gestiones de Alfonsín y Menem.* Buenos Aires: Universidad Torcuato Di Tella.

Brownlee, Jason. 2007. *Authoritarianism in an Age of Democratization.* Cambridge: Cambridge University Press.

Calvo, Ernesto, and Marcelo Escolar. 2005. *La nueva política de partidos en la Argentina. Crisis política, realineamientos partidarios y reforma electoral.* Buenos Aires: Prometeo-Pent.

Calvo, Ernesto, and Juan Pablo Micozzi. 2005. "The Governor's Backyard: A Seat-Vote Model of Electoral Reform for Subnational Multiparty Races." *Journal of Politics,* 67(4): 1050–74.

Cámara de Diputados. 2007. [cited 31-03-2007]. Available from <http://www.diputados.gov.ar>.

Cámara de Diputados. 2013. [cited 2013]. *Cámara de Diputados. Honorable Congreso de la Nación.* Available from <http://www.diputados.gob.mx/inicio.htm>.

Campos, Horacio Raúl. 2007. "Rodríguez Saá acusó al matrimonio K de 'atropellar el mundo de las ideas.'" *Diario Pérfil,* Sept. 9.

Caramani, Daniele. 2004. *The Nationalization of Politics: The Formation of National Electorates and Party Systems in Western Europe.* Cambridge: Cambridge University Press.

Casar, M. Amparo. 1999. "Las relaciones entre el poder ejecutivo y el legislativo. El caso de México." *Política y Gobierno XI,* 4(1): 83–128.

Castagnola, Andrea. 2010. "Rethinking Judicial Instability in Developing Democracies: A National and Subnational Analysis of Supreme Courts in Argentina." Doctoral dissertation, University of Pittsburgh.

Castagnola, Andrea. 2012. "I Want it All, and I Want it Now: The Political Manipulation of Argentina's Provincial High Courts." *Journal of Politics in Latin America,* 2: 39–62.

References

Castañeda, Jorge, and Héctor Aguilar Camin. 2007. "A Future for Mexico." <http://www.amazon.in/futuro-Mexico-Future-Ensayo-Lectura/dp/6071104009/ref=sr_1_2?s=books&ie=UTF8&qid=1411496501&sr=1-2>.

CECE. 1995. *El conflicto en torno a las relaciones financieras entre la Nación y las provincias. Primera parte: antecedentes de la ley 23548*. Buenos Aires: Centro de Estudios para el Cambio Estructural.

CECE. 1997. *Aportes del Tesoro Nacional. Discrecionalidad en la relación financiera entre la Nación y las provincias*. Buenos Aires: Centro de Estudios para el Cambio Estructural.

CEFP. 2007. *Política Fiscal. Tendencias del sistema tributario mexicano*. Mexico Ciy: Cámara de Diputados, Congreso de la Unión.

Census Data. 2010. *Censo 2010. Año del Bicentenario*. Buenos Aires: Instituto Nacional de Estadistica.

Centeno, Miguel Ángel. 1994. *Democracy within Reason: Technocratic Revolution*. Mexico City and University Park, PA: Pennsylvania State University Press.

Centro de Documentación, Información, y Análisis. 2006. *Compilación hemorográfica. Caso Marín: Desarrollo cronológico de su tratamiento*. Mexico City: Honorable Cámara de Diputados.

Cetrángolo, Oscar, and Juan Pablo Jiménez. 1997. *Aportes del Tesoro Nacional. Discrecionalidad en la relación financiera entre la Nación y las Provincias*. Serie Estudios CECE #21. Buenos Aires: Fundación CECE.

CEPAL. Various years. Estadísticas e Indicadores Económicos. Cuentas Nacionales.

Cetrángolo, Oscar, and Juan Pablo Jiménez. 2004. Las relaciones entre niveles de gobierno en Argentina. Raíces históricas, instituciones y conflictos persistentes. Serie Gestión Pública #47. Santiago de Chile: CEPAL/ILPES.

Cetrángolo, Oscar, Juan Pablo Jiménez, Florencia Devoto, and Daniel Vega. 2002. Las finanzas públicas provinciales. Situación actual y perspectivas. Serie Estudios y perspectival # 12. Santiago de Chile: CEPAL/ILPES.

CIDAC. 2008. *Base de Datos de Elecciones Locales 1980–2008*. Mexico City: Centro de Investigación para el Desarrollo en México.

Cleary, Matthew, and Susan Stokes. 2006. *Democracy and the Culture of Skepticism: Political Trust in Argentina and Mexico*. New York: Russel Sage Foundation.

Collier, David, and Robert Adcock. 1999. "Democracy and Dichotomies: A Pragmatic Approach to Choices about Concepts." *American Political Science Review,* 2: 537–65.

Collier, David, and Steven Levitsky. 1997. "Democracy with Adjectives: Conceptual Innovation in Comparative Analysis." *World Politics,* 49: 430–51.

Collier, David, and J. Mahon. 1993. "Conceptual 'Stretching' Revisited: Adapting Categories in Comparative Analysis." *American Political Science Review,* 87: 845–55.

Coppedge, Michael, and Wolfgang Reinicke. 1991. "Measuring Polyarchy." In Alex Inkeles (ed.), *On Measuring Democracy: Its Consequences and Concomitants,* 47–68. New Brunswick, NJ: Transaction Publishers.

Cornelius, Wayne. 1999. "Subnational Politics and Democratization: Tensions between Center and Periphery in the Mexican Political System." In Wayne Cornelius, Todd A. Eisenstadt, and Jane Hindley (eds), *Subnational Politics and Democratization in Mexico,* 3–18. La Jolla: Center for US-Mexican Studies, University of California San Diego.

References

Courchene, Thomas, and Alberto Díaz-Cayeros. 2000. "Transfers and the Nature of the Mexican Federation." In M. G. a. S. Webb (ed.), *Achievements and Challenges of Decentralization: Lessons from Mexico*, 200–36. Washington, DC: World Bank.

Cué, Gabino. n.d. *Oaxaca. Transición Democrática o Regresión Autoritaria. Lucha contra el fraude y la elección de Estado en el sur de México*. Oaxac: n. publ.

Dahl, Robert. 1971. *Poliarchy: Participation and Opposition*. New Haven: Yale University Press.

del Collado, Fernando. 2003. "Murat, retrato de un cacique. Entrevista con José Murat." *Enfoque* insert to Reforma, Oct. 19: 13–18.

De Luca, Miguel, Mark Jones, and María Inés Tula. 2002. "Back Rooms or Ballot Boxes? Candidate Nomination in Argentina." *Comparative Political Studies*, 35(4): 413–36.

Diamond, Larry, Jonathan Hartlyn, Juan Linz, and Seymour Martin Lipset, eds. 1999. *Democracy in Developing Countries: Latin America*. Boulder, CO: Lynne Rienner.

Diario Perfil. 2008. "Rodríguez Saá denunció a la Nación por 'discriminación'." *Diario Pérfil*, Apr. 6.

Diaz Montes, Fausto. 2009. "Elecciones y protesta social en Oaxaca." In Víctor Raúl Martínez Vásquez (ed.), *La APPO: ¿Rebelión o movimiento social? (nuevas formas de expresión ante la crisis)*, 247–74. Oaxaca: IISUABJO.

Díaz-Cayeros, Alberto. 2004a. "Dependencia fiscal y estrategias de coalición en el federalismo mexicano." *Política y Gobierno XI*, 2: 229–62.

Díaz-Cayeros, Alberto. 2004b. "Do Federal Institutions Matter? Rules and Political Practices in Regional Resource Allocation in Mexico." In E. L. Gibson (ed.), *Federalism and Democracy in Latin America*, 297–322. Baltimore: Johns Hopkins University Press.

Díaz-Cayeros, Alberto. 2006. *Federalism, Fiscal Authority, and Centralization in Latin America*. Cambridge: Cambridge University Press.

Dickovick, T. 2007. "Municipalization as Central Government Strategy: Central-Regional-Local Politics in Peru, Brazil, and South Africa." *Publius*, 37(1): 1–25.

DINE. 2012. "Dirección Nacional Electoral." Retrieved July 2012, from <http://www.mininterior.gov.ar/asuntos_politicos_y_alectorales/dine/infogral/dine.php>.

Dirección Nacional de Coordinación Fiscal con las Provincias, Ministerio de Economía de la República Argentina. 2013. Available from <http://www.mecon.gov.ar/hacienda/dncfp/index.html>.

Douglas, James W., and Roger E. Hartley. 2003. "The Politics of Court Budgeting in the States: Is Judicial Independence Threatened by the Budgetary Process?" *Public Administration Review*, 63(4): 441–54.

Durazo-Herrmann, Julián. 2010. "Neo-Patrimonialism and Subnational Authoritarianism in Mexico: The Case of Oaxaca." *Journal of Politics in Latin America*, 2(2): 85–112.

Eaton, Kent. 2001. "The Logic of Congressional Delegation: Explaining Argentine Economic Reform." *Latin American Research Review*, 3(2): 97–117.

Eaton, Kent. 2004. *Politics Beyond the Capital: The Design of Subnational Institutions in South America*. Stanford, CA: Stanford University Press.

Eisenstadt, Todd. 1999. "Electoral Federalism or Abdication of Presidential Authority? Gubernatorial Elections in Tabasco." In Wayne Cornelius, Todd A. Eisenstadt, and Jane Hindley (eds), *Subnational Politics and Democratization in*

Mexico, 269–93. La Jolla: Center for US-Mexican Studies, University of California San Diego.
Eisenstadt, Todd. 2004. *Courting Democracy in Mexico: Party Strategies and Electoral Institutions*. Cambridge: Cambridge University Press.
Eisenstadt, Todd. 2006. "Mexico's Postelectoral Concertacesiones: The Rise and Demise of a Substitutive Informal Institution." In G. Helmke and S. Levitsky (eds), *Informal Institutions and Democracy: Lessons from Latin America*, 227–48. Baltimore: Johns Hopkins University Press.
Eisenstadt, Todd, and Jennifer Yelle. 2012. "Ulysses, the Sirens, and Mexico's Judiciary: Increasing Commitments to Strengthen the Rule of Law." In Roderic Ai Camp (ed.), *Oxford Handbook of Mexican Politics*, 210–33. New York: Oxford University Press.
Elecciones Nacionales 2011. Dirección Nacional Electoral 2011 [cited 07-2011. Available from <http://www.elecciones.gob.ar>.
Ertman, Thomas. 1997. *Birth of the Leviathan: Building States and Regimes in Medieval and Early Modern Europe*. Cambridge: Cambridge University Press.
Escribanía de Gobierno, San Luis. 2006. Carta presentada al Gobierno Federal [Notary of Government, San Luis. Letter submitted to the federal government].
Evans, Peter. 1994. *Embedded Autonomy: States and Industrial Transformation*. Princeton: Princeton University Press.
Falleti, Tulia. 2005. "A Sequential Theory of Decentralization: Latin American Cases in Comparative Perspective." *American Political Science Review*, 99(3): 327–46.
Falleti, Tulia. 2010. *Decentralization and Subnational Politics in Latin America*. Cambridge: Cambridge University Press.
Falleti, Tulia. 2011. "Varieties of Authoritarianism: The Organization of the Military State and its Effects on Federalism in Argentina and Brazil." *Studies in Comparative International Development*, 46: 137–62.
Fenwick, Tracy Beck. 2010. "The Institutional Feasibility of National–Local Policy Collaboration: Insights from Argentina and Brazil." *Journal of Politics in Latin America*, 2(2): 155–83.
Figueroa Neri, Aimée, ed. 2009. *Cuenta Pública en México. Evaluando el laberinto legal de la fiscalización superior*. Guadalajara, Jalisco, México: Universidad de Guadalajara.
Fox, Jonathan. 1994. "The Diffucult Transition from Clientelism to Citizenship: Lessons from Mexico." *World Politics*, 46(2): 151–84.
FUNDAR. 2006. *Ingresos Petroleros y Gasto Público. La dependencia continúa*. Mexico City: Fundar, Centro de Análisis e Investigación, A.C.
FUNIF. 1999a. *Mapa productivo provincial. Caracterización productiva de la Provincia de San Luis, i*. San Luis: Talleres Gráficos Payne.
FUNIF. 1999b. *Mapa productivo provincial. Antecedentes, infraestructura económica-social y aspectos legales*, ii. San Luis: Talleres Gráficos Payne.
Garman, Christopher, Stephan Haggard, and Eliza Willis. 2001. "Fiscal Decentralization: A Political Theory with Latin American Cases." *World Politics*, 53: 205–36.
Geddes, Barbara. 1999. "What do we Know about Democratization After Twenty Years?" *Annual Review of Political Science*, 2: 115–44.

References

Geddes, Barbara. 2006. "Why Parties and Elections in Authoritarian Regimes?" Annual Meeting of the American Political Science Association. Washington, DC.

Geddes, Barbara. 2008. "Party Creation as an Autocratic Survival Strategy." Conference on Dictatorships: Their Governance and Social Consequences. Princeton University.

George, Alexander, and Andrew Bennett. 2005. *Case Studies and Theory Development in the Social Sciences*. Cambridge, MA: MIT Press.

Gerring, John. 2007. *Case Study Research: Principles and Practices*. Cambridge: Cambridge University Press.

Gerring, John, Jan Teorell, and Dominic Zarecki. 2013. "Scaling up: Demographics and Schumpeterian Democracy at Subnational Levels." Paper prepared for Annual Meeting, American Political Science Association, Chicago, Aug. 29–Sept. 1.

Gervasoni, Carlos. 2010a. "Measuring Variance in Subnational Regimes: Results from an Expert-Based Operationalization of Democracy in the Argentine Provinces." *Journal of Politics in Latin America*, 2(2): 13–52.

Gervasoni, Carlos. 2010b. "A Rentier Theory of Subnational Regimes: Fiscal Federalism, Democracy, and Authoritarianism in the Argentine Provinces." *World Politics*, 62(2): 302–40.

Gervasoni, Carlos. 2011. "A Rentier Theory of Subnational Democracy: The Politically Regressive Effects of Fiscal Federalism in Argentina." Doctoral dissertation, University of Notre Dame.

Gibson, Edward. 1997. "The Populist Road to Market Reform: Policy and Electoral Coalitions in Mexico and Argentina." *World Politics*, 49: 339–70.

Gibson, Edward. 2004. "Federalism and Democracy: Theoretical Connections and Cautionary Insights." In Edward Gibson (ed.), *Federalism and Democracy in Latin America*, 1–28. Baltimore: Johns Hopkins University Press.

Gibson, Edward. 2005. "Boundary Control: Subnational Authoritarianism in Democratic Countries." *World Politics*, 58(1): 101–32.

Gibson, Edward. 2010. "Politics of the Periphery: An Introduction to Subnational Authoritarianism and Democratization in Latin America." *Journal of Politics in Latin America*, 2 (Aug.): 3–12.

Gibson, Edward. 2013. *Boundary Control: Subnational Authoritarianism in Federal Democracies,*. Cambridge: Cambridge University Press.

Gibson, Edward, and Ernesto Calvo. 2001. "Federalism and Low-Maintenance Constituencies: Territorial Dimensions of Economic Reform in Argentina." *Studies in Comparative International Development*, 35(3): 32–55.

Gibson, Edward, Ernesto Calvo, and Tulia Falleti. 2004. "Reallocative Federalism: Legislative Overrepresentation and Public Spending in the Western Hemisphere." In E. L. Gibson (ed.), *Federalism and Democracy in Latin America*, 173–96. Baltimore: Johns Hopkins University Press.

Gibson, Edward, and Julieta Suarez-Cao. 2010. "Federalized Party Systems and Subnational Party Competition: Theory and an Empirical Application to Argentina." *Comparative Politics*, 43(1): 21–39.

Giraudy, Agustina. 2007. "The Distributive Politics of Emergency Employment Programs in Argentina (1993–2002)." *Latin American Research Review*, 42(2): 33–55.

References

Giraudy, Agustina. 2009. *Subnational Undemocratic Regime Continuity After Democratization: Argentina and Mexico in Comparative Perspective*. Chapel Hill, NC: Department of Political Science, University of North Carolina.

Giraudy, Agustina. 2010. "The Politics of Subnational Undemocratic Regime Reproduction in Argentina and Mexico." *Journal of Politics in Latin America*, 2(2): 53–84.

Giraudy, Agustina. 2013. "Varieties of Subnational Undemocratic Regimes: Evidence from Argentina and Mexico." *Studies in Comparative International Development*, 48(1): 51–80.

Giraudy, Agustina, and Germán Lodola. 2008. Base de Legislaturas Provinciales en Argentina: 1983–2008. Unpublished dataset.

Giraudy, Eugenia. 2006. *La racionalidad política en la distribución de los fondos federales para obras públicas. Los gobiernos de Menem y De la Rúa*. Buenos Aires: Universidad Torcuato Di Tella.

Goertz, Gary. 2006. *Social Science Concepts: A User's Guide*. Princeton: Princeton University Press.

Gordin, Jorge P. 2004. "Testing Riker's Party-Based Theory of Federalism: The Argentine Case." *Publius: The Journal of Federalism*, 34: 21–34.

Greene, Kenneth F. 2007. *Why Dominant Parties Lose: Mexico's Democratization in Comparative Perspective*. Cambridge: Cambridge University Press.

Guiñazú, María Clelia. 2003. *The Subnational Politics of Structural Adjustment in Argentina: The Case of San Luis*. Cambridge, MA: MIT Press.

Hagopian, Frances. 1996. *Traditional Politics and Regime Change in Brazil*. New York: Cambridge University Press.

Hartlyn, Jonathan. 1998. "Political Continuities, Missed Opportunities and Institutional Rigidities: Another Look at Democratic Transitions in Latin America." In S. P. M. a. A. Valenzuela (ed.), *Politics, Society and Democracy: Latin America, Essays in Honor of Juan J. Linz*, 101–20. Boulder, CO: Westview Press.

Heller, Patrick. 2000. "Degrees of Democracy: Some Comparative Lessons from India." *World Politics*, 52: 484–519.

Helmke, Gretchen. 2005. *Courts Under Constraints: Judges, Generals, and Presidents in Argentina*. New York: Cambridge University Press.

Hernández Rodríguez, Rogelio. 2008. *El centro dividido. La nueva autonomía de los gobernadores*. Mexico City: El Colegio de México.

Hernández Trillo, Fausto, Alberto Diaz-Cayeros, and Rafael Gamboa González. 2002. *Fiscal Decentralization in Mexico: The Bailout Problem*. Washington, DC: InterAmerican Development Bank.

Huber, Evelyne, and John Stephens. 2001. *Development and Crisis of the Welfare State: Parties and Policies in Global Market*. Chicago: Chicago University Press.

Huber, Evelyne, François Nielsen, Jennifer Pribble, and John D. Stephens. 2006. "Politics and Inequality in Latin America and the Caribbean." *American Sociological Review*, 71 (Dec.): 943–63.

Human Rights Watch. 2007. *World Report: Events of 2006*. New York and Washington, DC: HRW.

Hunter, Wendy, and Timothy J. Power. 2007. "Rewarding Lula: Executive Power, Social Policy, and the Brazilian Elections of 2006." *Latin American Politics and Society*, 49(1): 1–30.

References

Huntington, S. P. 1991. *The Third Wave: Democratization in the Late Twentieth Century*. Norman, Okla.: University of Oklahoma Press.

Iaryczower, Matias, Pablo T. Spiller, and Mariano Tommasi. 2002. "Judicial Independence in Unstable Environments, Argentina 1935–1998." *American Journal of Political Science*, 46(4): 699–716.

IFE. *Instituto Federal Electoral* 2013. Available from <http://www.ife.org.mx/portal/site/ifev2>.

INEGI. Various years. *Sistema de cuentas nacionales de México. Gobiernos estatales. Cuentas corrientes y de acumulación*. Mexico City: INEGI.

INEGI. Various years. *Finanzas públicas estatales y municipales de México* [Anexo A]. Mexico City: INEGI.

Inglehart, Ronald, and Christian Welzel. 2005. *Modernization, Cultural Change, and Democracy: The Human Development Sequence*. New York: Cambridge University Press.

Ingram, Matthew C. 2014. "Elections, Ideology, or Opposition? Assessing Competing Explanations of Judicial Spending in the Mexican States." *Journal of Law, Economics and Organization*, 29(1): 178–209.

Instituto Nacional de Estadística y Censos. 2007. Available from <http://www.indec.gov.ar>.

Jones, Mark P., Pablo Sanguinetti, and Mariano Tommasi. 2000. "Politics, Institutions, and Public Sector Spending in the Argentine Provinces." *Journal of Development Economics*, 61: 305–33.

Jones, Mark P., and Wonjae Hwang. 2005. "Provincial Party Bosses: Keystone of the Argentine Congress." In Steven Levitsky and María Victoria Murillo (eds), *Argentine Democracy: The Politics of Institutional Weakness*, 115–38. University Park, PA: Pennsylvania State University Press.

Jones, Mark P., and Scott Mainwaring. 2003. "The Nationalizatioin of Parties and Party Systems." *Party Politics*, 9(2): 139–66.

Kaufman, Robert M. 1999. "Threats to Judicial Independence: An Appeal from AJS Past President Robert M. Kaufman." <http://www.ajs.org/cji/cji_threats.asp>.

Keating, Michael. 1998. *The New Regionalism in Western Europe*. Cheltenham and Northampton, MA: Edward Elgar.

Lakin, Jason M. 2008. "The Possibilities and Limitations of Insurgent Technocratic Reform: Mexico's Popular Health Insurance Program, 2001–2006." Doctoral dissertation, Harvard University.

Langston, Joy. 2004. "Legislative Recruitment in Mexico." In Peter Siavelis and Scott Morgenstern (eds), *Pathways to Power: Political Recruitment and Candidate Selection in Latin America*, 143–63. University Park, PA: Pennsylvania State University Press.

Langston, Joy. 2005. *The Search for Principals in the Mexican Legislature: The PRI's Federal Deputies*. Documentos de Trabajo, Mexico City: CIDE.

Langston, Joy, and Javier Aparicio. 2008. *Legislative Career Patterns in Democratic Mexico*. Mexico City: CIDE.

Lankina, Tomila, and Lullit Getachew. 2012. "Mission or Empire,Word or Sword? The Human Capital Legacy in Postcolonial Democratic Development." *American Journal of Political Science*, 56(2): 465–83.

References

Lankina, Tomila, and Lullit Getachew. 2006. "A Geographic Incremental Theory of Democratization: Territory, Aid, and Democracy in Postcommunist Regions." *World Politics*, 58: 536–82.

LASA. 2007. *Violations Against Freedoms of Inquiry and Expression in Oaxaca de Juárez: Report by the Fact-Finding Delegation of the Latin American Studies Association on the Impact of the 2006 Social Conflict*. Oaxaca: LASA.

Lazarev, Valery. 2005. "Economics of One-Party State: Promotion Incentives and Support for the Soviet Regime." *Comparative Economic Studies*, 47(2): 346–63.

Leiras, Marcelo. 2006. *Parties, Provinces, and Electoral Coordination: A Study on the Determinants of Party and Party System Aggregation in Argentina, 1983–2005*. Notre Dame, IN: University of Notre Dame.

Leiras, Marcelo. 2007. *Todos los caballos del rey. La integración de los partidos políticos y el gobierno democrático de la Argentina, 1995–2003*. Buenos Aires: Prometeo-Pent.

Leiras, Marcelo, Guadalupe Tuñón, and Agustina Giraudy. 2012. *Who Wants an Independent Court? Political Competition and Supreme Court Instability in the Argentine Provinces (1984–2008)*. Buenos Aires: Universidad de San Andrés.

Levitsky, Steven. 2003. *Transforming Labor-Based Parties in Latin America: Argentine Peronism in Comparative Perspective*. Cambridge: Cambridge University Press.

Levitsky, Steven, and María Victoria Murillo, eds. 2005. *The Politics of Institutional Weakness: Argentine Democracy*. University Park, PA: Pennsylvania State University Press.

Levitsky, Steven, and Lucan A. Way. 2010. *Competitive Authoritarianism: Hybrid Regimes After the Cold War*. Cambridge: Cambridge University Press.

Ley, Sandra. 2009. *Electoral Institutions and Democratic Consolidation in the Mexican States, 1990–2004*. Mexico City: CIDE.

Lieberman, Evan. 2002. "Taxation Data as Indicators of State-Society Relations: Possibilities and Pitfalls in Cross-National Research." *Studies in Comparative International Development*, 36(4): 89–115.

Linz, J. J. 1975. "Totalitarian and Authoritarian Regimes." In F. I. Greenstein and N. W. Polsby (eds), *Handbook of Political Science*, 175–353. Reading, MA: Addison-Wesley.

Linz, Juan, and Alfred Stepan. 1996. *Problems of Democratic Transition and Consolidation: Southern Europe, South America, and Post-Communist Europe*. Baltimore: Johns Hopkins University Press.

Loaeza, S. 2003. "The National Action Party: From the Fringes of Power to the Heart of Political Change." In S. Mainwaring and T. Scully (eds), *Christian Democracy in Latin America: Electoral Competition and Regime Conflict*, 196–247. Stanford, CA: Stanford University Press.

Long, J. Scott, and Laurie H. Ervin. 2000. "Using Heteroskedasticity Consistent Standard Errors in Linear Regression Model." *The American Statistician*, 54(3): 217–24.

Lujambio, Alonso. 2000. *El poder compartido. Un ensayo sobre la democratización mexicana*. Mexico City: Editorial Océano de México, S.A. de C.V.

McMann, Kelly. 2006. *Economic Autonomy and Democracy: Hybrid Regimes in Russia and Kyrgyzstan*. Cambridge: Cambridge University Press.

Madrazo, Roberto. 2007. *La Traición*. Mexico City: Editorial Planeta.

References

Magaloni, Beatriz. 2005. "The Demise of Mexico's One-Party Dominant Regime: Elite Choices and the Masses in the Establishment of Democracy." In Frances Hagopian and Scott Mainwaring (eds), *The Third Wave of Democratization in Latin America: Advances and Setbacks*, 121–48. Cambridge: Cambridge University Press.

Magaloni, Beatriz. 2006. *Voting for Autocracy: Hegemonic Party Survival and its Demise in Mexico*. Cambridge: Cambridge University Press.

Magaloni, Beatriz, and Ruth Kricheli. 2010. "Political Order and One-Party Rule." *Annual Review of Political Science*, 13: 123–43.

Mainwaring, Scott. 1999. *Rethinking Party Systems in the Third Wave of Democratization: The Case of Brazil*. Stanford, CA: Stanford University Press.

Mainwaring, Scott, Daniel Brinks, and Aníbal Pérez-Liñán. 2007. "Classifying Political Regimes in Latin America, 1945–2004." In Gerardo Munck (ed.), *Regimes and Democracy in Latin America: Theories and Methods*, 123–62. Oxford and New York: Oxford University Press.

Mann, Michael. 1986. *The Sources of Social Power*, i. *A History of Power from the Beginning to A.D. 1760*. Cambridge: Cambridge University Press.

Martínez Vásquez, Víctor. 2006. "Movimiento magisterial y crisis política en Oaxaca." In Joel Vicente Cortés (ed.), *Educación, sindicalismo y gobernabilidad en Oaxaca* (Education, Unionism, and Governability in Oaxaca), 125–49. Oaxaca: SNTE.

Martínez Vásquez, Víctor. 2007. *Autoritarismo, movimiento popular y crisis política. Oaxaca 2006*. Oaxaca: IISUABJO.

Martínez Vásquez, Víctor, and Fausto Diaz Montes. 2001. *Elecciones municipales en Oaxaca*. Oaxaca, Mexico: Universidad Autónoma Benito Juárez de Oaxaca, Instituto Estatal Electoral.

Mazzuca, Sebastián. 2007. "Reconceptualizing Democratization: Access to Power Versus Exercise of Power." In Gerardo Munck (ed.), *Regimes and Democracy in Latin America: Theory and Methods*, 39–49. Oxford: Oxford University Press.

Mazzuca, Sebastián. 2010. "Access to Power versus Exercise of Power: Reconceptualizing the Quality of Democracy in Latin America." *Studies in Comparative International Development*, 45: 334–57.

MECON. Various years a. Cuenta de Inversión, 1993–2007. In *Boletín Fiscal 1993–2007*. Buenos Aires: Minsterio de Economía, República Argentina.

MECON. Various years b. *Cuenta de Inversión*, 1993–2009. Buenos Aires: Ministerio de Economía, República Argentina.

Melo, Marcus André, Carlos Pereira, and Carlos Mauricio Figueiredo. 2009. "Political and Institutional Checks on Corruption. Explaining the Performance of Brazilian Audit Institutions." *Comparative Political Studies*, 42(9): 1217–44.

Mickey, Robert. 2013. *Paths Out of Dixie: The Democratization of Authoritarian Enclaves in America's Deep South*. Princeton: Princeton University Press.

Micozzi, Juan Pablo. 2009. "The Electoral Connection in Multilevel Systems with Non-Static Ambition: Linking Political Careers and Legislative Performance in Argentina." Doctoral dissertation, Rice University.

Micozzi, Juan Pablo, Mark Jones, and Wonjae Hwang. 2009. "Government and Opposition in the Argentine Congress, 1989–2007: Understanding Inter-Party Dynamics through Roll Call Vote Analysis." *Politics in Latin America*, 1: 67–96.

References

Migdal, Joel S. 1992. "The Power and Limits of States: Struggles for Domination between States and Societies." In Volker Bornschier and Peter Lengyel (eds), *Waves, Formations and Values in the World System*, 213–33. New Brunswick, NJ: Transaction Publishers.

Migdal, Joel S. 1994. "The State in Society: An Approach to Struggles for Domination." In Joel S. Migdal, Atul Kohli, and Vivienne Shue (eds), *State Power and Social Forces: Domination and Transformation in the Third World*, 7–32. Cambridge: Cambridge University Press.

Ministerio de Economía, Secretaría de Programación Económica y Regional. 1999. *10 Años en la relación fiscal Nación, Provincias y Municipios*. Buenos Aires: Ministerio de Economía.

Ministerio de Economía y Producción. Centro de Documentación e Información (CDI). 2007. *Información Legislativa (Infoleg)* [cited 10-02-2007]. Available from <http://www.infoleg.gov.ar>.

Mizrahi, Yemile. 2003. *From Martyrdom to Power: The Partido de Acción Nacional in Mexico*. Notre Dame, IN: University of Notre Dame Press.

Montero, Alfred. 2007. "Uneven Democracy? Subnational Authoritarianism in Democratic Brazil." Latin American Studies Association Annual Meeting. Montreal, Quebec, Canada.

Montero, Alfred. 2010a. "No Country for Leftists? Clientelist Continuity and the 2006 Vote in the Brazilian Northeast." *Journal of Politics in Latin America*, 2(2): 113–53.

Montero, Alfred. 2010b. "Trading Spaces: The Endogenous Dynamics of Subnational Authoritarianism in Brazil." 2010 Congress of the Latin American Studies Association. Toronto.

Montero, Alfred. 2011. "The New Boss Same as the Old Boss? Incumbency and the Decline of Conservative Rule in the Brazilian Northeast." American Political Science Association Meeting. Seattle.

Montero, Alfred, and David Samuels, eds. 2004. *Decentralization and Democracy in Latin America*. Notre Dame, IN: University of Notre Dame Press.

Moraski, Bryon, and William Reisinger. 2003. "Explaining Electoral Competition across Russia's Regions." *Slavic Review*, 62(2): 278–301.

Munck, Gerardo. 2004. "Democratic Politics in Latin America: New Debates and Research Frontiers." *Annual Review of Political Science*, 7: 437–62.

Munck, Gerardo. 2009. *Measuring Democracy: A Bridge between Scholarship and Politics*. Baltimore: Johns Hopkins University Press.

Munck, Gerardo, and Jay Verkuilen. 2002. "Conceptualizing and Measuring Democracy." *Comparative Political Studies*, 35(1) (Feb.): 5–34.

Nichter, Simeon. 2008. "Vote Buying or Turnout Buying? Machine Politics and the Secret Ballot." *American Political Science Review*, 102(1): 19–31.

Niedzwiecki, S. 2012. "Non-Contributory Social Policies in Mendoza and San Luis." Paper presented at the American Political Science Association Meeting, New Orleans, LA.

Ochoa-Reza, Enrique. 2004. "Multiple Arenas of Struggle: Federalism and Mexico's Transition to Democracy." In E. L. Gibson (ed.), *Federalism and Democracy in Latin America*, 255–96. Baltimore: Johns Hopkins University Press.

References

O'Donnell, Guillermo. 1993. "On the State, Democratization and Some Conceptual Conceptual Problems: A Latin American View with Glances at Some Postcommunist Countries." *World Development*, 21: 1355–69.

O'Donnell, Guillermo. 1999. *Counterpoints: Selected Essays on Authoritarianism and Democratization*. Notre Dame, IN: University of Notre Dame Press.

Olmeda, Juan Cruz, and Julieta Suárez-Cao. n.d. "The Federal Connection: Organization Strategies and the Development of Conservative Parties in Mexico and Argentina." Unpublished.

Ordeshook, Peter C. 1996. "Russia's Party System: Is Russian Federalism Viable?" *Post-Soviet Affairs*, 12: 195–217.

Pardinas, Juan. 2005. "Mexico: Democracy without Accountability?" Doctoral dissertation, London School of Economics.

Petrov, Nikolai. 2005. "Regional Models of Democratic Development." In Michael McFaul, Nikolai Petrov, and Andrei Ryabov (eds), *Between Dictatorship and Democracy: Russian Post-Communist Political Reform*, 239–67. Washington, DC: Carnegie Endowment for International Peace.

Plümper, Thomas, Philip Manow, and Vera Troeger. 2005. "Panel Data Analysis in the Comparative Politics: Linking Method to Theory." *European Journal of Political Research*, 44: 327–54.

Población, Consejo Nacional de. 2012. Available from <http://www.conapo.gob.mx>.

Porto, Alberto. 2003. *Etapas de la coparticipación federal de impuestos*. Documento de Federalismo Fiscal, La Plata, Argentina: Universidad Nacional de la Plata, Facultad de Ciencias Económicas, Departamento de Economía.

Porto, Alberto, and Juan Sanguinetti. 1993. *Decentralización fiscal en América latina. El caso argentino*. Serie Política Fiscal, 45. Santiago, Chile: CEPAL.

Porto, Alberto, and Juan Sanguinetti. 2001. "Political Determinants of Intergovernmental Grants: Evidence from Argentina." *Economics and Politics*, 13(3): 237–56.

Przeworski, Adam. 1991. *Democracy and the Market*. Cambridge: Cambridge University Press.

Przeworski, A., M. Alvarez, J. A. Cheibub, and F. Limongi. 1996. "What Makes Democracies Endure?" *Journal of Democracy*, 7: 39–55.

Ragin, Charles. 1987. *The Comparative Method: Moving beyond Qualitative and Quantitative Strategies*. Berkeley-Los Angeles and London: University of California Press.

Ragin, Charles. 2000. *Fuzzy-Set Social Science*. Chicago: University of Chicago Press.

Rebolledo, Juan. 2011. "Voting with the Enemy: Democratic Support for Subnational Authoritarians." Doctoral dissertation, Yale University.

Reisinger, William, and Bryon Moraski. 2010. "Regional Changes and Changing Regional Relations with the Center." In Vladimir Gelman and Cameron Ross (eds), *The Politics of Sub-National Authoritarianism in Russia*, 67–84. Aldershot: Ashgate.

Remington, Thomas. 2009. "Democracy and Inequality in the Postcommunist Transition." Midwestern Political Science Association Conference. Chicago.

Remington, Thomas. 2010a. "Accounting for Regime Differences in the Russian Regions: Historical and Structural Influences." Annual Meeting of the Midwestern Political Science Association. Chicago.

Remington, Thomas. 2010b. *Politics in Russia*. Boston: Longman.

References

Revista En Marcha 2001. Available from <http://www.revistaenmarcha.com.mx>.

Rodden, Jonathan. 2003. *Breaking the Golden Rule: Fiscal Behavior with Rational Bailout Expectations in the German States*. Cambridge, MA: MIT.

Rodden, Jonathan. 2006. *Hamilton's Paradox: The Promise and Peril of Fiscal Federalism*. Cambridge: Cambridge University Press.

Rokkan, Stein. 1970. *Citizens,* Elections, Parties. Oslo and New York: Universitetsforlaget-McKay.

Rokkan, Stein, and Derek Urwin. 1982. *The Politics of Territorial Identity*. London: Sage Publications.

Rokkan, Stein, and Derek Urwin. 1983. *Economy, Territory, Identity: Politics of the West European Peripheries*. London: Sage Publications.

Rulers. 2012. <www.rulers.org>.

Saikkonen, Inga Liisa. 2011. *Sub-National Variation in Democratisation and Electoral Authoritarianism in the Russian Federation*. London: London School of Economics.

Samper, José. 2006. *San Luis. Entre el atraso y el autoritarismo*. Buenos Aires: Editorial Dunken; 1st publ. 1993.

Samuels, David. 2000. "The Gubernatorial Coattails Effect: Federalism and Congressional Elections in Brazil." *Journal of Politics in Latin America*, 62(1): 240–53.

Samuels, David. 2003. *Ambassadors of the States: Political Ambition, Federalism, and Congressional Politics in Brazil*. New York: Cambridge University Press.

Samuels, David, and Richard Snyder. 2001. "The Value of a Vote: Malapportionment in Comparative Perspective." *British Journal of Political Science*, 31(4): 651–71.

Sanguinetti, Juan. 1999. "Restricción de presupuesto blanda en los niveles subnacionales de gobierno. El caso de los salvatajes en el caso argentino." *Económica* (La Plata), 45(3): 361–99.

Sartori, Giovanni. 1970. "Concept Misformation in Comparative Politics." *American Political Science Review*, 64(4): 1033–53.

Sartori, Giovanni. 1987. *The Theory of Democracy Revisited*. Chatham, NJ: Chatham House.

Sawers, Larry. 1996. *The Other Argentina: The Interior and National Development*. Boulder, CO: Westview Press.

SHCP. 2007. *Diagnóstico integral de la situación actual de las haciendas públicas estatales y municipales*. Mexico City: Secretaría de Hacienda y Crédito Público.

SHCP. 2008. *El federalismo fiscal en México. Situación actual y retos hacia el futuro*. Mexico City: Secretaría de Hacienda y Crédito Público

SHCP. 2013. *Secretaría de Hacienda y Crédito Público. Unidad de coordinación con entidades federativas*. Mexico City: Secretaría de Hacienda y Crédito Público

Shirk, David A. 2000. "Vicente Fox and the Rise of the PAN." *Journal of Democracy*, 11(4): 25–32.

Shirk, David A. 2005. *Mexico's New Politics: The PAN and Democratic Change*. Boulder, CO: Lynne Rienner Publishers.

Slater, Dan. 2010. *Ordering Power: Contentious Politics and Authoritarian Leviathans in Southeast Asia*. Cambridge: Cambridge University Press.

Snyder, Richard. 1992. "Explaining Transitions from Neopatrimonial Dictatorships." *Comparative Politics*, 24(4): 379–99.

References

Snyder, Richard. 1999. "After the States Withdraws: Neoliberalism and Subnational Authoritarian Regimes in Mexico." In Wayne Cornelius, Todd Eisenstadt, and Jane Hindley (eds), *Subnational Politics and Democratization in Mexico*, 295–341. La Jolla: Center for US-Mexican Studies, University of California San Diego.

Snyder, Richard. 2001a. *Politics after Neoliberalism: Reregulation in Mexico*. Cambridge: Cambridge University Press.

Snyder, Richard. 2001b. "Scaling Down: The Subnational Comparative Method." *Studies in Comparative International Development*, 36(1): 93–110.

Soifer, Hillel. 2008. "State Infrastructural Power: Approaches to Conceptualization and Measurement." *Studies in Comparative International Development*, 3–4(43): 231–51.

Solnick, Steven L. 1995. "Federal Bargaining in Russia." *East European Constitutional Review*, 4: 52–9.

Solt, Frederick. 2003. *Explaining the Quality of New Democracies: Actors, Institutions, and Socioeconomic Structure in Mexico's States*. Chapel Hill, NC: Political Science, University of North Carolina at Chapel Hill.

Sorroza, Carlos. 2006. "Oaxaca. ¿Conflicto político o crisis de sistema?" In J. V. Cortés (ed.), *Educación, sindicalismo y governabilidad en Oaxaca*, 151–83. Mexico City: SNTE.

Sorroza, Carlos. 2011a. "Formación y despegue de regiones para el desarrollo social sustentable de Oaxaca." Unpublished.

Sorroza, Carlos. 2011b. *Gabino Cué Monteagudo. Ganó el gobierno y perdió la posibilidad del cambio social*. Oaxaca: UABJO.

Stepan, Alfred. 2000. "Russian Federalism in Comparative Perspective." *Post-Soviet Affairs*, 16: 133–76.

Stepan, Alfred. 2004. "A New Comparative Politics of Federalism, Multinationalism, and Democracy." In E. Gibson (ed.), *Federalism and Democracy in Latin America*, 29–84. Baltimore: Johns Hopkins University Press.

Suárez Godoy, Enrique Helio. 2004. *San Luis, una política social diferente. Plan de Inclusión Social*. San Luis: Talleres Gráficos Payne.

Suárez-Cao, Julieta. 2001. "Innovaciones constitucionales provinciales. Arquitectura institucional del Legislativo. Los casos de las provincias de San Luis y Tucumán." XXIII International Congress of the Latin American Studies Association. Washington, DC.

Tarrow, Sidney. 1978. "Introduction." In P. K. L. G. Tarrow (ed.), *Territorial Politics in Industrial Nations*, 13–15. New York and London: Praeger Publishers.

Tilly, Charles. 1990. *Coercion, Capital and the European States, A.D. 990–1990*. Cambridge, MA, and Oxford: Blackwell.

Tow, Andy. 2012. *Atlas electoral de Andy Tow*. Available from <www.towsa.com>.

Tudor, Maya, and Adam Ziegfeld. forthcoming. "Sub-national Democratization in India: Colonial Competition and the Challenge to Congress Dominance." In Laurence Whitehead and Jacqueline Behrend (eds), *Multiple Arenas: Territorial Variance within Large Federal Democracies*. Book currently under review, Johns Hopkins University Press.

Van Dyck, Brandon. 2013. "Why Party Organization Still Matters: The Workers' Party in Northeastern Brazil." Doctoral dissertation, Harvard University, Department of Government.

References

Van Evera, Stephen. 1997. *Guide to Methods for Students of Political Science*. Ithaca, NY: Cornell University Press.

Vanhanen, Tatu. 2000. "A New Dataset for Measuring Democracy, 1810–1998." *Journal of Peace Research*, 37(2): 251–65.

Ward, Peter, and Victoria Rodríguez, eds. 1995. *Opposition Government in Mexico*. Albuquerque, NM: University of New Mexico Press.

Ward, Peter, and Victoria Rodríguez. 1999. "New Federalism and State Government in Mexico: Bringing the States Back in." In *U.S.-Mexican Policy Report*, 1–206. Austin, TX: University of Texas at Austin.

Way, Lucan. 2005. "Authoritarian State Building and the Sources of Regime Competitiveness in the Fourth Wave: The Cases of Belarus, Moldova, Russia, and Ukraine." *World Politics*, 57(2): 231–61.

Weber, Max. 1976 [1925]. *Wirtschaft und Gesellschaft. Grundniss der verstehenden Soziologie*. Tübingen: J. C. B. Mohr.

Wibbels, Erik. 2005. *Federalism and the Market: Intergovernmental Conflict and Economic Reform in the Developing World*. Cambridge: Cambridge University Press.

Willis, Eliza, Christopher C. B. Garman, and Stephan Haggard. 1999. "The Politics of Decentralization in Latin America." *Latin America Research Review*, 34(1): 7–56.

Wuhs, S. (2006). "Democratization and the Dynamics of Candidate Selection Rule Change in Mexico, 1991–2003." *Estudios Mexicanos/Mexican Studies*, 22(1): 33–55.

Wuhs, Steve. 2008. *Savage Democracy: Institutional Change and Party Development in Mexico*. University Park, PA: Pennsylvania State University Press.

List of Interviews

The following list provides the information of all interviewees who explicitly agreed to disclose their names and positions. The interviewees who did not consent to have their names and positions disclosed are listed with numbers.

Acevedo, Sergio. Governor of Santa Cruz (2003–6). Ciudad de Buenos Aires. April 11, and May 22, 2008.
Aguilar Coronado, Humberto. Undersecretary of Legislative Coordination, Ministry of Interior (2003–5). Mexico City, July 10, 2007.
Agúndez, Miriam. General Secretary, Municipality of San Luis (1999–2003). San Luis City, June 6 and 15, 2008.
Alcántara, Jaime. Adjunct Secretary to the Presidency of the National PRI (2007). Mexico City, September 25, 2007.
Aldaz, Huberto. PAN federal deputy (Oaxaca) (2003–6). Oaxaca City, July 18, 2007.
Allende, Eduardo. General Attorney, Province of San Luis (2007–). San Luis City, June 3, 2008.
Altamirano. PAN mayor of Matías Romero, Oaxaca. Oaxaca City, July 17, 2007.
Bailón, Jaime. State Auditor (Oaxaca) (1992–5). Oaxaca City, July 19, 2007.
Barrionuevo, Chingolo. PJ provincial deputy (La Rioja). La Rioja City, May 7, 2008.
Bartlett, Manuel. Governor of Puebla (1992–8), Mexico City, September 24, 2007.
Bengolea, Jorge. Minister of Production, La Rioja province. La Rioja City, May 30, 2008.
Brodersohn, Mario. Secretary of the Treasury (1985–7). Ciudad de Buenos Aires, April 8, 2008.
Bruno, Alberto. High official from the Electoral Federal Court of La Rioja. La Rioja City, May 8, 2008.
Cafiero, Juan Pablo. Former PJ deputy, Grupo de los Ocho (1989–91). Ciudad de Buenos Aires, April 10, 2008.
Cao, Horacio. Member of Federal Intervention Delegation in Santiago del Estero (2004–5). Ciudad de Buenos Aires, February 21, 2008.
Carrasco, Diódoro. PAN federal deputy (Oaxaca) (2006–9). Mexico City, June 8, 2007.
Cetrángolo, Oscar. Secretary of Provincial Relations, Ministry of Economy (1999–2000). Ciudad de Buenos Aires, March 27 and April 23, 2008.
Cevallos, Walter. Secretary of Provinces, Ministry of Interior (1999–2001). Ciudad de Buenos Aires, June 11, 2008.
Chamía, Oscar. Secretary of Goverment, La Rioja (2003–6). La Rioja City, May 29, 2008.
Coeto, Contreras. PAN federal deputy (Puebla) (2006–9). Mexico City, September 20, 2007.

List of Interviews

Colmenares, David. Coordinator of the Fiscal Coordination Unit with the States (Ministry of Economy) (2000–6). Mexico City, June 8, 2007.
Corach, Carlos. Ministry of Interior (1995–9). Ciudad de Buenos Aires, April 14, 2008.
Cué, Gabino. Mayor of Oaxaca City (2001–4). Mexico City, June 12, 2007.
Dávila, Humberto. Former Secretary General of SNTE (Teacher's Union). Mexico City, September 20, 2007.
De Leonardi, Juan José. Secretary of Infrastructure and Public Works, La Rioja City. La Rioja City, May 29, 2008.
De los Santos, Joaquín. PRD federal deputy (Oaxaca) (2006–9). Mexico City, June 5, 2007.
Díaz Arnaudo, Graciela. High official, La Rioja Supreme Court. La Rioja City, 2008, May 31, 2008.
Díaz Pimentel, Juan. PRI President of the Oaxacan Legislature (1998–2000). Oaxaca City, July 16, 2007.
Douglas, Guillermo. UCR deputy of La Rioja (1983–7). La Rioja City, May 7, 2008.
Durán Sabas, Héctor. General Advisor to the Governor of La Rioja. La Rioja City, May 27, 2008.
Ehlinger, Jorge. President of the PAN in the state of Puebla. Puebla City, October 1, 2007.
Escobedo, Salvador. Mayor of Atlixco, Puebla (1996–9). Mexico City, October 12, 2007.
Esteva, Gabriel. Federal Delegate, Corett, Oaxaca. Oaxaca City, July 17, 2007.
Esteva, Luis Andrés. President of the PAN in the state of Oaxaca (2000–3). Oaxaca City, July 18, 2007.
Fernández, Alberto. Chief of Government (2003–9). Ciudad de Buenos Aires, June 2012.
Fraile, Francisco. Former President of the PAN in the state of Puebla. Puebla City, October 5, 2007.
Frigeri, Rodolfo. Secretary of the Treasury (1991), Secretary of Economic and Regional Planning, Ministry of Economy (1996–9). Ciudad de Buenos Aires, April 18, and May 12, 2008.
Galván, Raúl. UCR Senator of La Rioja (1995–2001). La Rioja City, May 9, 2008.
Garat, Pablo María. Advisor to the Federal Tax Commission (Comisión Federal de Impuestos). Ciudad de Buenos Aires, April 23, 2008.
Germán. Leader of the Popular Organization of Sombrero Rojo, Canoa (state of Puebla). Puebla City, October 3, 2007.
Gómez Nucamendi, Ericel. Director of *Noticias* Newspaper (Oaxaca). Oaxaca City, July 16, 2007.
González González, Felipe. PAN Governor of Aguascalientes (1998–2004). Mexico City, April 11, 2007.
Guadagni, Alieto. Minister of Public Works, province of Buenos Aires (1987–91). Ciudad de Buenos Aires, May 13, 2008.
Guerrero, Juan Pablo. Commisioner to the Instituto Federal de Acceso a la Información. Mexico City, March 29, 2007.
Guidotti, Pablo. Secretary of the Treasury, Ministry of Economy (1996–9). Ciudad de Buenos Aires, April 14, 2008.

List of Interviews

Hernández, Fausto. Undersecretary of Expenditures (1996–8). Mexico City, March 23, 2007.
Hernández y Génis, Antonio. Technical secretary to the PRI (Puebla). Puebla City, October 3, 2007.
Hinojosa, Gabriel. Mayor of Puebla City (1996–8). Puebla City, October 2, 2007.
Ibáñez, Carlos. Advisor to the Undersecretary of Legislative Coordination, Ministry of Interior (2003–5). Puebla City, October 3, 2007.
Interview 1. Top rank politician of La Rioja's opposition. La Rioja City, Argentina, May 30, 2008.
Interview 2. Advisor to Governor Maza of La Rioja. Ciudad de Buenos Aires, Argentina, May 5, 2008.
Interview 3. Advisor to Governor Maza of La Rioja. Ciudad de Buenos Aires, Argentina, May 14, 2008.
Interview 4. Advisor to Ricardo Quintela (mayor of La Rioja City 2003–7). La Rioja City, Argentina, May 26, 2008.
Interview 5. Top rank official of La Rioja's judiciary. La Rioja city, Argentina, May 27, 2008.
Interview 6. Member of the PJ Youth during the 3rd administration of Adolfo Rodríguez Saá. San Luis city, Argentina, June 2, 2008.
Interview 7. Advisor to Governor Maza. Ciudad de Buenos Aires, May 14, 2008.
Interview 8. Member of the PJ Youth during the 3rd administration of Adolfo Rodríguez Saá. San Luis City, June 3, 2008.
Interview 9. Top rank official of San Luis City municipality. San Luis City, June 5, 2008.
Interview 10. Top rank PRI politician. Mexico City, April 4, 2007.
Interview 11. Minister during Fox's administration (2000–6). Mexico City, July 27, 2007.
Interview 12. PRD federal deputy of Oaxaca (2006–9). Mexico City, June 26, 2007.
Interview 13. Top rank PRI politician. Mexico City, July 9, 2007.
Interview 14. Top rank PRI politician. Mexico City, June 22, 2007.
Interview 15. PRD federal deputy of Oaxaca (2006–9). Mexico City, June 29, 2007.
Interview 16. Top rank official at the Ministry of Interior. Mexico City, June 21, 2007.
Interview 17. Top rank official at the Ministry of Interior. Mexico City, April 18, 2007.
Interview 18. Top rank PRI politician and adviser to Roberto Madrazo. Mexico City, June 26, 2007.
Interview 19. Coordinator of advisors, Undersecretary of Legislative Coordination, Ministry of Interior (2005–6). Mexico City, June 27, 2007.
Interview 20. Top rank PRI politician. Mexico City, July 4, 2007.
Interview 21. Top rank PAN official. Mexico City, July 5, 2007.
Interview 22. Top rank Oaxacan politician. Mexico City, July 23, 2007.
Interview 23. Advisor to Santiago Creel (Minister of Interior) (2000–5). Mexico City, September 24, 2007.
Interview 24. Journalist. Puebla City, October 2, 2007.
Interview 25. Local top rank PAN politician. Puebla City, October 1, 2007.
Interview 26. Top rank official of La Rioja's Supreme Court. La Rioja City, May 31, 2008.

List of Interviews

Jiménez, Miguel Ángel. Coordinator of the PANAL federal congressional delegation (2006–9). Mexico City, September 18 and October 9, 2007.
Juárez, Horacio. General Secretary, Judiciary Employees Association of La Rioja. La Rioja City, May 9, 2008.
Kohan, Alberto. General Secretary of the Presidency (1996–9). Ciudad de Buenos Aires, April 16, 2008.
Laborda, Juan José. Provincial deputy Frente Juntos for San Luis. San Luis City, June 2 and 3, 2008.
Lanzilotto, Karim. Journalist (La Rioja). La Rioja City, May 7, 2008.
Lepine, Enrique. Coordinator of Advisers (Ministry of Social Development) (2006–). Mexico City, June 29, 2007.
Leyva, Marcos. NGO Director (Oaxaca). Oaxaca City, July 17, 2007.
López Lena, Humberto. Convergencia federal deputy (Oaxaca) (2006–9). Mexico City, June 8, 2007.
Luna Corso, José. Justice, La Rioja Supreme Court. La Rioja City, May 30, 2008.
Mantilla, Miguel Ángel. PAN Federal Delegate of the Secretaría de Economía, state of Puebla. Puebla City, October 3, 2007.
Marín, Hugo. Ministry of Economy and Public Works, San Luis province (1991–5). San Luis City, June 3, 2008, and Ciudad de Buenos Aires. June 11, 2008.
Martínez, Roberto. PRD federal deputy (Oaxaca) (2006–9). Mexico City, June 12, 2007.
Maza, Ada. Federal Senator of La Rioja. La Rioja City, May 8, 2008.
Maza, E. Ángel. Governor of La Rioja (1995–2003). La Rioja City, May 8, 2008.
Mejía, Mario Alberto. Journalist of Quinta Columna (Puebla). Puebla City, October 2, 2007.
Menem, Carlos. President of Argentina (1989–99). La Rioja City, May 9, 2008.
Mercado Luna, Gastón. UCR deputy of La Rioja (1995–9). La Rioja City, May 6 and 10, 2008.
Montero, Oscar. Secretary of Municipal Affairs, Government of San Luis (2007–). San Luis City, June 6 and 19, 2008.
Morales, Melquíades. Governor of Puebla (1998–2004). Mexico City, October 8, 2007.
Moreno Tello, Miguel Ángel. PRI federal deputy (Oaxaca) (2000–3). Mexico City, July 30, 2007.
Moreno Valle, Rafael. Secretary of the Treasury of Puebla (1999–2003). Mexico City, September 27, 2007.
Murat, José. Governor of Oaxca (1998–2004). Mexico City, October 11, 2007.
Murdochowicz, Alejandro. Official from the Secretary of the Treasury, Ministry of Economy (Alfonsín's administration). Ciudad de Buenos Aires, April 7, 2008.
Murillo Karam, Jesús. PRI senator (Hidalgo) (2006–12). Mexico City, June 20, 2007.
Nosiglia, Enrique. Ministry of Interior (1987–9). Ciudad de Buenos Aires, April 9, 2008.
Núñez Jiménez, Arturo. PRD federal senatror (Tabasco) (2006–12). Mexico City, April 16, 2007.
Ortiz, Claudia. Secretary of Economy, Treasury, and Finances of La Rioja City. La Rioja City, May 28 and 29, 2008..
Ortiz, Julieta. Vice-minister of Economy, San Luis Province 2007–). San Luis City, June 5, 2008.

List of Interviews

Otero, Mario. Journalist of San Luis province. San Luis City, June 4, 2008.

Palacios Alcócer, Mariano. President of the national PRI. Mexico City, July 12, 2007.

Pérez Audelo, Juan. Journalist of El Imparcial (Oaxaca). Oaxaca City, July 19, 2007.

Pessino, Carola. Advisor to Roque Fernández, Ministry of Economy (1996–9). Ciudad de Buenos Aires, April 21, 2008.

Poggi, Claudio. Minister of Economy of San Luis Province. San Luis City, June 2, 2008.

Poiré, Alejandro. Advisor to President Calderón. Mexico City, July 11, 2007.

Porrás, Analía. Legal advisor to the legislature of La Rioja. La Rioja City, May 26, 2008.

Quintela, Ricardo. Mayor of La Rioja City (2003–). La Rioja City, May 29, 2008.

Rivera Domínguez, Noe. Top advisor to Elba Esther Gordillo. Mexico City, September 19, 2007.

Rodríguez, Jesús. Ministry of Economy (1989). Ciudad de Buenos Aires, April 8, 2008.

Rodríguez Prats, Juan José. PAN federal deputy (Tabasco) (2006–9). Mexico City, April 16, 2007.

Rodríguez Uresti, Enrique. PANAL federal deputy (San Luis Potosí) (2006–9). Mexico City, September 19, 2007.

Rueda, Arturo. Journalist La Quinta Columna (Puebla). Puebla City, October 2, 2007.

Salinas, Bulmaro Rito. PRI federal deputy (Oaxaca) (2000–3). Oaxaca City, July 19, 2007.

Samper, José. Former General Attorney, San Luis Government. San Luis City, June 3, 2008. June 4, 2008.

Solís Barrera, Alejandro. Direction of Coordination with States and Municipalities, Instituto Federal de Acceso a la Información. Mexico City, April 18, 2007.

Souto, Oscar. Chief of Staff, Secretary of Assistance to the Reform of Provincial Economies, Ministry of Interior (Menem's first administration). Ciudad de Buenos Aires, March 27 and April 4, 2008.

Szterenlicht, Edmundo. High official from the Consejo Federal de Inversiones. Ciudad de Buenos Aires, April 15, 2008.

Taurant, Elías. Supreme Court Justice (1994–6). San Luis City, June 4, 2008.

Trejo, Abel. PRI federal deputy (Oaxaca) (2003–6). Oaxaca City, July 19, 2007.

Vacchiano, Rodolfo. Secretary of Provinces, Ministry of Interior (1997–9). Ciudad de Buenos Aires, Argentina, May 15, 2008.

Varela Laguna, José Luis. Convergencia federal deputy (Oaxaca) (2006–9). Mexico City, June 19, 2007.

Velázquez, Felipe. Mayor of Atlixco (Puebla) (2002–5). Mexico City, September 28, 2007.

Index

administration
   bureaucratic 12–13, 117, 158, 176
   patrimonial 12–13, 25–8, 31, 34, 45, 47, 77, 81, 86, 88, 99, 100–2, 122, 128–9, 133–43, 147, 151–6, 166, 168–72, 176–7, 183, 185–7
Alfonsín, Raúl, *see* presidents
Alianza, *see* political parties
aportaciones 63–5, 67, 81, 138, 142, 148, 150, 154, 156, 168
APPO 147, 157
authoritarian(ism) 7, 30, 33–8, 52, 174
autocrat(s)
   Argentina
      San Luis 110–12, 114–18, 120–2
      La Rioja 96, 97–104, 106–10
   Mexico 2–4, 6–12, 14–24, 26–32, 34–6, 38, 42, 44–8, 50–2, 54–6, 58, 60, 62, 64, 66, 68, 70, 72, 74–80, 82–6, 88–96, 98–104, 106–12, 114–18, 120, 122–9, 131–4, 136–44, 146–56, 158–76, 178
      Oaxaca 143–4, 146–56, 158–9
      Puebla 131–4, 136–43

Bartlett, Manuel, *see* governors
Beder Herrera, Luis, *see* governors
Behrend, Jacqueline 24, 33, 35–7, 113, 123–4, 166
Benton, Allyson 14, 30, 33, 144, 153, 173
boundary
   control 2–3, 17, 22, 26, 46, 77, 128, 175
   opening 3, 144, 176
breakdown, *see* SUR
Brownlee, Jason 29–30
bureaucracy 69, 72, 102, 116, 134, 149, 151, 164

Cacho, Lydia 133, 137–8, 143, 168, 171
Calderón, Felipe, *see* presidents
Calvo, Ernesto 15, 36, 54, 70–1, 78, 81, 90, 98–9, 103, 180–1
Carrasco, Diódoro, *see* governors
Castagnola, Andrea 15, 19, 100

Cetrángolo, Oscar 81, 118
Convergencia por la Democracia, *see* political parties
cooptation 10, 54, 73, 125
coordinación, *see* Ley de Coordinación Fiscal (LCF)
coparticipation 56, 58–60, 67, 73, 100–1, 105, 110, 115, 118, 120, 186
copartisan 4, 6–7, 21, 23–4, 67–70, 72–4, 78–80, 83, 85, 88, 92, 126, 150, 152, 164, 172–3
Coppedge, Michael 37–8
Cué, Gabino 144, 146, 153, 156, 159, 168, 172–4

debt 50, 81–2, 87, 95, 105–7, 117–19
De la Rúa, Fernando, *see* presidents
democracy 2–3, 5–10, 14–18, 21–22, 26, 28–49, 51–53, 57, 64, 66–7, 74, 77–8, 84–6, 91–2, 95, 97–9, 104, 111–12, 115, 118, 127, 129, 131–2, 136, 140, 142, 144–5, 147, 158, 161–4, 168–9, 173–5, 177–83; *see also* subnational democracy
democratization 1–2, 15–16, 18, 30, 39, 42, 44, 46, 72, 80–1, 91, 99, 140, 160, 164, 177
Diaz-Cayeros, Alberto 20, 22, 25, 49, 55, 62, 79, 81, 153
Dickovick, Tyler 22, 24
Duhalde, Eduardo, *see* presidents

Eaton, Kent 22, 55, 57, 59, 119
Eisenstadt, Todd 2, 14, 33, 88, 131, 135, 152–3, 183
Ertman, Thomas 25, 45–6
Evans, Peter 25, 45–6

Fenwick, Tracy 22, 24
Fiscal Dependence 24–5, 27, 49, 106, 108, 136, 147–9, 162, 166, 185
Fiscal Discretion 1, 22–3, 25–7, 29, 46, 50, 56, 61–7, 74, 92, 100–2, 115–16, 138, 148, 155, 162, 168

211

Index

Fox, Vicente (president), *see* presidents
Front of Victory (FpV), *see* political parties

Geddes, Barbara 31, 37, 176
Gervasoni, Carlos 5, 7–8, 14–16, 18, 33, 35–8, 44, 50, 53, 174–5, 183
Getachew, Lullit 14, 16, 33, 43
Gibson, Edward 2, 5, 8, 14–15, 17, 19–20, 22, 24, 26, 30, 33, 35–6, 39, 44, 46, 50, 54, 70–1, 77–8, 81, 88, 90–1, 98, 102–3, 128, 144, 150, 155–6, 158, 165, 169, 173, 175, 180
Goertz, Gary 179–80, 183, 185
governors
  Mexico
    Oaxaca
      Diódoro Carrasco 152, 158–9
      José Murat 1–2, 13, 79, 88, 141, 144, 146–59, 167, 172
      Ulises Ruiz 1–2, 13, 79, 144, 146–51, 153–9, 167, 172–4
    Puebla
      Manuel Bartlett 134–7, 168, 171
      Melquíades Morales 13, 131, 134–8, 140–1, 143–4, 168, 171
      Mario Marín 13, 116–17, 120, 131–4, 137–8, 140–1, 143–4, 168–72
  Argentina
    San Luis
      Adolfo Rodríguez Saá 71, 103, 111, 113–15, 117, 123
      Alberto Rodríguez Saá 12, 71, 97, 107, 109, 111, 113, 121, 124
    La Rioja
      Ángel Maza 12, 97, 100–2, 106–10, 166
      Luis Beder Herrera 12, 97, 100–1, 109–10, 166
Guiñazú, María Clelia 112, 116, 119, 123–4, 166

Haggard, Stephan 3, 34, 47–8
Hagopian, Frances 14, 19, 78, 165
Huber, Evelyne 85

Industrialization 119, 123–4; *see also* Industrial Promotion Regime
Industrial Promotion Regime (RPI) 96, 118–19, 123–4
Ingram, Matthew 186–7
instruments 9, 11–12, 18, 22–6, 54–67, 72–4, 93, 102–4, 114, 120, 142, 162, 164
  fiscal 9, 11, 13, 22, 24, 55–66, 74
  partisan 9, 11–13, 20, 23, 25, 67–74
Institutional Revolutionary Party (PRI), *see* political parties

Jones, Mark 20, 23, 67, 69–71, 78–9, 89, 103

Kirchner
  Cristina Fernández, *see* presidents
  Néstor, *see* presidents

Lakin, Jason 144, 148, 150
Leiras, Marcelo 15, 19, 23, 7071, 98, 103, 187
Levitsky, Steven 7, 23–4, 29–31, 37, 67–9, 92, 103, 181, 183
Ley, Sandra 15, 19, 35
Ley de Coordinación Fiscal (LCF) 50, 63–4, 105–6, 117–19
Lujambio, Alonso 152, 182

Madrazo, Roberto 88, 90, 138, 158–9, 168, 172
Magaloni, Beatriz 29–31, 39, 81, 131–2, 145, 182
Mazzuca, Sebastián 25, 36, 45–6
McMann, Kelly 6–7, 14–15, 33, 35–6, 44, 53, 174
Menem, Carlos, *see* presidents
Micozzi, Juan Pablo 15, 36, 82, 98–9, 110, 121, 180
Morales, Melquíades, *see* governors
Murat, José, *see* governors
Murillo, María Victoria 183

National Action Party (PAN), *see* political parties
National Treasury Funds (ATN) 58, 81–2, 85, 87, 89
Niedzwiecki, Sara 45
non-patrimonial state administration
  Mexico 88
    Oaxaca 48, 129
    Puebla 13, 129, 133, 135, 139, 142, 166, 172, 175
  Argentina 88
    San Luis 114–16, 122, 175
    La Rioja 48

O'Donnell, Guillermo 14, 33, 177

partisan 1, 6, 8–9, 11–13, 19, 21–4, 26–8, 31–2, 42, 44–5, 54–5, 57, 67–8, 70, 72–5, 77–8, 81–2, 84, 86, 89, 91–2, 94, 102–3, 116, 123, 126–9, 136, 139–40, 143, 151, 153, 160–5, 167, 169, 172, 174, 177, 180
  instrument, *see* instrument
  power 6, 8–9, 13, 24, 26, 31, 55, 68, 70, 72–3, 75, 77–8, 92, 94, 126–8, 139–43, 151, 162, 164–9, 172, 174

party elite unity 4, 7–8, 19, 30–32, 71, 103, 123–4, 129, 157–9, 161, 167, 170, 172–3
Party of the Democratic Revolution (PRD), *see* political parties
Party Nationalization 70–2, 74, 103, 110, 164
pathway 3–5, 9–14, 18–19, 22, 28–9, 32, 54, 92–3, 125–7, 159–63, 165–6
patrimonialism 2, 11–13, 25–8, 31, 34, 45–9, 77–8, 81–2, 85–6, 88, 94, 99–102, 114–16, 122, 128–9, 133–9, 141–3, 147–9, 151, 153, 156, 162, 166–9, 172, 175–7, 183, 185–7
  Mexico
    Puebla 134–43, 168–72
    Oaxaca 136, 147–9, 151, 153, 156, 172–5
  Argentina
    La Rioja 99, 166
    San Luis 114–16, 122
Peronist Party (PJ), *see* political parties
political parties
  Alianza 71, 103, 108, 170
  Convergencia por la Democracia 150, 168, 170, 173
  FpV 70–1, 92, 103, 108–9, 121
  PAN 1–3, 42–3, 55, 63, 69–70, 72, 74, 83–4, 88–90, 126, 134–44, 150–6, 164, 167–71, 173
  PJ 42, 54–5, 69–71, 74, 95, 97, 108–9, 111–12, 120, 123–4, 164
  PRD 135–7, 140, 144, 150, 152–4, 168–70, 173
  PRI 1–2, 13, 39, 42–3, 71–2, 79, 83, 88, 90, 129, 131–6, 138–41, 144, 146–50, 152–3, 155–9, 168–74, 180
  the Radical Party (UCR) 42, 70, 97, 111–112
presidents
  Mexico
    Carlos Salinas 88, 154, 157, 159
    Ernesto Zedillo 63, 71, 88, 143, 158
    Felipe Calderón 10–12, 55, 63, 65–6, 69, 71, 73–4, 126–7, 131, 138–41, 143–4, 151, 153, 155–6, 160, 164, 166–7, 169–70, 172, 174
    Vicente Fox 1–2, 10–12, 14, 33, 55, 63, 65–6, 69, 71, 73–4, 88–90, 126–7, 131, 138–44, 150–1, 153–6, 160, 164, 166–7, 170, 172, 174
  Argentina
    Carlos Menem 11–12, 54, 58–9, 70–1, 74, 83–4, 90, 97, 100, 103, 107–9
    Cristina Fernández de Kirchner 10, 55, 69–71, 73, 92–4, 97, 103, 107, 111, 116, 120–1
    Eduardo Duhalde 1–2, 55, 59, 62, 71, 74, 87, 103, 107, 164

Fernando De la Rúa 12, 55, 59, 62, 71, 87, 164
Néstor Kirchner 10–12, 42, 55, 60, 62, 69, 71, 73–4, 84, 90, 92–4, 97, 102–4, 107–11, 116, 120–2, 125, 164, 166
Raúl Alfonsín 11, 55, 57, 66, 71, 163
presidential power 3, 6, 9–13, 18–22, 24–29, 31, 54–5, 57, 59, 61, 63, 65, 67, 69, 71–7, 83, 86, 88, 90–6, 102–3, 108–9, 121, 125–7, 140, 143, 152, 154, 159–60, 162–3, 165, 169, 172
Przeworski, Adam 36–8, 99, 133

Radical Party, the (UCR), *see* political parties
Rebolledo, Juan 14–15, 19–20, 33, 35, 132–3, 135, 173, 140–3, 156, 168, 170–1, 173–5
regime 2–11, 13–15, 17–19, 21, 24, 26, 28–39, 42–9, 51–4, 57, 68, 76–7, 80, 84–6, 91–9, 111–12, 114–15, 118, 122–9, 131–4, 142–4, 147, 149, 155–7, 159–61, 163, 165–7, 169–77, 179–80, 186
  continuity 3–13, 15–19, 22, 28, 31–4, 44–7, 53–4, 75–7, 91–9, 111–15, 118, 122–9, 131–4, 142–4, 155–67, 172–7
  reproduction 4–7, 9–13, 16, 18–19, 21, 28–9, 31–2, 76–81, 83, 85–6, 89–91, 93–5, 97, 103, 111, 125, 127–9, 131, 144, 160–1, 165–7, 172–3, 175–6
  weaken(ing) 2–4, 9, 11, 18, 31–2, 68, 76, 80, 93, 95, 110, 122–5, 129, 142, 155–8, 160–1, 163, 165–7, 169–70, 172, 174
Rodden, Jonathan 23, 25, 50, 54, 68
Rodríguez Saá, Adolfo and Alberto, *see* governors
Ruiz, Ulises, *see* governors

Soifer, Hillel 179
Solt, Frederick 14, 33, 53, 174–5
Stephens, John 85
Suárez-Cao, Julieta 70–2, 103, 112, 124
subnational 2–57, 59, 61, 64–70, 72–81, 83–4, 86, 88–9, 91–5, 102–3, 114–16, 118, 120, 123, 125–9, 131, 134, 137, 140–3, 154, 159–66, 169–70, 173–83, 185
  democracy 8, 15–16, 37–44, 48–53, 95, 118, 129, 142, 174–5, 177, 179–83
  politics 21, 43
  undemocratic regime (SUR), *see* SUR(s)
SUR(s) 2–23, 25–39, 41–55, 75–81, 83–6, 88–95, 97–9, 101–3, 105, 107, 109–17, 119, 121–9, 131–3, 135–9, 141–4, 147–9, 151, 153, 155–63, 165–70, 172–7, 183–4

213

Index

Argentina
    La Rioja 10, 12–13, 40–8, 51, 84, 92–112, 114–15, 118, 121–2, 125–6, 165–6, 176–7
    San Luis 110, 12–13, 40–52, 71, 92–97, 111–26, 165–6, 170, 175–7
    breakdown 8, 13, 30, 32, 161, 163, 167, 170, 172–174
Mexico
    Puebla 1–3, 8, 13, 41–7, 49, 127–33, 135–9, 141–4, 148, 155, 159–60, 163–72, 174, 177
    Oaxaca 1–3, 8, 10, 13, 41–7, 52, 79, 88, 126–31, 135–6, 139, 141–4, 145–60, 163, 165, 167–8, 172–7
    weakening, *see* regime, weakening
sustainability 7, 45, 91, 110

Tarrow, Sidney 17
territorial politics/control 10, 14, 17, 22–7, 31, 46, 49, 68, 70–5, 89, 102–3, 108, 116, 126–8, 136–40, 143, 149, 153, 155, 166–7, 176

territorialization 72, 74, 103
territory(-ies) 3, 17, 22, 26, 46, 71–3, 77, 99, 102, 108, 128, 151, 155, 164, 177
trajectories 5, 9, 11, 31, 45, 75, 93–4, 127–8, 161, 165, 167; *see also* pathways
Tudor, Maya 18–20, 165
Tuñón, Guadalupe 15, 19, 187

UCR, *see* political parties

Van Dyck, Brandon 24, 68
Verkuilen, Jay 37, 179

Weber, Max 25, 45, 48, 176
Wibbels, Erik 22–5, 31, 48–50, 54–5, 68, 77, 86

Zedillo, Ernesto *see* presidents
Ziegfeld, Adam 18–20, 165